To Do the Right and the Good

ELLIOT N. DORFF

To Do the Right and the Good

A JEWISH APPROACH TO MODERN SOCIAL ETHICS

5762   2002

The Jewish Publication Society
Philadelphia

The Jewish Publication Society
2100 Arch Street
Philadelphia, PA 19103

Design and composition by Varda Graphics

Manufactured in the United States of America

02 03 04 05 06 07 08 09 10 10 9 8 7 6 5 4 3 2 1

LIBRARY OF CONGRESS CATALOGING-IN-PUBLICATION DATA

Dorff, Elliot N.
  To do the right and the good: a Jewish approach to modern
social ethics / Elliot Dorff. — 1st ed.
     p.   cm.
Includes bibliographical references and index.
ISBN 0–8276–0715–6
  1. Judaism and social problems.   2. Social ethics.   3. Ethics,
Jewish.   I. Title.
  HN40.J5 D67 2002
  289.3'6—dc21

2002001912

In honor of my teacher,
dissertation adviser,
and mentor in philosophy
for four decades:
Professor David Sidorsky

"I instruct you in the way,
of wisdom,
I guide you in the way
of ethics."

Proverbs 4:11

The publication of this book

was made possible by the generosity of

MARILYN ZIERING

in memory of her beloved

SIGI ZIERING

Table of Contents

Preface

You shall do the right and the good in the eyes of the Lord.

—Deuteronomy 6:18

This refers to compromise [rather than judgment according to strict law] and conduct beyond the requirements of the Law. The intent of this is that initially [in Deuteronomy 6:17] God had said that you should observe the laws and statutes that He had commanded you. Now God says that, with respect to what He has not commanded, you should likewise take heed to do the right and the good in His eyes, for He loves the good and the right. This is a great matter, for it is impossible to mention in the Torah all of a person's actions toward his neighbors and acquaintances, all of his commercial activity, and all social and political institutions. So, after God had mentioned many of them . . . He continues to say generally that one should do the right and the good in all matters through compromise and conduct beyond the requirements of the Law.

—Nahmanides on Deuteronomy 6:18

One glance at the contents of this book amply explains why anyone would be interested in its topics: Communal relations, interfaith relations, national policy, procedural justice, poverty, war, and forgiveness among individuals and communities are issues that have deeply affected human life from its very inception. The modern world's instant communication over any distance; its internationally interwoven economy; its capabilities of mass destruction; and its simultaneous potential for true global learning, understanding, and enrichment make these age-old issues all the more compelling. Some of the old answers seem to do just fine in our modern world, whereas others seem to be woefully inadequate. In some cases, we are not even sure how to apply ancient wisdom to the new circumstances in which we find ourselves. New explorations of these issues, then, are clearly in order.

Why, though, should we try to apply the Jewish tradition to these matters? Jews may be interested in doing so simply as an expression of their self-identity, of who they are. Such a discussion would then strengthen their self-understanding and pride.

That is a powerful motivation for Jews to plumb the Jewish tradition for its approach to these issues, but it is certainly not the only one for engaging in this inquiry. Another important reason—one applicable to both Jews and non-Jews—is that Judaism, like other religions, presents a particular picture of the world as it is and as it ought to be. The word "religion," in fact, comes from the same Latin root from which we get the English word "ligament." The root means a "tie, link, or bond." Religions provide us, among other things, with a view of our ties to other people in our family, our circle of friends, our community, humanity at large, the environment, and the transcendent (imaged in the Western world as God). The various secular philosophies of the world (Western liberalism, Marxism, existentialism, etc.) do that, too; but religions are generally connected to living communities whose members try to live by the vision their religion presents.

The important thing to note is that no human being can be a completely objective observer, none of us can attain the vantage point that Judaism ascribes to God in His omniscience. Instead, *each of us must look at the world from a particular perspective, through a particular set of lenses.* We both can and should learn about other people's perspectives—we can try on other people's or other religion's eyeglasses, as it were—but ultimately we must come to recognize that each religion and secular philosophy suggests a different way to think and act based on its specific way of seeing who we are and who we ought to be. Moreover, each perspective, as a human product, inevitably has its strengths and weaknesses; even the religions, or the forms of religions, that claim to be revealed directly by God ultimately have to be interpreted by human beings with their particular limits and assets, insights and prejudices.

Thus there is no way to escape the ultimate perspectivism of human knowledge. (What commonly passes as a secular approach these days is, in reality, just the viewpoint of a particular philosophy, namely, Western liberalism.) Moreover, each viewpoint has its own inherent strengths and weaknesses. Both Jews and non-Jews might be interested in reading about a Jewish approach to the topics in this book so that they can learn from Judaism's experience, faults, and insights in seeking to deal with what are some very hard issues.

I come to these issues with these same limitations of human knowledge and wisdom that every other human being has. I find the Jewish tradition's approach to moral questions interesting, first, because it is my own tradition. Although I have studied most of the major religions of the world and many secular philosophies with some serious rigor and sympathy, and although I tried to learn from each of them what I found to be true and wise, I cannot pretend to be any more objective than anyone else can. In the end, I was and am biased by my own tradition.

That is not just because it is my own. In addition to that ethnic reason, I indeed believe that God really wants Jews, and perhaps all humanity, to abide by this tradition. I discuss such theological claims and, in particular, why I am nevertheless far from being a fundamentalist in my books *Knowing God: Jewish Journeys to the Unknowable* and *Conservative Judaism: Our Ancestors to Our Descendants,* and so I will not repeat the discussion here. Suffice it to say, I am committed to a Jewish approach to moral matters not only for ethnic or cultural reasons but for religious ones.

Still, I think that I can suggest some reasons why those who are not Jews and those Jews who have severe doubts about God or Judaism might also want to examine the material in this book. First, the Jewish tradition is one long-standing tradition among the six or eight major religions of the world, and it has its own distinctive way of looking at the world and responding to it. Judaism is, in other words, minimally one of the perspectives that must be taken seriously by anyone interested in the major ways in which human beings have tried to make sense of their lives and to live morally.

Second, the Jewish tradition has close to four thousand years of experience in trying to understand individuals and communities and in motivating them to act rightly and aspire to the good. Experience, of course, does not guarantee wisdom; after all, that could have been four thousand years of terrible mistakes! Jews, though, have historically made some morally crucial contributions to the world as well as many intellectual, cultural, and scientific ones; that track record alone suggests that there is some notable substance here, something worth learning.

Third, the biblical tradition and, even more, the rabbinic tradition embody the experience of judges who see the highs and lows of human life each day in their courtrooms. This has enabled the Jewish tradition, based on these sources, to arrive at a truly remarkable combination of a realistic assessment of human beings with a strong sense of mission to push human life to ever greater moral, social, and intellectual heights. That recipe makes Judaism neither Pollyannaish nor cynical about this life but rather realistic and hopeful. These qualities also argue for a serious consideration of what the Jewish tradition has to offer in addressing all our old and new ethical questions.

This book is specifically *a* Jewish approach to social ethics, not *the* Jewish approach, because the Jewish tradition is much too rich and varied for any articulation of it to legitimately make the latter claim. I nevertheless maintain that I present a fair reading of the Jewish tradition in these matters—that is, I present a Jewish approach to the topics included and not just my own idiosyncratic views—and I try to support that claim by affording the reader a rich set of classical materials along with the reasons for my interpretations of those materials. I fully expect that other readers of the tradition will argue with me on specific points by adducing other texts or other readings of the same texts, together with the justifications for those interpretations. Indeed, I sincerely hope that my work stimulates such discussion, because then we can all learn and grow.

At the same time, I have not taken the Jewish component of my task lightly; I mean to present a Jewish understanding of the topics, deeply rooted in Jewish sources, along with a careful judgment of how to apply those sources. I describe the issues involved in choosing an appropriate way to gain moral guidance from the tradition in the appendix to my book *Matters of Life and Death: A Jewish Approach to Modern Medical Ethics,* and more of that meta-ethical thinking is incorporated in the appendices to this book.

To Do the Right and the Good is divided into eight chapters. In Chapter One, I describe the fundamental convictions of the Jewish tradition that guide its approach to specific moral matters. Because many Jews presume that all peoples of the world think and act as Jews do (!), I have included some comparisons to the fundamental convictions of two other world traditions: Christianity and American secularism (that is, the specifically American version of Enlightenment thought). These comparisons illustrate clearly that the Jewish perspective on how the world is and ought to be is by far not the only possible one, that intelligent and morally sensitive people have chosen to dedicate their lives to fulfilling different concepts and values. These comparisons prepare the reader for more specific discussions in later chapters on, for example, interfaith relations, religion and state, and poverty.

Chapter Two focuses on relationships within the Jewish community. I discuss a variety of views that have been proposed by others about the ground rules for relating to other Jews, together with the theological reasons for those approaches. Then I suggest my own defense of pluralism, together with historical, philosophical, and theological reasons to embrace it.

In Chapter Three I take that analysis one step further in my discussion of interfaith relations. Relating to Christians and Muslims poses one set of problems, because each of Judaism's daughter religions has asserted that it supersedes the parent: Judaism may have been fine in the past, but it now must bow to the greater authority of a later representative of God, whether His Son (Jesus) or ultimate Prophet (Muhammad). Ancient and medieval Jewish texts raise some theological questions about the extent to which the doctrine of the Trinity compromises Christianity's claim to monotheism, but current relations with both Christians and Muslims are more troubled because of the oppression and deaths that Jews have suffered by the proponents of its daughter religions historically and by the ongoing developments in the modern State of Israel. On the other hand, when we consider Hinduism, Buddhism, and other Asian religions, Jews have few negative historical memories to overcome, but there are many theological questions about the (at least) apparent idolatry manifest in some of these religions.

How, then, should Jews interact with the adherents of other religions? I deepen the line of reasoning developed in Chapter Two, as I present historical and theological grounds for good interfaith relations—together with the limits of such discussions and activities.

In Chapter Four, I turn to the avowedly secular community that is the United States and ask how American Jews should act both as Americans and as Jews. I suggest that American ideology itself requires that we know our tradition and bring it to bear in our discussions of national policy whenever we think that it can be helpful, knowing all the time that our religion has no right to determine national policy unilaterally any more than any other religion does. Still, we owe it to America to bring Jewish concepts and values to the American marketplace of ideas.

The next chapters of the book address our social goals of both procedural and substantive justice and the realities of how we face our failures to attain those goals—through war and, if we can, the much better alternatives of individual and communal forgiveness. Chapter Five defines procedural justice as the Jewish tradition understands it. In many ways, Jewish law is much more demanding than other traditions in its insistence on ways to guarantee procedural justice. The chapter also discusses the pitfalls of using the law to resolve every dispute and the alternatives of arbitration and mediation. It also explains Judaism's understanding of the connections between justice and love.

Chapter Six moves on to substantive justice—that is, the effort to make sure, whatever procedures society uses to make its legislative and judicial decisions, that ultimately people gain their due. As creatures of God, all people, according to the Jewish tradition, have a right to basic minimums of food, clothing, and shelter. The chapter describes how classical Jewish texts understand the obligations of the community—and both the rich and the poor individuals within it—to make sure that the basic minimums are provided to all. It also explores how to take those texts and apply them intelligently to the conditions within our modern context—a task in which methodological concerns are critical. The chapter is rooted in a discussion of the reasons why we do not—and maybe should not—want to help the poor together with the Jewish reasons why we should.

Chapter Seven addresses situations in which substantive justice falls apart altogether or threatens to do so. These are conditions in which it is not just the poor who will not get their due, but actually everyone will be threatened by outside invaders. The chapter discusses a Jewish approach to the ethics of war in general and of international intervention (military, economic, or political) in particular.

Chapter Eight takes up an alternative way of resolving a lack of justice—namely, forgiveness. In this chapter, I reproduce a set of discussions about reconciliation and forgiveness initiated by the Priest–Rabbi Dialogue of Los Angeles, a group that I have been a part of since 1973 and the co-chair of for about ten years. The priests finally felt sufficiently secure in our dialogue to ask what it would take for Jews to forgive Catholics for the atrocities of the past for which the Church was responsible directly (for example, the Crusades and the Inquisition) and possibly indirectly (for example, the Holocaust) and also for the Church's inaction when it should have intervened to stop oppression of the Jews (the Holocaust is probably the most poignant example). That led to a series of discussions about communal forgiveness and reconciliation, including the differences between the two, the criteria for deciding when either is warranted, and the parties who can extend both the request and the offer. Although I focus on interfaith reconciliation in this chapter, its principles also apply to reconciliation among ethnic and national groups, a particularly hot topic in the modern world of Arab–Israeli conflicts and genocides in Africa, Asia, and Europe.

Finally, in the appendices I address two philosophical issues that are somewhat more abstract (and hence their placement in appendices) but crucial for understanding important elements that underlie the discussion presented in the chapters. I discussed two such topics in the appendix of my book *Matters of Life and Death: A Jewish Approach to Modern Medical Ethics*. There I explore the relationship between religion and morality and legal versus nonlegal methods of accessing the Jewish tradition for its moral guidance. In the first appendix of this book, I discuss the differences between judging something as right versus judging it as good, together with a proposed theory to explain the differences between the right and the good. The second appendix examines the relative strengths and weaknesses of identifying moral norms using Catholic, Protestant, American secular, and Jewish methods. Although my presentation in this appendix is necessarily limited and ignores some of the philosophical niceties and variations within each of the groups I discuss, the points are, I think, both substantially correct and significant for understanding some of the foundations on which social ethics is built.

Before concluding this preface, I want to thank a number of people who helped me write this book. I have already mentioned the priests of the Los Angeles Priest–Rabbi Dialogue, who motivated me to think through the material given in Chapter Eight. Reverend Hans Ucko of the World Council of Churches invited me to give a paper on the theological underpinnings of interfaith relations at a conference he held in Cochin, India, and Chapter Three is a slightly revised version of that paper.

Professor R. Bruce Douglass, dean of the faculty of Georgetown College, and Professor Joshua Mitchell, both members of the political science department at Georgetown University, included me in their project on the relationship between religion and state in the United States, and Chapter Four is the paper I wrote for the group of scholars they assembled. I want to thank them and all the members of the group for their important input to that paper.

The Rabbinical Assembly—the organization of Conservative rabbis—has played a significant role in my writing by stimulating me to take on projects for its Committee on Jewish Law and Standards, its Commission on Human Sexuality, its Social Action Commission, and its Torah Commentary Commission. I have thoroughly enjoyed my participation on those committees and commissions, and my sincere thanks go to my colleagues in those groups for their significant input in the projects that I undertook that became the source of chapters of this book. Specifically, I would like to thank Rabbi Charles Feinberg and the members of the Rabbinical Assembly's Social Action Committee, which he chaired, for their help in developing Chapter Six, which is a revised form of my *"You Shall Strengthen Them": A Rabbinic Letter on the Poor,* published by the Rabbinical Assembly. The core of that chapter originated as work I did for the American Jewish Committee's Commission on Poverty in 1986. I would like to thank my good friend and one of my favorite intellectual sparring partners David Gordis, president of Boston's Hebrew College and then executive director of the American Jewish Committee, for appointing me to that commission, and Gary Rubin, who organized the work of the commission and wrote an important chapter in *The Poor among Us: Jewish Tradition and Social Policy,* published by the commission.

I have always been blessed with family and friends who stimulate me to think about new things in new ways and who provide the encouragement to carry on. Rabbi Moshe Rothblum of Adat Ariel in North Hollywood, California, and Professor Arthur Rosett of the University of California at Los Angeles School of Law have been constant goads in my side for some three decades, pushing me forward; if they were not such wonderful people, I might have resented that! As it is, they both have my sincere thanks and love.

My wife, Marlynn, the love of my life, has graciously let me have the time to complete this project, and I have much appreciated her acute questions and wise suggestions about some of this material. Our children, Tammy, Michael, Havi, and Jonathan, and now Havi's husband, Adam, Jonathan's wife, Mara, and our granddaughter, Noa Yarden, are the unrivaled treasures of my life who give life itself love and meaning.

I have chosen to dedicate this book to Professor David Sidorsky of Columbia University. He was my instructor for my first undergraduate course in ethics, a course that has had more influence on my life than either he or I could possibly have known at the time. He, more than anyone else, taught me how to write through the many papers he assigned for his history of philosophy course and through the senior seminar paper on the philosophy of science that I wrote for him. As a graduate student, I took his course in social philosophy, and he was my dissertation adviser. A sparkling mind, a great wit, a dedicated and consummate teacher, and a warm, wonderful friend, David—with his patent enthusiasm for philosophical discussions and his strong interest in Judaism and the Jewish people—is a true mentor for me and a great blessing for me and his many students and admirers.

Elliot N. Dorff
Los Angeles, California
November 16, 2001

Acknowledgments

M Y THINKING ABOUT THE MORAL AND ETHICAL TOPICS OF this volume has spanned many years. It is, therefore, not surprising that some sections of this book have appeared in earlier forms. I would like to thank the sponsors and publishers of my earlier work for giving me the opportunity to be published and for their permission to revise and reprint the original articles.

Chapter Two is based on my chapter "Pluralism," in *Frontiers of Jewish Thought*, ed. Steven Katz (Washington, DC: B'nai Brith, 1992), 213–234, which was reprinted in a somewhat revised form as "Pluralism: Models for the Conservative Movement," *Conservative Judaism* 48, no. 1 (fall, 1995): 21–35.

Chapter Three is a revision of my chapter "A Jewish Theology of Jewish Relations to Other People," in *People of God, Peoples of God: A Jewish-Christian Conversation in Asia*, ed. Hans Ucko (Geneva: World Council of Churches, 1996), 46–66.

Chapter Four, in its earliest form, was my chapter "Jewish Tradition and National Policy," in *Commandment and Community: New Essays in Jewish Legal and Political Philosophy*, ed. Daniel H. Frank (Albany: State University of New York Press, 1995), 85–109; a later revised version appeared as "The King's Torah: The Role of Judaism in Shaping Jews' Input in National

Policy," in *A Nation Under God? Essays on the Fate of Religion in American Public Life,* ed. R. Bruce Douglass and Joshua Mitchell (Lanham, MD: Rowman & Littlefield, 2000), 203–222.

Chapter Five is based in part on my essay "Justice," in *Etz Hayyim,* ed. David Lieber (Philadelphia: Jewish Publication Society; New York: Rabbinical Assembly and United Synagogue of Conservative Judaism, 2001).

Chapter Six appeared in two earlier forms: "Jewish Perspectives on the Poor," in *The Poor among Us: Jewish Tradition and Social Policy,* ed. Gary Rubin (New York: American Jewish Committee, 1986), 21–55, and *"You Shall Strengthen Them": A Rabbinic Letter on the Poor* (New York: Rabbinical Assembly, 1999).

Chapter Seven is a revised version of my monograph *"A Time for War and a Time for Peace": A Jewish Perspective on the Ethics of International Intervention* (University Papers, vol. 6, no. 3) (Los Angeles: University of Judaism, 1987).

Chapter Eight first appeared as "Individual and Communal Forgiveness," in *Autonomy and Judaism: The Individual and the Community in Jewish Philosophical Thought,* ed. Daniel H. Frank (Albany: State University of New York Press, 1992), 193–218.

CHAPTER ONE

Fundamental Beliefs That Guide Jewish Social Ethics

I N A NATIONAL POLL OF AMERICAN JEWS CONDUCTED BY THE *LOS Angeles Times*,[1] fully half of the respondents listed a commitment to social equality as the most important factor in their Jewish identity, whereas only 17 percent cited religious observance and another 17 percent noted support for Israel. Those deeply committed to Judaism may find these results disturbing, for they mean that Jews are mistaking the fruit for the tree. After all, in classical Jewish sources, Judaism's commitment to social equality stems from its more fundamental convictions regarding God, covenant, and mitzvot. Thus Jews not only should include those elements in their Jewish identity but should see them as central.

Nevertheless, the 50 percent of respondents who singled out social equality as the most critical factor in their Jewish commitment were not wrong in identifying that as an important Jewish conviction. A number of the laws and theological tenets of the Torah articulate that principle, and later Jewish law and thought expand on that base. As Jews were accepted more fully into general society in post-Enlightenment times, they became all the more interested in making society as a whole not only fair and equitable but also supportive and, as much as possible, ideal.

This book speaks to the social aspect of the Jewish tradition. It explores intrafaith and interfaith relations, justice, poverty, war, and forgiveness. Because its social message is a significant part of Judaism, and because, as the *Los Angeles Times* survey indicates, it is the fundamental mainstay of the Jewish identity of half of America's Jews, this book will help many Jews understand the foundations and directions of their Jewish social commitments.

From the Torah's point of view, the task of discerning the right and the good and then acting on that knowledge is not just central to Jewish identity; it is what God demands of us: "Do what is right and good in the sight of the Lord."[2] Many philosophical questions immediately arise from that verse: What is meant by the terms "right" and "good" in the first place, and how are they different from each other? How does one determine the courses of action that are right or good? And how is God related to moral discernment and action?

These questions, fundamental as they are, do not speak directly to Judaism's understanding of social ethics, and so I have placed my responses to the questions of definition and method in Jewish moral theory in the appendices to this book. This frees up the body of the text to deal specifically with issues in social ethics. I urge readers who are philosophically curious, though, to tackle the material in the appendices, so that they can understand some of the theoretical underpinnings of the normative, social ethics that I explore in this book.

Before I begin the discussion of specific topics in Jewish social ethics, let me describe the underlying aspects of the Jewish perspective on life that govern all of the following discussions. What is Judaism's conception of the individual? What is Judaism's understanding of the community? What are the goals of human existence? Because all issues in social ethics depend on these fundamental commitments and because Judaism's view of these matters differs significantly from that of many of the world's other religions and secular philosophies, it is important to understand at the outset Judaism's perspective.

Most Jews tend to assume that everyone in the world thinks and acts as they do. This includes not only what Jews believe and how they live their lives but also the argumentative, and yet humorous, way in which they conduct themselves. It is thus helpful to clarify the underlying assumptions of Jewish ethics by comparing them to those of Christianity and American secularism, the two other traditions that American Jews are likely to know. The same kind of comparison elucidates the discussions of specific topics in the chapters that follow. These comparisons are not intended to be invidious, aimed at denigrating either of the other systems of thought and action; they are rather designed to highlight the ways in which the Jewish tradition has something distinctive to say about the ethics of social issues.

The Central Stories of Jews, Christians, and Americans

Many traditions articulate their fundamental assertions about the nature of life in their central stories, the tales describing their founding and many of their basic convictions. Judaism's central story, for example, is Exodus–Sinai; Christianity's is the Passion–Resurrection of Jesus; and the central story of the United States is the American Revolution and the adoption of the Constitution and Bill of Rights. When core commitments are described in story form, it is easy for adherents to understand the affirmations, to remember them, and to apply them to daily life. At the end of this chapter, I describe exactly how the Jewish, Christian, and American secular stories graphically portray each tradition's beliefs about the individual, society, and the goal of living. At the outset, though, it is helpful to remember the stories and to keep them in mind as I go through the more abstract ideas embedded in the Jewish, Christian, and American secular views.

In the beginning of the Bible, there is Genesis, in which we hear about Creation and meet the Patriarchs and Matriarchs. The central Jewish story, though, comes later: It is the Exodus from Egypt to meet God at Sinai and to continue to the Promised Land. The last four of the five books of the Torah all revolve around the Exodus from Egypt, the trek to Sinai, the Revelation there, the forty years in the wilderness, and the anticipated end of reaching the Promised Land, together with the laws and theological concepts that are announced along the way.

Like the Torah, much of the later Jewish tradition also concentrates on these events. Thus the Exodus from Egypt is the paradigm that is repeatedly invoked when the authors of traditional Jewish prayers wanted to demonstrate that God acts in history and that God has been, and will be, our redeemer. Passover, of course, focuses on the Exodus story, and, at least in rabbinic tradition, Shavuot does as well, marking the time when the Revelation at Sinai occurred. The Torah also connects Sukkot, the harvest festival, to this story, asserting that the festival should remind us of the huts in which the Israelites lived as they wandered through the wilderness on their way to Israel.[3] Even the Sabbath, first announced in the Torah as a reminder of Creation, shifts in focus in the Book of Deuteronomy to the redemption from slavery in Egypt.[4] Thus the story is not only a prime feature of Jewish sacred Scripture but also permeates Jewish liturgy and holidays. As I explore Jewish conceptions of the individual, the community, and life's ultimate purpose, then, think of how these ideas are reflected in the Torah's account of the Israelites' trek from Egypt to Sinai to the Promised Land.

The central Christian story is the Passion and Resurrection of Christ. Here again, that is not the first story. The birth of Jesus, celebrated prominently at Christmas, is full of hope and expectation, but that hope and expectation are realized only in the Good Friday and Easter story, marking the end of Jesus' life in his crucifixion (Passion) and his rising from the dead (Resurrection). As I discuss Christian concepts of the individual, the community, and the purpose of life, think of how they are reflected in the Christian Passion and Resurrection story.

Finally, secular America (a term I use to describe the United States, according to common custom, with apologies to our neighbors in North, Central, and South America) begins with the stories of the Puritans and others who fled religious persecution in Europe during the colonial period. But the central story is the American Revolution and the framing of the U.S. Constitution. In U.S. high school courses, George Washington, Thomas Jefferson, James Madison, Benjamin Franklin, and others are presented as hero figures. We hear of the Boston Tea Party; the Minutemen, Paul Revere, and "One if by land, two if by sea"; the somber decision, filled with personal and communal danger, to write and sign the Declaration of Independence; the tough winter at Valley Forge; the crossing of the Delaware; and the ultimate surrender of the British. Students learn about the Whiskey Rebellion and the other problems that plagued the new government under the Articles of Confederation; the long, hot summer in Philadelphia that culminated in the Constitution; the addition of the Bill of Rights in 1791; and the last attempt of Britain to assert its rule in the War of 1812.

These events, told in story and song, accompany Americans as they grow up, and they are invoked again and again whenever Americans recite the Pledge of Allegiance, sing "The Star Spangled Banner," celebrate the Fourth of July, and read about constitutional matters in the news. What concepts of the individual, the community, and life's ultimate purpose underlie these events and documents?

I will return to these stories at the end of the chapter to see how they represent each group's fundamental convictions and make them memorable. First, I present and compare the fundamental convictions themselves.

The Nature of the Individual

The Jewish Concept

Jewish tradition places strong emphasis on the worth of the individual. Human worth derives first from being created in God's image, a concept that the Torah repeats three times in the opening chapters of Genesis to ensure that we take note of it:

> And God created the human being in His image, in the image of God He created him: male and female He created them.[5]

> This is the record of Adam's line. When God created man, He made him in the likeness of God; male and female He created them. And when they were created, He blessed them and called them Human.[6]
>
> Whoever sheds the blood of man, by man shall his blood be shed; for in His image did God make man.[7]

As this last verse indicates, the divine image in each of us is not only a philosophical conception but also justifies and explains specific laws. The most obvious, the one in Genesis 9, is that murder is to be banned because human beings have divine worth. Even murderers, though, are created in the divine image, as are others guilty of a capital offense. The Torah, therefore, prescribes that after we execute such people for their crimes, we must honor the divinity of their bodies (and the holiness of the Land of Israel) by burying them quickly:

> If a man is guilty of a capital offense and is put to death, and you impale him on a stake, you must not let his corpse remain on the stake overnight, but must bury him the same day. For an impaled body is an affront to God; you shall not defile the land that the Lord your God is giving you to possess.[8]

The Rabbis[9] took this further. That we were created in God's image is a manifestation of God's love for us; our awareness of the divine image within us is a mark of yet more divine love:

> Beloved is man, for he was created in the image of God; but it was by a special love that it was made known to him that he was created in the image of God, as the Torah says, "For in the image of God He made man."[10]

Exactly which feature of the human being reflects this divine image is a matter of debate within the tradition. The Torah itself seems to tie it to humanity's ability to make moral judgments—that is, to distinguish good from bad and right from wrong, to behave accordingly, and to judge one's own actions and those of others on the basis of such moral knowledge.[11] Another human faculty connected by the Torah and by the later tradition to divinity is the ability to speak.[12] Maimonides (1135–1204), undoubtedly the most influential medieval Jewish philosopher, claimed that the divine image resides in our capacity to think, especially discursively.[13] Locating the divine image within us may also be the Torah's way of acknowledging that we can love, just as God does[14] or that we are at least partially spiritual and thus share God's spiritual nature.[15]

In the biblical account, humanity not only was created in the divine image but was created, initially, in the form of one human being: Adam. In an oft-quoted passage in the Mishnah, the Rabbis, in describing how the judges in a capital case are to be warned, spell out several implications of God's creating first a single human being. Two of those ramifications add further to the worth of each individual.

First, killing one person is also killing all of his or her potential descendants—indeed "an entire world." Conversely, someone who saves an individual "saves an entire world." That makes murder of any one individual all the more serious—and, conversely, saving a human life all the more praiseworthy. It also ascribes value to each of us as the possible progenitor of future generations.

Second, when people use a mold to create coins, the image on each coin is exactly the same. God, however, made each human being unique. In accordance with the laws of supply and demand, a one-of-a-kind thing demands a far higher price than something that is plentiful on the market. Think, for example, of the comparative value of a Picasso original, of each of a few hundred prints of that work, and, finally, of a photograph of that work: The fewer copies of the product, the greater its value. The fact that each of us is unique imparts immense value to the individual.

How were witnesses [in capital cases] inspired with awe? . . . [The judges told them this:] Know that capital cases are not like monetary cases. In civil suits, one can make restitution [for false testimony] and thereby effect atonement, but in capital cases the false witness is held responsible for the accused's blood and the blood of his [potential] descendants until the end of time. For thus we find in the case of Cain, who killed his brother, that it is written, "The bloods of your brother cry out to Me"[16]—not [just] the blood of your brother, but the bloods of your brother, i.e., his blood and the blood of his [potential] descendants. . . . For this reason was man created alone: to teach you that with regard to anyone who destroys a single soul [of Israel], Scripture imputes guilt to him as though he had destroyed a complete world; and with regard to anyone who preserves a single soul [of Israel], Scripture ascribes merit to him as though he had preserved a complete world. Furthermore, [man was created alone] for the sake of peace among men, that one might not say to his fellow, "My father was greater than yours." And [man was created alone] so that the sectarians might not say, "There are many powers in heaven." Additionally, [man was created alone] to proclaim the greatness of the Holy One, blessed be He: for if a man strikes many coins from one mold, they all resemble one another, but the Supreme King of kings, the Holy One, blessed be He, fashioned every person in the stamp of the first person, and yet not one of them looks the same as anyone else. Therefore every single person is obligated to say: "The world was created for my sake."[17]

Thinking that the world was created for your sake can, of course, produce more than a little arrogance. The following lovely Hasidic saying introduces an appropriate balance:

A person should always carry two pieces of paper in his or her pockets. On one should be written, "For me the world was created," and on the other, "I am but dust and ashes."[18]

Thus we must have humility before God and before other people, while still appreciating our own immense worth and that of every other human being by virtue of our creation in the image of God.

The Rabbis, like the Torah before them, invoked the doctrines that God created humans in the divine image and uniquely not only to *describe* aspects of our nature but also to *prescribe* behavior. Specifically, the Rabbis maintained that because humans are created in God's image, they affront God when they insult other people.[19] Conversely, "one who welcomes his friend is as if he welcomes the face of the Divine Presence."[20] Moreover, when we see someone with a disability, we are to utter this blessing: "Praised are you, Lord our God, *meshaneh ha-briyyot*, who makes different creatures," or "who created us different." Precisely when we might recoil or when we might thank God for not making us deformed or incapacitated, the tradition instead bids us to embrace the divine image in such people—indeed, to bless God for creating some of us so.[21] Finally, the non-utilitarian basis of the Rabbis' assertion of human worth is graphically illustrated in their ruling that no one person can be sacrificed to save even an entire city unless that person is named by the enemy or guilty of a capital crime:

> Caravans of men are walking down a road, and they are accosted by non-Jews who say to them: "Give us one from among you that we may kill him; otherwise we shall kill you all." Though all may be killed, they may not hand over a single soul of Israel. However, if the demand is for a specified individual like Sheva, son of Bikhri [who, according to 2 Samuel 20, was also subject to the death penalty], they should surrender him rather than all be killed.[22]

Even when a person is named by the enemy and condemned to capital punishment, the Rabbis were not convinced that the people within the city should hand him or her over to the enemy:

> Ulla, son of Qoseb, was wanted by the [non-Jewish] government. He arose and fled to Rabbi Joshua ben Levi at Lydda. They [troops] came, surrounded the city, and said: "If you do not hand him over to us, we will destroy the city." Rabbi Joshua ben Levi went up to him, persuaded him to submit and gave him up [to them]. Now Elijah [the prophet], of blessed memory, had been in the habit of visiting him [Rabbi Joshua], but he [now] ceased visiting him. He [Rabbi Joshua] fasted several fasts and Elijah appeared and said to him: "Shall I reveal myself to informers [betrayers]?" He [Rabbi Joshua] said: "Have I not carried out a *mishnah* [a rabbinic ruling]?" Said he [Elijah]: "Is this a ruling for the pious [*mishnat hasidim*]?" [Another version: "This should have been done through others and not by yourself."][23]

The various positions in this ruling are complex, and I discuss them elsewhere.[24] Suffice it to say here, though, that the underlying premise of the debate embedded in all the positions of this ruling is that every life has a supreme claim on us; that individual value is not a function of a person's social position, wealth, or skills; and that no life can be sacrificed even for the survival of many others, except under specific conditions—and some say not even then.

There is one other aspect of the Jewish conception of the individual that is important for our understanding of Jewish social ethics. In Jewish theology, we are not born as machines, programmed either to obey or disobey God's commandments. We are instead born with the abilities to discern what is right and wrong and good and bad, to make moral choices, and to act on them. That is, we are born with free will. That is one understanding of the image of God within us. Moreover, all of the commandments in the Torah and the rewards and punishments attached to them make logical and moral sense only if we have the freedom to obey or disobey. Thus the assumption of free will and the responsibility that goes with it run very deep in the Jewish understanding of the individual.

The Rabbis articulated this in a graphic way. We each have, according to them, two impulses: one for good and one for evil.[25] The evil impulse we inherit at birth; the good impulse we gain at age thirteen, by which time we have presumably learned the Torah's norms and become responsible for obeying them.[26] The good impulse controls the righteous, the evil impulse governs the wicked, and most of us are subject to them both.[27]

That simple description, however, does not tell the whole story. Even though the Rabbis used the terminology "*yetzer hara*" (literally: the evil impulse), it is clear from several rabbinic sources that the evil impulse is not wholly so. Thus the Rabbis noted that in the Creation story in Genesis 1, God declares each day's creation "good"; but the sixth day's work, in which Adam was created, is "very good." Why so? Because animals have no moral sense and hence no evil impulse,[28] but human beings have both. But then, it is asked, is the evil impulse good—indeed, very good? Yes, is the answer, for "were it not for that impulse, a man would not build a house, marry a wife, beget children, or conduct business affairs."[29] Similarly, the Rabbis said, "Come let us ascribe merit to our ancestors; for if they had not sinned, we should not have come into the world."[30] Clearly, "sinned" here cannot be taken literally, for it is not a sin but rather a very good thing for married couples to fulfill the commandment to procreate. Thus the Talmud there must mean that during sexual intercourse couples are under the influence of the evil impulse.

The evil impulse, then, simply refers to natural—and especially sexual—instincts, which are not evil in themselves but which, when unguided by the laws of the Torah, can lead people to sin. Hence the Rabbis could understandably say that the Torah's commandment to "Love the Lord your God with all your heart"[31]—where the word for "heart" is spelled unusually with two Hebrew letter *bet*s rather than with just one—refers to loving God "with both impulses—the good and the evil."[32] That is, we should serve God with both our natural instincts and with our moral consciousness.

The trick, then, is not to root out our sexual and other desires altogether but rather to channel them to good purpose, as defined by the Torah. The Rabbis harbored no illusions that this is easy; indeed, rabbinic literature abounds in descriptions of how difficult it is to live a moral life.[33] They also prescribed a variety of methods for overcoming temptation when it occurs, including, but not limited to, engaging in study of the Torah, God's "antidote" to the evil impulse.[34] Moreover, when someone does something wrong, the Jewish tradition prescribes a specific path of *teshuvah* (literally: return) to the proper moral path and to the good graces of God and those he or she has wronged.[35] Thus, in the end, the moral life, with its choices, its responsibilities, its missteps, and its modes of repair, is an integral part of what it means to be human.

The factors that I discussed concerning the Jewish concept of the individual have a direct impact on issues in social ethics. If we are inherently worthwhile as unique creations of God in the divine image, then we must respect ourselves and each other, regardless of our age, gender, race, creed, or abilities. That does not mean that we must or should tolerate any behavior whatsoever; on the contrary, we may, and should, establish and enforce laws to ensure that proper behavior is clearly defined and practiced. Moreover, on the moral plane, we can distinguish the right from the wrong and the good from the bad, and we have both the ability and the duty to act on that knowledge. When someone acts immorally or illegally, an inherent respect must underlie our corrective treatment of such a person. Conversely, we must seek the welfare of others as part of our respect for the divine image within them. These aspects of the Jewish concept of the individual, then, establish a strong ideological and motivational foundation for social action.

The Christian Concept

In Christian theology, each of us is born with Original Sin. We cannot escape the effect of Original Sin or any of the sins we commit through deeds; only faith can bring salvation. The required faith is in Jesus as Savior and Redeemer. The various denominations of Christianity define that belief in different degrees of specificity, and they differ on some aspects of that belief, for example, in whether Mary has a role in salvation, too. Christian faith for most denominations, however, involves affirming some tenets of belief, as articulated in each denomination's creed. Even if born and raised in a Christian family, people can remain Christians only if they continue to affirm belief in the salvational power of Jesus as defined by their particular church's creed.

What Jesus saves human beings from is sin and its wages, damnation. Beginning with Paul in the New Testament,[36] many Christian authors have seen the body as a primary source of sin. The body's drives can be overcome only by devoting ourselves to the spirit. Ideally, we should do that as much as possible, and hence the long history of Christian asceticism and chastity. If we cannot suppress the body's lusts to that extent, then we should at least contain them as much as possible. In regard to sex, "it is better to be married than to burn with passion."[37] Marriage, though, is a compromise, for it is better to remain single so that we can devote ourselves totally to God. One price of engaging in the marital compromise is that divorce is not allowed, and another, developed by the later Church, is that nothing may be used to impede marriage's redeeming quality of producing the next generation.[38] (Protestant churches have modified both of these stands.)

Even with its strong emphasis on faith, Christianity, as Christian theologian Durwood Foster once told me, does not amount to "cheap salvation," by which all that is required of Christians is repeated declarations of Christian beliefs. Rather, believers are expected to act in accordance with their beliefs. Exactly what Christians are supposed to do in response to their faith, though, is not spelled out in detail in most Christian denominations, not nearly as much as it is in Judaism. Still, patterns of action, including social activism, have a role in most forms of Christianity.

In "The Nature of the Community," later in this chapter, I explore what this means for Christian communal organizations. But here, where I am looking at the individual, note that individual Christians are expected to model themselves after Jesus, acting charitably toward others. Ultimately, though, a Christian's salvation does not depend on that, nor can a Christian earn God's grace through charitable acts alone. Thus the individual's involvement in social betterment is, within Christianity, an individual response to his or her faith, and it is to be prized as such. It is not, however, a commanded act or even one that ultimately figures in the central Christian concept of salvation, according to which only faith in Jesus can avail.

The American Secular Concept

The American secular ideology, with deep roots in the Enlightenment, sees us, first, as isolated individuals endowed by our Creator (whether that be God or Nature[39]) with "certain unalienable Rights, and among these are Life, Liberty, and the pursuit of Happiness." We may choose to give up some of those rights to gain the benefits of communities and governments, but the ultimate truth is that we are individuals with rights first and citizens with duties second.

Thus, when it comes to the individual's role in social ethics, American ideology is sparse. Any of us may *choose* to help others; that might, in fact, be part of our own pursuit of happiness if we happen to enjoy the good that we do. We do not, though, have any *duty* to help others, except to the extent that we have voluntarily entered into agreements to do so. Such agreements might include formally consecrated ones like marriage or informal ones like friendships. Then our duties derive from the nature of the relationship and/or the specific agreements we have made with each other. Otherwise, though, we need only look out for our own "Life, Liberty, and . . . pursuit of Happiness."

Some recent American thinkers, called "communitarians," have challenged the Enlightenment view. They point out, among other things, that some of our duties, like family obligations, are not of our own choosing. We may choose our mate and the number of children we have, but we do not choose our parents or siblings, and we nevertheless have significant obligations toward them. Similarly, just by living among one another in a given neighborhood and in a particular state and nation we are part of a community to which we owe at least some things. Some of those expectations are articulated in law; others come from the sheer proximity of our living arrangements. Certainly American domestic policy, at least since the New Deal, has provided a partial safety net for the most needy. Have we done this because we do not want beggars on the streets to bother us? Or is our motive less pragmatic and more moral—for example, because it is not right for the richest country in the world to ignore or abandon its destitute?

It is particularly among communitarians that we nowadays hear not only about individual *rights* but also about *entitlements* that the government is obliged to give us as members of the national community. Entitlements include direct government action to provide such things as a decent education and health care as well as government regulation of private individuals or companies to protect our air and water from pollution and, through gun-control legislation, to safeguard life itself.

However one comes out in the debate between American libertarians and communitarians, American pragmatism has another important role to play in this discussion. In marked contrast to the Jewish position, which sees all individuals as possessing divine worth regardless of their level of capacity or incapacity, the American way of thinking is thoroughly pragmatic: A person's value is a function of what that person can *do* for himself or herself and others. Self-sufficiency thus becomes a major goal, and power is prized. It is this view, so deeply ingrained in American culture, that prompts Americans to value individuals who have unusual abilities, who *succeed*— and, conversely, to devalue those who are disabled in some way, even questioning whether someone with severe disabilities should continue to live when his or her condition becomes burdensome and expensive. Particularly in end-of-life care, such utilitarian criteria for judging the value of a given person's life are often embedded in "quality-of-life" discussions in America, not only when insurers or others are making the judgment but even when the disabled person is doing so for his or her own health care. Life becomes "futile," on such utilitarian criteria, when the person loses specific capacities.

These three ideologies, then, depict the individual in vastly different ways. The Jewish conception, with its assertion of the mission to improve life and one's ability to act with God in carrying it out, directly and strongly promotes social action. The Christian view, with its emphasis on imparting faith in Christ to individuals so that they can merit a life to come, only indirectly fosters social action, largely as imitating the model of Jesus. The American secular tradition, with its own individualistic vision of people with rights, treats social action either as a pragmatic step to accomplish one's own ends or as a duty that stems from one's previous relationships or promises. Although adherents of all three ideologies have made important contributions to improving human life, Judaism provides a much stronger ideological foundation for such efforts.

The Nature of the Community

The three ideologies that I am considering have radically different understandings of community. I discuss Christianity first because its view is least likely to be assimilated by American Jews. Then I compare the Jewish and secular American views of community, showing exactly why American Jews have such trouble balancing and integrating these disparate views. Finally, in each of the two parts of this section, I note the effects of these conceptions of community on the social ethics of those who adhere to one of these particular ideologies.

Christianity

The individual is very much the focus of Christianity. It is, after all, the individual who is saved or damned, just as it was an individual, Jesus, who died on the Cross. Missionary activities are, therefore, directed at converting not only the leaders of nations but each and every person.

What, then, happens to the community in Christian thought and action? The earliest Christian community was tight-knit:

> The faithful all lived together and owned everything in common; they sold their goods and possessions and apportioned the proceeds among themselves according to what each one needed. They went as a body to the Temple every day but met in their houses for the breaking of bread; they shared their food gladly and generously; they praised God and were looked up to by everyone. Day by day the Lord added to their community those destined to be saved.[40]

Similar Christian communities exist to this day in monasteries and in the various orders of Catholic clergy. The vast majority of Christians, though, experience Christian community through what goes on at their churches. Some churches succeed in creating a strong sense of camaraderie among their members through a broad range of religious, educational, social, charitable, and recreational activities.

Ultimately, though, the community in the Christian conception is only an administrative entity, designed to organize the faithful so that Christian worship, education, and social action can go on. These are clearly very important functions, but they do not impart to the community any theological status. Ultimately for Christianity, it is the individual who is saved or damned, not communities.

Even so, some Christian communities have a proud record of achievement in social thought and ethics. One cannot help but be stimulated by the thoughtful pastoral letters issued by the American Catholic bishops on social issues, even if one disagrees with their approach or conclusions, and some Protestant groups have produced similar documents. Moreover, Catholic Social Services and Catholic hospitals provide a wide range of social and medical services to the community, and the same can be said for agencies created and run by many Protestant denominations. Many Christian denominations also sponsor programs to aid the poor. In many cases, especially in developing countries, these efforts are intertwined with missionary programs; but whatever the motive, these undertakings must be appreciated for the social good that they do.

It is the exception to the rule, though, for these efforts to be linked theologically to the purposes of Christianity. One such exception is the "social gospel" groups at the end of the nineteenth century and the beginning of the twentieth.[41] Another is Catholic liberation theology, especially as developed in Latin America.[42] Protestant and Catholic leaders' negative reaction to these efforts as being unduly political and theologically misguided stems from the fundamental Christian doctrine that salvation comes from faith, not deeds. Nevertheless, Jesus' own acts of charity have served as a model and inspiration for significant Christian social thinking and service.

Judaism and Secular America

We hold these truths to be self-evident, that all men are created equal, that they are endowed by their Creator with certain unalienable Rights, that among these are Life, Liberty, and the pursuit of Happiness.—That to secure these rights, Governments are instituted among Men, deriving their just powers from the consent of the governed.[43]

See, this day I set before you blessing and curse: blessing, if you obey the commandments of the Lord your God that I enjoin upon you this day; and curse, if you do not obey the commandments of the Lord your God.[44]

Jews in the United States are the product of both the American and the Jewish culture, each with a radically different understanding of community. Am I, as the Declaration of Independence proclaims, a creature born with inalienable rights within a community that exists only at the pleasure of those who give up some of their rights? Or am I, as Deuteronomy would have it, a person born into a host of obligations that are as "unalienable" as the Declaration's rights? The two are not mutually contradictory, but they certainly present two very different ways of thinking of oneself and of one's community.

The clashes between Judaism and American democratic theory appear in several forms. The first, as I have been suggesting, concerns the assumptions that I as a human being and a citizen make about myself and others. If rights are the primary reality of my being, the burden of proof rests on anyone who wants to deprive me of those rights or restrict them. Because other people are born with the same rights, there are times when my rights are legitimately restricted, and there are even times when I have a positive duty to others. In each case, however, the duty arises out of a consideration of the other person's rights.

If, on the other hand, the prime fact of my being is that I have obligations, as it is in Judaism, then the burden of proof rests on me to demonstrate that I have a right against another person as a result of his or her duties to me. My rights exist only to the extent that others have obligations to me, not as an innate characteristic of my being.

The source and purpose of my obligations also divide Judaism from American democracy. It is "We, the people" who create the Constitution of the United States; the government must be "*of* the people" and "*by* the people," according to President Abraham Lincoln's Gettysburg Address, not just "*for* the people."[45] The reason is the underlying assumption articulated in the passage from the Declaration of Independence quoted at the start of this section: "To secure these rights, Governments are instituted among Men, deriving their just powers from the consent of the governed." Rules are instituted to secure rights; American individualism can be set aside only by American pragmatism, in this case the practical need to ensure that all can enjoy what is theirs by right. The source of authority of the law is the consent of the governed, who presumably see the practical need for imposing a law that restricts freedom.

For Judaism, on the other hand, the author of the commandments is God, not the governed. The Bible delineates several reasons to obey God's laws: to avoid divine punishment and/or to receive divine reward; to fulfill the promises of our ancestors to abide by the covenant, promises to which we, too, are subject; to have a special relationship with God, thereby becoming a holy people; and, as the opening passage of this section from Deuteronomy declares, to express our love for God.[46] None of these aims, however, is to secure rights. Judaism and American democracy differ completely, then, in the initial assumptions of the legal system (rights vs. obligations), the source of the law (the people vs. God), and the goals of the law (securing rights vs. participating in the covenantal relationship with God).

Moreover, the way in which a person views the world in the two systems of thought is different. In the one, I owe God; in the other, the world, or at least the government, owes me. In Judaism, I begin with the assumption that things can be expected of me; in the American system, I begin with the assumption that I have an unalienable right to life, liberty, and the pursuit of happiness, which the government has been established to secure. In his 1961 inaugural address, President John F. Kennedy said, "Ask not what your country can do for you; ask what you can do for your country"; but those lines are memorable precisely because they are so surprising in an American context.

All of these differences between Jewish and American ideology derive at least in part from disparate, basic assumptions about the relationship of the individual to the group. With the possible exception of some right-wing Orthodox groups, all modern Jews see the world through Enlightenment glasses in which the individual is the fundamental reality. All individuals are independent agents who may or may not choose to associate themselves with others for specific purposes. Religious congregations of all faiths in the United States, for example, are voluntary associations to which individuals belong and from which they may dissociate themselves at any time. That is one manifestation of the enduring individuality of existence in the American system of thought; for even when people join groups, they do not lose their primary identity and privileges as individuals. That is why the rights of seventeenth-century philosopher John Locke and Declaration of Independence author Thomas Jefferson are "unalienable" by any government. Another corollary of this view is that the actions of another member of any group to which I belong are none of my business, unless all members of the group have specifically undertaken duties to care for each other in some way or unless another person's actions have a direct effect on me.

This perspective stands in stark contrast to the traditional Jewish view, shared with most Western pre-Enlightenment theories, in which the individual is defined by his or her membership in the group.[47] This membership is not voluntary and cannot be terminated at will; it is a metaphysical fact over which those born Jewish have no control. God speaks to the entire People Israel at Sinai; it is the people as a whole with whom God makes the covenant and it is the people as a whole who will be punished or rewarded according to their adherence to that covenant. It is the community's leaders who know the covenant and who thus bear the responsibility and have the right to interpret and apply God's word in each generation; and it is the People Israel who will ultimately be redeemed in messianic times. Thus, contrary to the concept of the group in Christianity or American secular thought, in Jewish thought the community has not only practical but also theological status.

These tenets have important implications in practice. For example, because membership in the People Israel is not voluntary for those born Jewish, Jews who convert to another religion lose their *privileges* as Jews—for example, they may not be married or buried as Jews and they do not count as part of a prayer quorum (minyan)—but even as apostates (*meshumadim*) they retain all the *responsibilities* of Jews! The same is true for converts to Judaism: They clearly choose to convert, but once they have completed the conversion process, from the perspective of Judaism they become an organic part of the People Israel and cannot leave the Jewish fold any more than can one born Jewish. Moreover, this indissoluble linkage between the individual and the group means that each individual is responsible for every other[48] without any specific assumption of that duty by the individual Jew and even against his or her will. Furthermore, virtually everything that one does is, in Judaism's view, everyone else's business. As the Talmud puts it:

> Whoever is able to protest against the wrongdoings of his family and fails to do so is punished for the family's wrongdoings. Whoever is able to protest against the wrongdoings of his fellow citizens and does not do so is punished for the wrongdoings of the people of his city. Whoever is able to protest against the wrongdoings of the world and does not do so is punished for the wrongdoings of the world.[49]

At the same time, the communal view of traditional Judaism does not swallow up the individual's identity; it actually enhances it by linking it to the larger reality of the group. Law professor and legal philosopher Milton Konvitz has expressed the resulting viewpoint well:

> The traditional Jew is no detached, rugged individual. Nor is his reality, his essence, completely absorbed in some monstrous collectivity which alone can claim rights and significance. He *is* an individual but one whose essence is determined by the fact that he is a brother, a *fellow Jew*. His prayers are, therefore, communal and not private, integrative and not isolative, holistic and not separative. . . . This consciousness does not reduce but rather enhances and accentuates the dignity and power of the individual. Although an inte-

gral part of an organic whole, from which he cannot be separated, except at the cost of his moral and spiritual life, let each man say, with Hillel, "If I am here, then everyone is here."[50]

The principal philosophical and legal differences between American democracy and Judaism are thus viewing one's fundamental identity as an independent individual against being an organic part of a group, the idea of voluntary association and disassociation with any group vs. integral membership within an organic community with no possibility of leaving, and the resultant status of one's duty to care for others in the group. These differences make it difficult for American Jews to integrate the two parts of their identity. As I discuss in the chapters that follow, the tensions American Jews feel often manifest themselves in many issues in social ethics, with American ideology pulling in one direction and Judaism pulling in another. This opposition, though, should not be exaggerated. In a number of ways, American Jews' Jewish and American identities converge and reinforce each other. These factors explain the high degree of comfort Jews feel in America.

On a practical level, Jews have fared much better politically and economically under American democracy than they have under the stratified societies of the Middle Ages and under most of the dictatorships of past or present. Jews in America have been legally protected from infringement in the free exercise of their religion, and they have enjoyed unprecedented political, cultural, and economic opportunities. The open, pluralistic view of community inherent in American ideology, while markedly different from most other societies' view of community and, indeed, from Judaism's own view, has provided a welcoming and nurturing context for Jews. Assimilation and intermarriage are real contemporary concerns for American Jews, but they are further proof of America's sincerity in creating an open society free from religious discrimination.

Theoretical affinities also link the Jewish and American visions of community. Although Judaism places strong emphasis on the solidarity of the community, it has gone a long way to protect individuals and minorities. Rabbinic Judaism respects the rights of non-Jews to live as such, as long as they obey the seven laws given, according to tradition, to the descendants of Noah.[51] In many passages, the Bible boldly proclaims equality in law between Jew and alien; for instance, "There shall be one law for you and for the resident stranger; it shall be a law for all time throughout the ages. You and the stranger shall be alike before the Lord; the same ritual and the same rule shall apply to you and to the stranger who resides among you."[52] Although the attitude of Jews toward non-Jews varied according to the specific conditions of their interaction, and although there were exceptions to the general principle of equal treatment, the Rabbis applied the principle not only to the ritual context in which it appears most often in the Bible but to broad areas of civil legislation as well.[53] Furthermore, Judaism does not missionize, except by example.[54] It even reserves a place for righteous gentiles in the World to Come.[55] In all these ways, Jewish law and theology protect the rights of individuals and minorities and parallel in many ways the protections offered by American law and ideology.

Jewish law also protects the rights of individual Jews and of minorities within the Jewish community. As I will discuss in some detail in Chapter Six, treatment of the poor in Jewish law and in actual practice has historically been truly remarkable in its level of service and humanity, and that continues to our own day.[56] Jews are enjoined from tormenting the handicapped by, for example, insulting the deaf or placing a stumbling block in front of the blind, and, with the exception of a few functions that specific handicaps make it impossible to perform, the handicapped are treated in Jewish law like everyone else.[57]

In addition to protecting individuals and minorities from physical abuse or abandonment, Jewish law, like American law, safeguards an individual's right to express his or her own opinion, however unpopular. Although Judaism does not recognize the right of Jews to adopt another religion, it does preserve the other First Amendment rights—and, for that matter, many of the privileges embodied in the other sections of the Bill of Rights.[58] These rights are not just theoretical; they are broadly used. Thus people who read the Talmud from the perspective of other cultures are often amazed at the high degree of tolerance in the Jewish tradition for questioning and disagreement. Ultimately, a rule of law must be established, but individuals are free to question it and argue against it, and all "are the words of the living God."[59]

These similarities between the ideologies of Judaism and the United States are rooted in a broader doctrine that they share, specifically, that we are human beings first and citizens second. The Declaration of Independence refers to "all men" and the Bill of Rights applies to all "people," not just to citizens. Similarly, in the Bible, God creates the progenitors of all human beings in the divine image long before establishing a special relationship with the Jewish People through the covenant. Both traditions are thereby asserting the inherent dignity of all human beings independent of membership in a nation. Their shared, moral affirmation is that people are not merely means for some social or theological goal; they are ends and are to be treated as such.[60] It is no accident, then, that both traditions seek to protect individuals and minorities, and both cherish and vigorously exercise individual freedoms.

Another, important manifestation of the sanctity of the individual over the group in both ideologies is the overpowering emphasis that they both put on the rule of law. Kings, presidents, military leaders, and even individual judges do not determine the rules; there is a law by which even they must abide.[61] Thus in a poignant passage the Torah requires the king to own a copy of the Torah, to keep it nearby, and to "read it all his life. . . . Thus he will not act haughtily toward his fellows or deviate from the Instruction to the right or to the left."[62] Similarly, to ensure that judges are not lured into thinking that they are the source of the law, they are advised by the Mishnah not to judge cases on their own. As Rabbi Ishmael, son of Rabbi Yose, said, "Do not judge by yourself, for there is only One who [appropriately] judges by Himself."[63]

Insistence that the law must govern has engendered great effort in both systems to extend it to cover every contingency.

Jewish law became, as the Talmud put it, a veritable sea, and American law is now even more extensive. The United States may well be the only nation in the world that has centered its civilization around law as much as the Jews have.[64]

There are even some similarities in the sources of the law. As indicated earlier, one major distinction between American democracy and Judaism is that American documents assert that the source of the law is the will of the people, and its ultimate claim to authority is the consent of the governed. In contrast, Jewish sources declare both the origin of the law and its claim to authority to be the will of God. Although that difference is real, one should not exaggerate it. After all, according to the Declaration of Independence governments are instituted among men to secure rights given them by their Creator. Government in this theory is thus not only a pragmatic mechanism to take care of the practical needs of the society but also an instrument to accomplish divine purpose. Conversely, while classical Judaism understands God to be the author of the law, the judges of each generation have both the right and the obligation to interpret and apply it—even to the extent of revising it outright. Over the centuries, these judges have been guided significantly, and sometimes openly, by the needs and customs of the people.[65] Thus American law cannot be reduced to populism, and Jewish law cannot be reduced to divine authoritarianism. Both traditions involve both elements—albeit in significantly different degrees and forms.

Thus the Jewish and American understandings of the nature of community and of the status of the individual within the community have some important similarities. In the minds of many American Jews, these mask the significant differences between the two concepts. Indeed, many American Jews *want* to believe that their Jewish self and their American self fit neatly together, like hand in glove, with no contradictions or even tensions. As we have seen, though, American ideology depicts the community in a "thin" sense, by which membership is completely voluntary and may be revoked by the individual at any time and by which the purpose of the community is predominantly pragmatic. In contrast, Judaism's sense of community is "thick," which means that its members are organically part of the communal corpus and cannot sever themselves from it and that the purpose of the community, while partially pragmatic, is essentially theological, to be "a kingdom of priests and a holy nation."[66]

The Goals of Human Existence

In classical Christianity, the ultimate goal of human existence is to be saved from sin through belief in Jesus Christ. Those saved inherit eternal bliss in a life after death, whereas all others are damned to hell. Thirteenth-century Italian poet Dante, in his *Paradisio* and *Inferno,* graphically depicted the medieval Christian understanding of what awaits us after death as God's response to our faith in Jesus or our lack thereof.

His description of the Christian vision must be modified to some extent by recent developments in Christian theology. The Second Vatican document, *Nostra Aetate,* represented a completely new understanding of the status of non-Christians in Catholic practice and eschatology, and the Catholic Church has subsequently created other documents that expand on that base. Salvation may be best achieved through Jesus, but not exclusively so. Pope John Paul II's outreach to the Jewish community has been especially impressive. Some Protestant denominations have followed suit. The Evangelical Lutheran Church in America has even taken the remarkable step of officially repudiating the anti-Semitic statements of its founder, Luther—although the Missouri and Wisconsin synods of the Lutheran Church have yet to do likewise. With all this progress in interfaith relations, though, the Christian vision of the goal of human existence remains the same: namely, salvation in a life after death.

Because American ideology is avowedly secular, its vision of the goals of human existence are, not surprisingly, this-worldly. The ideal end time is one in which each individual's rights to life, liberty, and the pursuit of happiness are secured and the general welfare is achieved. This vision, embedded in the Declaration of Independence and the U.S. Constitution, presumes a voluntaristic, pluralistic society joined together for common purpose. Later American documents articulate another element of this American ideal—namely, technological development. The conquest of the West (which was itself understood as America's "manifest destiny") built into American self-understanding the drive to conquer other frontiers—in space, technology, medicine, and in all other areas in which human effort can improve life. Underlying this is a supreme self-confidence and an almost cocky optimism. American individualism, then, is joined to American pragmatism to form the American ideal of a world that we can shape to our desires, if we only try.

The Jewish tradition combines some of the other-worldliness of Christianity with the this-worldliness of American ideology. American Jews often prefer to ignore the other-worldly elements in the Jewish vision of the future to conform more closely with American this-worldliness. The Jewish tradition, though, was shaped by the Pharisees, the people the later tradition called "the Rabbis," who definitely envisioned not only the end of human history but also a life after death.[67]

Why did the Pharisees believe in a life after death? Largely because they were deeply bothered by the injustice of the world, in that the righteous suffer and the evil prosper (*tzaddik vera lo, rasha vetov lo*; literally, "the righteous person has it bad, the wicked person has it good").[68] The poverty of many of the Pharisees made this issue impossible for them to ignore, for they saw instances of this every day. At the same time, they believed in a just God. To square the injustice of people's desserts in this life with God's justice, they posited a life after death in which people's accounts would be rectified:

> Rabbi Joseph, the son of Rabbi Joshua ben Levi, was ill and fell into a coma. When he recovered, his father asked him, "What did you see?" He replied, "I beheld a world the reverse of this one; those who are on top here were below there, and *vice versa*." He said to him, "My son, you have seen a corrected world. But what is the position of us students of the Torah there?" He answered, "We are

the same as here. I heard it stated, 'Happy is he who comes here possessed of learning'; I further heard it said that martyrs occupy an eminence that nobody else can attain."[69]

Human beings best qualify themselves for the world to come through a combination of studying Torah and good deeds:

He who has acquired for himself words of Torah has acquired for himself life in the world to come.[70]

At the time of a person's death, neither silver, nor gold, nor precious stones, nor pearls will accompany him, but only his [learning of] Torah and [his record of] good deeds, as it is written, "When you walk, it [the Torah] will lead you"—in the world, "when you lie down, it will watch over you"—in the grave, "when you awake it will talk with you"—in the world-to-come.[71]

Thus even the belief in the world to come is, in Judaism, a motivator to study Torah and to perform good deeds in this world. Very much contrary to Christianity, salvation is not only or even primarily through faith; it is rather through one's study of God's will and the efforts to fulfill it in action. In this way the other-worldly and the this-worldly tendencies in Judaism complement each other.

Human worth, then, stems not only from God's creation of us as unique human beings fashioned in the divine image but also from the mission that God has assigned to us. Our purpose in life is to glorify our Creator by following the rules of the Torah:

All creatures that are formed from heaven [for example, angels], both their soul and their body are from heaven; and all creatures that are formed from earth [for example, animals], both their soul and their body are from earth, with the exception of man, whose soul is from heaven and whose body is from earth. Therefore, if a man obeys the Torah and does the will of his Father in heaven, he is like the creatures above, as it is written, "I had taken you for divine beings, children of the Most High, all of you." But if he does not obey the Torah and does not perform the will of his Father in heaven, he is like the creatures below, as it says [in the next verse], "but you shall die as men do."[72]

Rabbi Yohanan ben Zakkai said: If you have learned much Torah, do not take credit for yourself, for you were created for that purpose.[73]

The Rabbis articulate their conception of the human mission to improve the world in several ways. The Jewish tradition does not justify the commandment for every Jewish male to be circumcised in medical terms; instead, the Torah sees it as the sign of the covenant between God and Abraham and his descendants. The Rabbis add to the meaning of circumcision, though, maintaining that Jewish boys were not born circumcised specifically because God created the world such that it would need human fixing.[74] Thus circumcision is also a symbol of the role that God has assigned to human beings to fix the world. Similarly, although God causes illness and brings healing, we must not leave the healing process totally to God; on the contrary, "just as if one does not weed, fertilize, and plow, trees will not produce fruit . . . so with regard to the body: drugs and medicaments are the fertilizer, and the physician is the tiller of the soil."[75] Ultimately, in the rabbinic phrase, human beings are God's "partners" in the ongoing divine effort to improve this world and to bring justice to it,[76] a role that gives us honor but also responsibility. With this conception of the individual, Jews' heavy involvement in social action makes sense.

Despite the secularism of American ideology, these tenets of Judaism concerning ultimate human purpose link American Jews' Jewish identity to their American identity in additional, important ways. American individualism has always been accompanied by American idealism and pragmatism, and those elements are at the heart of Judaism as well.

American idealism appears in the very first documents of the nation. It is clearly not "self-evident" that all men are created equal; it is, in fact, patently false. Similarly, it is not the case that all human beings enjoy the "unalienable" rights of life, liberty, and the pursuit of happiness; many are ruled by despots, who can deprive them of their liberty and their very lives on a whim, and many others live under inherently miserable conditions. Jefferson knew this, but he inserted these lines in the Declaration of Independence to articulate the ideals for which this new nation would strive. The Jewish people also have such statements, descriptions of a time in which there would be neither want nor war, in which all nations would learn of God's word from Jerusalem and follow it.[77]

Although these statements in both traditions do not describe realities, they are not empty dreams either, for both ideologies are marked by a heavy dose of pragmatism. That is part of the reason for the emphasis on law in both societies; law is understood as one instrument to achieve an ideal society. As former vice-chancellor of the Jewish Theological Seminary Rabbi Simon Greenberg pointed out, the Declaration of Independence is to the Constitution very much as the *aggadah* (Jewish lore) is to the *halakhah* (Jewish law); in both cases the first element is the ideal that the second endeavors to articulate in real terms.[78]

The combination of idealism and pragmatism that characterizes and unites Judaism and Americanism is ultimately rooted in a positive attitude toward the material in life, an attitude that assumes that physical conditions can and should be improved. The Declaration of Independence itself speaks most about the colonists' specific grievances against the king, including many economic concerns. Moreover, Jefferson altered Locke's formula, making the pursuit of happiness, rather than of property, a prime goal of the American social contract. Similarly in Judaism, each person must give an account on the day of judgment of every good, permissible thing that he or she might have enjoyed but did not.[79] Jews living in difficult times sometimes despaired of the possibility of making life on this earth better and turned inward, using mysticism and even ascetic practices to cope with life and find meaning in it. The rubric of the Torah's commandments and the theological depiction of human beings as the agents and partners of God, however, have historically made most Jews active participants in the effort to improve life on earth. Thus, contrary to significant strands within Christianity and other cultures that embrace a bifurcation between body and soul and a renunciation of the body to cultivate the soul, Jewish and American ideology and practice have instead tried to infuse the physical with the ideal, seeing the physical as much as any other aspect of existence as the creation of God. This positive attitude toward the world lies at the bottom of the idealism and pragmatism that the two traditions share;[80] and those features, in turn, motivate both systems' emphasis on law.

Finally, the aggressive attitude that Americans and Jews take toward improving life is at least partly the reason that, as Cornell University professor emeritus of law Milton Konvitz notes, Americans and Jews are the only nations on earth that feel it necessary to justify their existence as nations. Other nations simply exist, but these two live in pursuit of ideals by which they and others measure them.[81] That instills in Americans and Jews alike a sense of urgency about life, a sense of challenge, and a sense of mission.

> The span of our life is seventy years,
>   or, given the strength, eighty years;
>   but the best of them are trouble and sorrow.
> They pass by speedily, and we are in darkness. . . .
> Teach us to count our days rightly,
>   that we may obtain a wise heart. . . .
> May the favor of the Lord, our God, be upon us;
>   let the work of our hands prosper,
>   O prosper the work of our hands![82]

Rabbi Tarfon taught: The day is short, the task is great, the workers indolent, the reward bountiful, and the Master pushes us on. He further used to say: You are not obliged to finish the task, but neither are you free to neglect it. If you have studied much Torah, your reward will be abundant. Your Employer can be relied upon to reward you [also] for your labors. Know, however, that the reward of the righteous is in a future time.[83]

Reprise: The Fundamental Concepts
As Articulated in the Central Stories

At the beginning of this chapter, I suggested that one fruitful way to think about the fundamental beliefs of Judaism, Christianity, and American secularism—and to remember them—is to analyze their central stories. Now that I have examined these concepts comparatively in some detail, it is helpful to return to their articulation in those stories.

Jesus dying on the Cross and undergoing divine resurrection symbolizes significant truths for Christians. Human beings, like Jesus, are ultimately individuals who are burdened with Original Sin as well as all the sins accumulated during life. Our actions cannot atone for those sins. However, God has through His mercy sent His Son to die for our sins and give us new life. The individual's ultimate purpose in life, then, is to believe in Jesus' intercession, which promises eternal life. Individuals should also missionize to spread the good news because believing in Jesus as Christ is the only way—or at least the most effective way—that people can be saved from their sins. The community should support such individual faith and missionary work. In this life, individuals should also imitate the charitable actions of Jesus in their lives.

The American story of the Revolution and the creation of the U.S. Constitution emphasizes the individual as well. Courageous individuals, honored and virtually worshiped as hero figures, overcame all odds in defeating the British and declaring their independence. They also devised a particularly wise form of government, with checks and balances, so that individuals would be given the best chance possible to enjoy their rights and to flourish. The story tells individuals to be resourceful and brave. It envisions the community as a pragmatic tool to protect individual rights and to promote the general welfare. As such, the government is ever subject to criticism and change by the people themselves. Moreover, unless they have committed a crime, individuals may leave the community at any time. Simultaneously, American ideology trusts law as the vehicle to fulfill the purposes of government. The ultimate purpose of life is for individuals to enjoy life, liberty, and the pursuit of happiness and, toward those ends, to change the world through exploration and technology—very much along the lines of Benjamin Franklin's and Jefferson's many inventions. Technological know-how, mastery over nature, and material success are big parts of the American Dream.

Finally, what is the nature of the individual, the community, and the purpose of life as described in Judaism's Exodus–Sinai story? We do not hear much about individuals; they seem to be glossed over in favor of the People Israel as a whole. We read, though, that Moses risks his life and position to save a Hebrew slave,[84] thus indicating the inherent worth of each person regardless of status. Similarly, later Jewish tradition has us dampen our joy at the Israelites' release, quoting God as saying to the angels, "My children are drowning in the sea, and you are singing songs?"[85] Since then, we diminish our cup of joy at the Seder table by extracting one drop of wine for each of the plagues that the Egyptians had to suffer. Non-Jews as well as Jews have inherent, divine worth.

Later Jewish tradition credits Nahshon ben Aminadav with taking the first steps into the sea when all the other Israelites refused to do that lest they drown.[86] Moreover, we hear of individuals who take leadership roles—Moses, Aaron, Miriam, Jethro, and later Joshua and Caleb, together with their triumphs and failures. These stories, like the American stories of the Founding Fathers, exalt people who take responsibility and model the qualities of good leadership. They also demonstrate the Jewish conviction that people have the freedom both to act responsibly and to choose a less desirable path.

The emphasis in the biblical story, though, is on God's covenantal relationship with the People Israel. We leave Egypt, we cross the sea, we stand at Sinai, and we march toward the Promised Land all as a group. Moreover, the Torah revealed at Sinai speaks to us as a community, and its punishments and rewards, therefore, are those that apply to a community—rain or drought, victory or defeat in battle, and so on.[87] God's covenant is also with the People Israel as a whole, and the goal is to make them "a kingdom of priests and a holy nation."[88] Thus later Jewish sources would have us see our own individual actions as adding to one side or the other of the scale by which God will judge the People Israel—and, indeed, the entire world—as a group.[89] In the Jewish story, then, individual identity is tightly intertwined with and defined by membership in the People Israel.

The ultimate goal is the Promised Land, described in the Torah both as "a land flowing with milk and honey" and as a holy land.[90] The Israelites, then, were to aspire to both physical and spiritual fulfillment, the goal of our own lives to this day. The prophet Isaiah later spells out this part of the story when he foretells that Jerusalem in the time to come will be both a place of physical safety and a place of moral instruction for all the world:

> In the days to come, the Mount of the Lord's House shall stand firm above the mountains and tower above the hills; and all the nations shall gaze on it with joy. And the many peoples shall go and say: "Come, let us go up to the Mount of the Lord, to the House of the God of Jacob; that He may instruct us in His ways, and that we may walk in His paths." For instruction shall come forth from Zion, the word of the Lord from Jerusalem. Thus shall He judge among the nations and arbitrate for the many peoples, and they shall beat their swords into plowshares and their spears into pruning hooks: nation shall not take up sword against nation; they shall never again know war.[91]

The mission of the Jews is nothing short of creating such a world in partnership with God, a world in which justice and peace prevail. As the *Los Angeles Times* poll cited at the beginning of this chapter demonstrates, contemporary Jews, however religious or secular in orientation, overwhelmingly remain committed to that task.

In the chapters that follow, I discuss how the Jewish tradition understands its mission in a number of specific arenas of life. As I do, I make a number of comparisons to the positions taken by Christians and secular Americans. Sometimes the perspective of two or all three of the traditions on a given issue is the same and sometimes Judaism takes its own distinctive stance. Even when there is agreement on a particular norm, the reasoning behind that norm and the motivation to promote it may differ. Often the master story of each of the three traditions plays a significant role in justifying and explaining a given norm and in motivating adherence to it. The underlying assumptions and goals that I described in this chapter and the stories that express and shape them continually reappear in one guise or another in the delineation of each tradition's specific moral norms.

CHAPTER TWO

Pluralism within the Jewish Community

T HE ESSENCE OF PLURALISM IS THAT JUST AS YOU ENJOY THE
freedom to have your own opinions and to act on them,
you must grant that liberty also to others.[1] Clearly, no
society can permit absolutely everything; but within the limits
of conformity necessary to enable a society to exist, a pluralistic community allows its members to act according to their individual conscience and desires. Indeed, those who affirm pluralism as an ideal maintain that society will flourish most if it
fosters an open marketplace of ideas and experiments, and so a
pluralistic society not only tolerates such diversity but appreciates and nourishes it, encouraging its members to think creative-
ly and independently.

Such an open-minded stance, as familiar and attractive as it
is to an American audience, entails some serious problems.
Specifically, how can I justify my own view while granting legitimacy to others? Will admitting the validity of other views
diminish what I am prepared to sacrifice for my own? Are there
any boundaries to the legitimacy I should extend to others? That
is, when, if ever, should I cease to accept what another says and
does and actively fight against it, perhaps even militarily? On
the other hand, if I am not pluralistic, how can I have anything
but hostile relations with anyone outside my own group? For

Jews, the issue exists on two levels: how they should interact with their fellow Jews who differ from them in how they understand and practice Judaism and how Jews should understand and relate to people of other faiths or of no faith.[2] I will address relations with fellow Jews in this chapter and relations with non-Jews in the next.

While the philosophical questions entailed in pluralism have been the same for millennia, recent disagreements within the Jewish community have heightened interest in both the practical and the theoretical sides of this issue. Family law problems have attracted the most attention—varying definitions of Jewish status and conversions, marriages, and divorces that some recognize and some do not, both in North America and in Israel.[3] The efforts within the Reform, Reconstructionist, and Conservative movements to expand the scope of women's participation in the synagogue and in Jewish communal life and to alleviate the disabilities that women suffer in Jewish law have been another source of public dispute among Jews. Since the 1980s, the standards for Jewish identity, the ordination of women as rabbis, mutual recognition of marriages and divorces, and the debate about homosexuality have especially tested the pluralism among the streams of Judaism and, in some cases, within the Conservative movement itself. These practical problems underscore the need for a theory of pluralism that explains how and why one could adopt a given view and yet be willing to respect as Jews those who have different views—at least within some bounds—and to continue to work together for the common good.

Rabbinic Approaches to Diversity

The Need for Unity

Why do we need to hold together in the first place? That is, why is *Kelal Yisrael*, the Jewish community as a whole, a value for the Jewish tradition and for us? The need for unity is, in part, political and social. Only a cohesive community can prevent anarchy and plan joint action to protect and enhance Jewish life.

For the Rabbis, though, the motivation is also theological. A play on words based on Deuteronomy 14:1 leads the Rabbis to the principle that Jews should not split into factions.[4] Unity thus accords with God's commandments, and it also is required for God's recognition and glory: "When Israel is of one mind below, God's great name is exalted above, as it says, 'He became King in Jeshurun when the heads of the people assembled, the tribes of Israel together' (Deuteronomy 33:5)."[5] If, on the other hand, communities are splintered, the various groups look as if they were guided by two different Torahs or even by two different gods.[6] This can undermine respect for religious institutions and, ultimately, for religion itself. Furthermore, a divided Jewish community cannot effectively accomplish its religious mission of being "a light of nations" in perfecting the world under the dominion of God.[7]

Those who hold unity as the exclusive or paramount goal sometimes seek to attain it by claiming that there is only one correct view and that all others should be shunned or even attacked. Unfortunately, there is ample precedent for this approach in Jewish history. One account of the relationships between the first-century School of Shammai and its rival School of Hillel, for example, depicts the former as ambushing and killing all but six members of the latter.[8] In the eighteenth century, eastern European Jewry was split between Hasidim and *mitnagdim* who issued bans of excommunication against each other and prohibited members of each group from engaging in communication or commerce with members of the other.

Rabbinic Endorsements of Pluralism

But that is not the only—and certainly not the predominant—Jewish model for attaining unity. In Deuteronomy 17, God commands that we abide by the decisions of the contemporary court, and that is the basis for judicial authority and communal conformity.[9] That demand, though, is effectively balanced by another commandment in that same book of the Torah that we "fear no man, for judgment is God's."[10] Traditional sources accordingly document a dynamic pluralism *within* the Jewish community. There are seventy faces to each passage in the Torah, according to the Rabbis, and Moses was not told the final decision on each matter of law "so that the Torah may be capable of interpretation with forty-nine points *pro* and forty-nine points *contra*."[11] People should listen to each other and be prepared to change their minds on legal matters, says the Mishnah, and the opinion of a dissenting judge is recorded because in a later generation the court may revise the law to agree with him.[12] Just as the manna tasted different to each person, so too, say the Rabbis, each person hears God's Revelation according to his own ability.[13] The long tradition of finding a variety of rationales for the laws and suggesting a variety of interpretations of the biblical stories is the sum and substance of the Midrash *aggadah,* and the very methodology used in Jewish law encourages debate.[14] One should, therefore, study with at least two rabbis to learn their diverse approaches to Judaism and the techniques for analyzing competing positions: "One who studies Torah from [only] one teacher will never achieve great success [literally, 'a sign of blessing']."[15]

Some of the classical Rabbis, of course, did not like diversity of opinion. In the second century, Rabbi Jose complains that it makes the Torah seem like multiple Torahs, and he attributes the lack of conformity to insufficient study and/or overweening pride on the part of contemporary scholars.[16] Ten centuries later, though, Maimonides pointed out that multiple interpretations are inevitable due to the varying temperaments and intellectual capabilities of the Torah's many interpreters.[17] Rabbi Menahem ben Solomon Meiri (1249–1316) maintained that disagreement is not only inevitable, but desirable as an integral part of establishing the truth, for without dispute people are not challenged to test and refine their own position.[18] The talmudic section most quoted on this issue, one that presents a totally different view of the disputes between the schools of Shammai and Hillel from the one cited above, understands scholarly arguments as not only rationally but also *theologically* necessary, for all sides bespeak "the words of the living God":

> Rabbi Abba stated in the name of Samuel: For three years there was a dispute between the School of Shammai and the School of Hillel, the former asserting, "The law agrees with us," and the latter contending, "The law agrees with us." Then a Heavenly Voice announced, "The utterances of both are the words of the living God, but the law agrees with the School of Hillel." Since "both are the words of the living God," what was it that entitled the School of Hillel to have the law fixed according to them? Because they were kindly and modest, they studied their own rulings and those of the School of Shammai, and they [were even so humble as to] mention the opinions of the School of Shammai before theirs.[19]

The goal is thus to educate people to be open to learning from others, similar to the School of Hillel, and to respect those with whom they disagree—so much so as to cite them first. One wants learning with manners, commitment to finding the truth together with respect for others and love of peace.[20]

If each answer is the word of God, though, why exert oneself in the process of defining one's own position? After all, does this not mean that the Rabbis were subjectivists, arguing that there was no objective truth but only individual opinions—or, at best, truths for individuals?

Clearly, the very fact that the Rabbis spend so much time and energy arguing with each other indicates that they did *not* think that anything goes. They held, on the contrary, that what one thinks, says, and does in fact makes a great difference. They argued so vehemently about the meaning of the Torah precisely because they believed that divine pronouncements and commands establish an objective basis for the true and the good. We may not think, say, or do whatever we want; we must rather do what God wants of us.

The problem, though—a problem of which they themselves were keenly aware—is the epistemological one: On any given matter, how can we *know* what the will of God is? A number of the biblical leaders simply asked God and received what were, to their minds, clear and dependable answers.[21] Already in biblical times, though, people were not sure how to distinguish a true prophet from a false one, for absolutely anyone could claim that a given position was not only his or her own opinion but was rather a message from God. This was not just a theoretical possibility; Jeremiah, in particular, complains often and bitterly of an abundance of false prophets misleading the people.[22] The Book of Deuteronomy twice tries to suggest a way to discern the difference between true and false prophets, once claiming that true prophets are known by their ability to predict what will happen (Deuteronomy 18:9–22) and the other time proclaiming that true prophets are those who simply reinforce the traditional adherence to God (Deuteronomy 13:1–6). But the latter criterion reduces prophets to good preachers, for no true prophet, by that measure, can tell us anything new. Moreover, although the biblical prophets certainly do not suggest that Jews worship other gods, a number of them do announce new rules.[23] The other criterion for true prophecy—that the prophet foretells events correctly—also fails as a test, for according to the Bible's own testimony, several of the prophets accepted as true predict things that do not come to be.[24]

This practical problem of distinguishing a true prophet from a false one, coupled with the conviction of several prophets' that God's punishment of the people for disobedience would include not only the destruction of the Temple but also the cessation of prophecy,[25] together meant that by the end of the biblical period prophecy was no longer seen as the vehicle for knowing God's will. Indeed, the prophet Zekhariah already foresees a time when "every 'prophet' will be ashamed of the 'visions' [he had] when he 'prophesied,' " and the prophet's own mother and father will say to the prophet, "You shall die, for you have lied in the name of the Lord" and they themselves "will put him to death when he 'prophesies.' "[26]

This, however, did not remove the statements of God as the objective criterion that would determine the true and the good. The way that we would know God's will, however, changed: It would now be through the interpretation and application of the Torah, the one text that all Jews accepted as true Revelation from God. Study, in other words, became the postbiblical form of God's Revelation,[27] making it a religious experience as well as an educational and legal one. It is for this reason that Jewish law obligates Jews to study the Torah throughout their lives, even if they are poor and even if such study involves them in debates with their teachers or parents, for nothing less than knowing God's will is at stake. Rabbis, who gain their authority at least in part from their expertise in the texts and traditions of Judaism, would often differ with each other in discerning the will of God, and that might be frustrating at times; but one must learn to live with that indeterminacy and open one's mind to the multiplicity of meanings inherent in both the law and lore of the Torah:

> Lest a person say, "Since some scholars declare a thing impure and others declare it pure, some pronounce it to be permitted while others declare it forbidden, some disqualify an object [as ritually fit] while others uphold its fitness, how can I study Torah under such circumstances?" Scripture states, "They are given from one shepherd" (Ecclesiastes 12:11): One God has given them, one leader [Moses] has uttered them at the command of the Lord of all creation, blessed be He, as it says, "And God spoke *all* these words" (Exodus 20:1). You, then, should make your ear like a grain receiver and acquire a heart that can understand the words of the scholars who declare a thing impure as well as those who declare it pure, the words of those who declare a thing forbidden as well as those who pronounce it permitted, and the words of those who disqualify an object [as ritually fit] as well as those who uphold its fitness. . . . Although one scholar offers his view and another scholar offers his, the words of both are all derived from what Moses, the shepherd, received from the One Lord of the universe.[28]

Rabbinic Limitations on Pluralism

The Talmud includes many fractious disputes, in which virtually anything could be questioned, but there were some limits to this general picture of uninhibited debate. When the Sanhedrin existed, rabbis could challenge decisions in debate, even vigorously, but in practice they had to conform to the Sanhedrin's majority ruling.[29] Furthermore, there were rules of propriety governing how the debates themselves should be held with colleagues and, all the more so, with teachers or parents.[30] So, for example, rabbinic sources strive to differentiate the high level of dissent to which the Rabbis were accustomed and which they thought healthy from that of the biblical figure Korah, whose rebellion the Torah condemns. Korah's dissent, the Rabbis said, was not "for the sake of Heaven" but rather for his own power and love of victory, whereas the disputes of Hillel and Shammai were for the sake of Heaven—that is, to identify God's will. Because that was the case, rabbinic disputes will continue for all time, but Korah's dispute died with him.[31] Thus disputants must argue for the right reasons while following the practice determined by the majority.

These rules were enforced, for rabbinic literature speaks of Jews whose mode of dissent led the community to exclude them. These include the *min* (sectarian) and the *apikoros* (heretic). In view of the wide latitude of rabbinic debate, one can understand why there is considerable discussion in classical and contemporary literature about exactly what these people held or did that made their modes of dissent unacceptable.[32] Rashi (1040–1105), for example, said that one feature of admissible debate is that "Neither side of the conflict cites an argument from the Torah of another god, but only from the Torah of our God."[33]

In addition to such individuals, there have been groups that splintered off from the Jewish people. These include Christians, Hebrew Christians (who existed from the first through the fifth centuries), Karaites (from the eighth century to the present), and Sabbetaians (in the late seventeenth and early eighteenth centuries). Thus, with all their commitment to pluralism, rabbis throughout the centuries have drawn some clear lines defining acceptable method and content.

Rabbinic Modes of Accommodation in Practice

How, though, were those who remained part of the Jewish people supposed to interact with those within the field with whom they disagreed?

One rabbinic source addresses the degree to which a community can tolerate diversity of practice. In interpreting the play on words based on Deuteronomy 14:1 that leads the Rabbis to the principle that Jews should not split into factions,[34] Rabbi Yohanon (third century, Israel) and Abayye (fourth century, Babylonia) proclaimed that that principle precludes multiple practices in one locale, but communities in distinct areas could follow disparate rulings in observing the law. Rava, Abayye's contemporary and sparring partner, was more permissive. For him the principle only prohibits the members of a given court from issuing conflicting rulings; they may disagree in discussion, but they ultimately have to make one, coherent decision. Two courts, however, even within the same city, could issue conflicting rulings without violating the principle. In tolerating this, Rava may have been thinking of the circumstances in large cities, where differing groups of Jews may live in close proximity to each other but practice Jewish law in distinct ways.[35]

Members of the schools of Shammai and Hillel, however, served on the same courts. How did they agree on a ruling—and even permit each others' children to marry one another? According to one talmudic opinion, since the Hillelites were in the majority, the Shammaites accepted their authority in practice while remaining opposed in theory. Pluralism, on this model, stops with thought; uniformity is necessary in action, and that must be determined by the majority of the rabbis charged with making the decision. A second talmudic solution is that God prevented any cases prohibited in one view but not in the other from occurring. The third explanation is that both parties kept each other informed of problematic cases, and thus marriages between the families associated with the two schools could continue.[36] In other words, they trusted the majority, they trusted God, or they trusted each other.[37]

Modern Approaches to Diversity

The rabbinic sources, as we have seen, tolerate a wide spectrum of opinion and even of practice within the Jewish community, but that community shared a commitment to the fundamental beliefs and practices of Judaism. For contemporary Jews, of course, that no longer is the case. Even if Jews believe in God, they rarely feel commanded to observe the dictates of Jewish law. Thus only a small percentage of the barely half who belong to synagogues observe the dietary or Sabbath laws.[38] Classical Jewish law defines a Jew as one born to a Jewish woman (or one converted to Judaism), but in 1985 the Reform movement voted to accept as Jewish the child of a non-Jewish mother but a Jewish father, provided that the child is raised as a Jew ("patrilineal descent"); thus in our time the very definition of who is a Jew is at issue.

On the other hand, the Holocaust and the State of Israel have demonstrated that, for better or worse, Jews *are* one, although not on religious grounds. Moreover, the contemporary Jewish community is clearly distinct from the various Christian and secular communities in America, and it has rejected the "Jews for Jesus" (or "Messianic Jews") as a legitimate expression of Judaism. Thus while the Jewish community cannot be defined nearly as neatly as it was before the Enlightenment, it nevertheless remains a distinct, identifiable community.

Any modern theory of pluralism, then, must take account of these new, complicating realities. Specifically, it must explain how we can justify a pluralism within the Jewish community much broader than the rabbinic sources ever contemplated while at the same time excluding those who are not accepted as Jews.

I will now review several contemporary proposals for negotiating these new realities, and then I will suggest my own theory for how and why we can and should be pluralistic in thought and in practice.

Modern Orthodox Rejectionism

Some modern refuse to engage in the effort to create a viable pluralism among Jews: They maintain that their view is the only correct one. Most of Orthodoxy has taken this tack, including even the modern Orthodox movement. Thus Rabbi Norman Lamm, president of Yeshiva University, has claimed that pluralism is not a sacred principle within Judaism. Moreover, "a pluralism which accepts everything as co-legitimate is not pluralism, but the kind of relativism that leads . . . to spiritual nihilism. If everything is kosher, nothing is kosher."[39] Similarly, Rabbi Walter Wurzburger, past editor of the modern Orthodox journal *Tradition*, said: "Religious pluralism borders on religious relativism, if not outright nihilism. It rests on the assumption that no religion can be true and that it does not really matter what kind of myth we invoke in order to provide us with a sense of meaning and purpose."[40]

Nevertheless, Orthodox spokesmen acknowledge the fact that, as the Talmud puts it, "A Jew, even if he sins, is [still] a Jew."[41] They may not recognize the conversions of non-Orthodox rabbis, but they are also not willing to cut themselves off from those born Jewish. Wurzburger states this positively and passionately:

> Ahavat Yisrael [love of fellow Jews] is a religious imperative which, according to Rabbi Akiva, constitutes the most inclusive principle of the entire Torah and must be extended to every Jew, regardless of his religious persuasion. . . . But our love for . . . fellow Jews by no means precludes our commitment to Torah as *Torat Emet* [a Torah of truth], which entails the rejection of any article of faith or practice which contravenes the teachings of the Torah.[42]

How, then, should an Orthodox Jew relate to the non-Orthodox movements? Rabbi Avi Shafran of Providence, Rhode Island, put the position of most Orthodox spokesmen succinctly: The Reform and Conservative "movements are not, to me, branches of Judaism. Jewish, perhaps, like B'nai B'rith or the Jewish War Veterans, but not Juda*ism*. That position has long been filled."[43]

Other Orthodox spokespeople create theoretical frameworks that soften the starkness of Shafran's statement but do not alter its substance. Their theories provide for cooperation and even a degree of appreciation of the other movements but deny them legitimacy as expressions of God's will.

Lamm, for example, says that the non-Orthodox movements have "functional validity" and maybe even "spiritual dignity," but not "Jewish legitimacy." Noting that the word "validity" comes from the Latin *validus*, meaning "strong," he points out that it is simply a fact that the non-Orthodox movements have both numbers and strength. Lamm further notes:

> From a *functional* point of view, therefore, non-Orthodox rabbis are *valid* leaders of Jewish religious communities, and it is both fatuous and self-defeating not to acknowledge this openly and draw the necessary consequences, e.g., of establishing friendly and harmonious and respectful relationships, and working together, all of us, towards the Jewish communal and global goals that we share and which unite us inextricably and indissolubly.[44]

Like Orthodox rabbis, non-Orthodox rabbis, according to Lamm, may or may not have *spiritual dignity*, depending on the sincerity with which they struggle to have their conduct conform to the principles of their faith. Non-Orthodox forms of Judaism and their representatives, however, cannot have Jewish *legitimacy*, for legitimacy (derived from *lex*, "law") is a normative and evaluative term, the criterion for which is

> acceptance of Halakhah [Jewish law] as transcendentally obligatory, as the holy and normative "way" for Jews, as decisive law and not just something to "consult" in the process of developing policy. . . . At bottom, any vision of the truth excludes certain competing visions. And so does the Torah commitment.[45]

Wurzburger's use of the words "validity" and "legitimacy" is apparently the exact opposite of Lamm's (different definitions of terms is an ongoing problem in these discussions), but his position is similar:

> While I cannot recognize the validity of procedures or practices which contravene *Halakhic* [Jewish legal] norms, I do not seek the delegitimization of non-Orthodox movements. On the contrary, I firmly believe that they can make significant contributions to the extent that they champion causes which reflect the values of our religious tradition.[46]

It is interesting to note that the same kind of rejectionism does not generally characterize the more liberal Jewish movements.

Reform and Conservative Jews clearly have principles that, in some measure, contradict those of the Orthodox. Nevertheless, they are not rejectionists in the sense used above because they would continue to view Orthodoxy as a valid (legitimate), although wrong, version of Judaism.

Covenant of Fate, Covenant of Destiny

A second model also comes from Orthodox spokespeople, but it differs considerably from the first. Rabbi Joseph Soloveitchik suggested in the 1950s that all Jews are bound by two covenants: a covenant of fate and a covenant of destiny (which he also called the covenant of Egypt and the covenant of Sinai).

The covenant of fate is the inescapable unity that binds Jews because of their shared fate in history. This covenant is involuntary; Jews are part of it whether they want to be or not. There are four components to this covenant: shared historical events (Jews feel that they are part of everything that happens to other Jews), shared suffering (the anguish and pain inflicted on some Jews are experienced as others' too), shared responsibility (a sense of obligation to help other Jews and a willingness to do so), and shared actions (activities with and for other Jews).

The covenant of destiny, by contrast, is voluntary. It is the act of commitment of the individual Jew and the Jews as a whole to realize Jewish values, goals, and dreams in history. There are significant differences among Jews as to how best to accomplish this, but such arguments must be carried on within the framework of all those who share the covenant of fate.

Soloveitchik devised this model to explain the ties of religious Jews to secular Zionists, but Rabbi Irving Greenberg suggests applying it to intermovement relationships as well. Note how the slippery words "legitimacy" and "validity" here take on yet another set of meanings:

> I would generalize Soloveitchik's insight: one must learn to distinguish validity and legitimacy. Legitimacy is derived from and applies to all groups that share the covenant of fate. Once having extended that legitimacy, one has every right to criticize and disagree

with the validity of actions by groups that "violate" the covenant of destiny. .... All communities, as all marriages, can exist with fights—even hard fights—as long as the fundamental legitimacy of the relationship is not challenged.[47]

Greenberg says that applying this model would rule out Jews for Jesus because by joining Christianity they have separated themselves from Jewish fate. It also suggests that the Satmar Hasidim, Neturei Karta, radical assimilationists, and anti-Zionist universalists be excluded because of their dissociation from the fate of Jews in Israel.

This analysis examines and articulates more clearly than the rejectionist view the reasons why all Jews feel strong connections to each other and why they should have empathy for other views while also explaining how various groups of Jews can think the others wrong. We not only should feel responsibility for each other (the covenant of fate) but should genuinely appreciate the many ways in which Jews devote themselves to realizing the covenant of destiny.

A Pedagogic Covenant

Rabbi Irving Greenberg suggests another way of justifying pluralism. In the Bible, he points out, God is the dominant partner in the creation and definition of the covenant. Rabbinic literature elevates human beings to a role equal to that of God in determining the law. No voice from heaven can do that; only the deliberation of the rabbis.[48] Their decisions, however, must be tied to God's Revelation in the Written or Oral Torah, and so both God and human beings have a role. In our own time, Greenberg argues, after the Holocaust and the State of Israel, the dominant role has shifted to humanity. The Holocaust has made us question God's willingness (or ability) to intervene in our lives, and the State of Israel has demonstrated that we must take responsibility for ourselves as a people. It is as if God, the ultimate parent, has now given us free rein to make our own decisions, however much we stumble. "To enable people to mature, the teacher/parent/authority must allow them experimentation, even differing judgments, and even the right to err."[49]

In Soloveitchik's model one effectively says of others who differ, "You are wrong, but you are part of my people;" in this model, one says, "We both may be right."[50] The extra bonus in this approach, then, is the positive emotional atmosphere it creates: We share not only mutual responsibility but also a mutual effort to articulate God's will in our time.

Embracing Diversity

As the Orthodox tend to have a low tolerance for diversity, liberals have a high tolerance for it. This is clearly a matter of degree: Everyone wants *some* unity and *some* diversity. Moreover, philosophical commitments, as well as psychological temper, determine where one fits on this spectrum.

Reconstructionist Rabbi Jacob Staub, for example, denies the centrality of Jewish law in linking the Jewish people historically: "I do *not* regard commitment to the halakhic system to be the tie that has always united all Jews. The surviving halakhic sources represent, I believe, the views of a very small minority of the rabbinic elite." Certainly in our post-emancipation world, when "Jews have been freed from halakhic authorities," we should expect and rejoice at the multiple approaches to Jewish life that have emerged. "I believe that Jews have always been, and will continue to be, divided—that *davka* [indeed] it is because of the passion that motivates our diversity that we are likely to survive with vibrancy."[51]

Aside from the obvious need to coordinate efforts on some matters, this view has at least one other disadvantage, one that Staub himself notes. Jews working to implement conflicting views of what modern Jewish life should be cannot help but affront each other: "[B]y our very existence, some Jews are offensive and insulting to others—on all sides." He speaks personally about the disappointment and pain his Orthodox relatives feel about his beliefs and practices, and vice versa. Therefore, he says that we must "apply ourselves to recognizing, acknowledging, and bemoaning the inadvertent pain we cause to those whom we love so dearly—even as we remain steadfastly committed to the principles we cherish."[52]

Identifying Shared Convictions

Some theorists justify pluralism by pointing out how many convictions Jews share; diversity in the areas that remain is then perceived not as deleterious but as enriching and enlivening.

Rabbi David Hartman, for example, says that religious and nonreligious Jews share the goals of developing character and rejecting idolatry in all its forms, even if they do not agree on appropriate methods or reasons for doing so. They can thus share both behavioral goals and a common theological language.[53] Rabbi Reuven Kimelman claims that all Jews search for retaining Jewish authenticity within contemporary civilization; they seek a share in holiness through living as part of the Jewish community; they know that separation from the Jewish community is detachment from the covenant with the God of Israel; and they participate in discovering the grandeur of the Jewish tradition and the cultural heroes who emerge from it.[54] Rabbi Eugene Lipman stresses that Jews share a mission, that our purpose is not simply Jewish survival but the creation of God's kingdom on earth.[55]

Those who take this tack often maintain that to the extent that varying positions do exist, they complement each other— a point that, of course, is available to the other theories as well. Thus Rabbi Abraham Kook, former chief rabbi of Israel, appreciates differing views for revealing different aspects of the truth: "For the building is constructed from various parts, and the truth of the light of the world will be built from various dimensions, from various approaches, for 'these and those are the words of the living God.' "[56]

Kimelman points out that, if synagogue options are reduced, affiliation rates are likely to fall even below 50 percent, which is where they now stand. Moreover, Reform Jews were the first to establish a synagogue movement and synagogue-centered youth groups, Conservative Jews pioneered religiously centered camping and teenage pilgrimages to Israel, and the Orthodox sponsored day schools before the other movements did. The movements, though, have learned from each other, and so these institutions now exist in all three movements to the benefit of all.[57]

God Wants Pluralism

Rabbi Simon Greenberg suggests a theological justification for pluralism. He defines pluralism as "the ability to say that 'your ideas are spiritually and ethically as valid—that is, as capable of being justified, supported, and defended—as mine' and yet remain firmly committed to your own ideas and practices."[58] Notice his definition of "valid"; it is not a term of power, as it is for Lamm, or conformity to a covenant, as it is for Irving Greenberg, but rather one designating intellectual credibility and worthiness. Moreover, in contrast to both Lamm and Irving Greenberg, Simon Greenberg uses "legitimacy" as a synonym for "validity."[59]

But what bestows legitimacy on different views such that a person should be pluralistic? Political pluralism, as mandated in the Bill of Rights, can be justified, as James Madison does, by pragmatic considerations of the need to live together in peace, despite our differences. What, though, legitimizes a spiritual or ethical pluralism? Greenberg says that he knows of no philosophic justification for pluralism, for that would entail the legitimation of accepting a position and its contrary or contradictory position. There is, however, a religious justification: God *intended* that we all think differently.

Greenberg learns this from, among other sources, the Mishnah, which asks why God initiated the human species by creating only one man. One reason, the Mishnah suggests, is to impress on us *the greatness of the Holy One, blessed be He,* for when human beings mint coins, they all come out the same, but God made one mold (Adam) and no one of us is exactly like another. This physical pluralism is matched by an intellectual pluralism for which, the Rabbis say, God is to be blessed: "When one sees a crowd of people, he is to say, 'Blessed is the Master of mysteries,' for just as their faces are not alike, so are their thoughts not alike." The Midrash supports this further when it says that when Moses was about to die, he said to the Lord: "Master of the Universe, You know the opinions of everyone, and that there are no two among Your children who think alike. I beg of You that after I die, when You appoint a leader for them, appoint one who will bear with [accept, *sovel*] each one of them as he thinks [on his own terms, *lefi da'ato*]." We know that Moses said this, the Rabbis said, because Moses describes God as "God of the *ruhot* ("spirits" [in the plural]) of all flesh."[60] It is even the case that righteous non-Jews have a portion in the world to come, for it is only "the nations who ignored God" who will be denied that—again, a theological consideration.[61] Thus God wants pluralism so that people will constantly be reminded of His grandeur.

These classical rabbinic sources also indicate that pluralism is a divine creation; human beings have difficulty imitating it. To achieve the ability to be pluralistic is, in fact, the ultimate ethical and spiritual challenge, according to Greenberg. Just as "love your neighbor as yourself"—which, for Rabbi Akiva, is the underlying principle of all the commandments[62]—requires a person to go beyond biologically rooted self-love, pluralism requires a person to escape egocentricity. It is not possible for human beings totally to love their neighbors as themselves, and neither is it possible to be totally pluralistic; we are by nature too self-centered fully to achieve either goal.

The tradition, however, prescribes methods to bring us closer to these aims. Many of its directions to gain love of neighbor appear in that same Chapter 19 of Leviticus in which the commandment itself appears. The later tradition's instructions on how to become pluralistic are contained, in part, in the talmudic source quoted earlier describing the debates of Hillel and Shammai; one must, like Hillel, be affable and humble and teach opinions opposed to one's own, citing them first.[63]

Relativity, Not Absolutism or Relativism: Historical, Epistemological, and Theological Grounds for Pluralism

Finally, I suggest my own approach. It is based on historical, epistemological, and religious rationales for pluralism.

HISTORICAL GROUNDS FOR PLURALISM   When speaking historically, we must first remember the organic nature of all communities, including the Jewish one. Every community grows like an organism; it changes over time in response to both internal drives and external circumstances. As a result, we cannot establish limits on the ideology or practice of a community with any degree of confidence in their accuracy or durability; even Moses could not understand the Jewish tradition as expounded in the school of Rabbi Akiva, according to the Talmud.[64] That does not mean that the community is incoherent; we are a community partly because we share a history and its heroes, partly because we are aware of ourselves and are perceived by others as a community, partly because we work together as a community, and partly because we have shared goals—a shared vision and mission. All the legal and intellectual attempts to define the limits and content of Jewish identity gain whatever degree of authority they have from that shared life.

This broad, historical perspective should impart a degree of humility to those trying to set definite bounds and should make one somewhat less earnest in doing so. The community *will* define itself in time in the organic, logically haphazard way it has always used; theoretical attempts to do this are *post facto* rationalizations of what happens in a largely irrational way. That does not mean that thinking hard about Jewish identity is worthless; on the contrary, efforts to give communal life rational form can contribute immensely to the community's self-awareness and its plans for the future. One should just not exaggerate the degree to which human beings can devise a communal definition adequate to ever-changing historical facts.

EPISTEMOLOGICAL GROUNDS FOR PLURALISM   If we have difficulty putting the facts of human history in intelligible form, how much more do we realize our limits when it comes to discovering God and defining what God wants of us. We are not, of course, totally at a loss in either situation; God has given us intellectual faculties and the Torah to guide us. But we each, as the Rabbis recognized, will understand God and His will according to our own individual abilities and perspectives.[65] "Every way of man is right in his own eyes, but the Lord weighs the hearts";[66] as Rashi explained, this verse means that God judges each of us by our intentions, because a human being cannot be expected to know the truth as God knows it.

The philosophical problem with the Orthodox positions that I described above is that they all assume that we have only two choices: absolutism or relativism. That is, *either* the Torah articulates indisputable, universal truths and moral norms *or* no such truths or norms exist, and so each society can and must determine what *it* thinks is true and good.

Some Orthodox thinkers state the contrast even more starkly as one between absolutism and subjectivism. The latter position holds that even groups have no standing to establish truths and norms; only individuals can do that. Thus something is either universally and indisputably true or right (absolutism), or otherwise it is only true or right *for me* (subjectivism).

There are, however, epistemological options between absolutism and relativism, and I espouse one of them—namely, epistemological *relativity*. That is, I believe that there are objective truths and norms, but no human being can know what they are because no person shares in God's omniscience. To claim that some person has such omniscience is to make an idol of him or her, for it is to assert that a human being knows what God knows; to maintain that I myself have such knowledge is to add the sin of haughtiness to that of idolatry.

Instead, each of us must view the world from our own vantage point, which is heavily influenced by our own personal histories, skills, talents, fears, and hopes. Albert Einstein taught us that we cannot know the objects and forces of nature absolutely because we inevitably view what we see from our own vantage point; I am suggesting that the same is true for all factual and moral statements. Thus the philosophically correct position is *neither* absolutism *nor* relativism *nor* subjectivism; it is *relativity*.

That understanding of human knowledge gives pluralism a strong philosophical base. We must each look at the world through our own individual glasses and through those of our community, the people who largely share how we see the world and react to it. But we must also acknowledge that *nobody* can legitimately claim knowledge of the absolute truth. To assert that one can ignores the limits of human knowledge and the inescapable *relativity* of our many *perspectives* on the world. We instead should acknowledge that we approach all matters from our own perspective, with its inherent strengths and weaknesses.

Moreover, in forming our view, we can and should learn from what others discern. In particular, we should pay attention to the members of our own community, with whom we share a history, a future, and many convictions. We should also broaden our horizons to learn from other communities. We will not necessarily adopt what others within our group or outside it say, and we may even fight against it vehemently if we think it is wrong-headed, immoral, or downright dangerous. Relativity does *not* entail accepting any position or even respecting all positions; you do not have to be an absolutist to declare Nazi ideology, for example, both false and immoral. A humble recognition of the limits of what we as individuals or as societies can know, however, should impel us to seek to learn from others and, except in extreme cases like Nazi ideology, to respect others' views even when we disagree.

Let me put this point from the opposite direction, for in arguing for epistemological relativity I am denying the truth not only of absolutism but also of relativism and subjectivism. The many ways in which individuals and groups differ from each other should not blind us to the numerous commonalities human individuals and communities share. Einstein shook our faith in our ability to know anything about the natural world with absolute certainty: We will always have to take our vantage point into account. German physicist Werner Karl Heisenberg went further: We must recognize that even with regard to natural objects and forces, our perspective may distort reality, for in the very process of trying to fix on something, we change how it acts in the dynamic reality of life. At the same time, neither scientist maintained that nature is whatever a given society says it is. Each molecule of water consists of two atoms of hydrogen and one of oxygen no matter where we live and no matter how much a particular society might wish it were otherwise. In this and in a whole host of other areas, we *can* gain scientific *knowledge* (not just opinion or belief) because there *is* an objective world out there that we are each seeing from our own perspective.

It is undoubtedly harder both to know and to gain consensus on the less concrete issues studied by the humanities and social sciences than on the topics of the natural sciences, and it is harder still to know and to gain consensus on transcendent matters—those issues that go beyond what we can examine and test with our five senses. Such issues, the ones treated by philosophy and theology, are no less important than the topics treated by the natural sciences, social sciences, and humanities. In some ways, they are even more important, for they deal with our *ultimate* perceptions and commitments—how we understand ourselves as individuals, as a family, as a community, as a nation, as the human species, as part of nature, and as part of God's plan; how we interpret and apply moral values such as justice and honesty; what we mean by aesthetic qualities such as beauty and suggestiveness; and even what we fear and hope for.

But the fact that it is hard to learn about these matters and justify claims about them does *not* mean that we lack all reason to prefer one stance about them to another, that any position is as good as any other. We may not be able to provide indisputable, watertight proofs for our claims, but we can give—and we should be expected to give—grounds for them. Those grounds are based on what we have come to know about life through our individual and collective experiences with each other, with nature, and with God (or with the transcendent element of our lives, however that is imaged).[67]

Because these matters are both complex and complicated, groups of human beings can understandably and legitimately view them differently. That is the reason that pluralism makes sense.

But the complexity and difficulty of these matters does not make it impossible to take *reasoned, grounded positions* (even if not indisputably proven ones). On the contrary, people *must* think through their positions on a whole host of issues to live life with a degree of self-understanding, with a framework for planning the future, and with a proper degree of responsibility. They may even be convinced of the truth and significance of their stance to the point of being willing to risk their lives in defending it. They can ground their positions on a variety of topics by pointing to many features of the reality we share, including its physical, mental, emotional, moral, aesthetic, psychological, spiritual, social, and economic aspects. That grounding available in epistemological (and moral) relativity is its major advantage over epistemological (and moral) relativism or subjectivism.

Epistemological relativity, then, does not amount to wishy-washiness in what one believes, much less complete inability to take a stand. It demands instead a recognition of the relativity in the epistemological status of everyone's claims, including one's own, a status that makes it possible to state and ground a position but not to assert it with absolute certainty. Epistemological relativity also demands an appreciation, although not necessarily an acceptance, of others who see the world from a different vantage point and who draw different conclusions about how to live wisely. In a word, epistemological relativity demands pluralism.

THEOLOGICAL GROUNDS FOR PLURALISM   Commitment to pluralism is motivated by theological considerations as well. Many of the theological points Rabbi Simon Greenberg noted in his discussion of pluralism, described earlier, I would include in my own approach as well. I would add, though, a few other grounds for pluralism found in traditional sources and doctrines.

God intentionally, according to the Rabbis, reveals only a part of His truth in the Torah; the rest must come from study and debate.[68] Even with study, there is a limit to human knowledge, for, as the medieval Jewish philosopher Joseph Albo said, "If I knew Him, I would be He."[69] God as understood in the Jewish tradition thus wants pluralism not only to demonstrate His grandeur in creating humanity with diversity but also to force human beings to realize their epistemological creatureliness, the limits of human knowledge compared to God's. One is commanded to study; one is supposed to be committed to learning as much about God, His world, and His will as possible. But one must recognize that a passion for truth does not mean that one has exclusive possession of it; indeed, it is humanly impossible to have full or sole ownership of it.

Furthermore, we should understand that everyone's quest for religious knowledge is aided by discussion with others, because different views force all concerned to evaluate and refine their positions. The paradigmatic disputants, the School of Hillel, reverse their position a number of times in the Talmud, in contrast to the School of Shammai, which did so at most once; the Hillelites understood the epistemological and theological value of plural views and the need to learn from others.

Conversely, absolutism is, as I stated earlier, tantamount to idolatry, for it asserts that I alone (or some other person[s] alone, or we as a group alone) know what is true and good. I (or he or she or we) might *say* that it is God who tells us what we aver, but no human being can know that for sure. The Bible's problems with false prophets are with us yet today. The claim to absolute knowledge of God's will, then, amounts to a theologically improper egotism and/or idolatry. People certainly have the right to their convictions; indeed, I would argue that we all have the *duty* to think through what we believe and commit our lives to. But we must all acknowledge that our convictions are what I (or we) *think* is the truth, given our history, values, fears, hopes, personalities, associations, and perspectives.

Thus an appropriate degree of religious humility before God leads us to engage in spirited, spiritual argumentation; we should not assume that we alone know the truth and attempt to exclude others by fiat or social pressure. We can and must take stands, but we should do so while remaining open to being convinced to the contrary. We should also recognize that others may intelligently, morally, and theologically both think and act differently. From the standpoint of piety, then, pluralism emerges not from relativism but from a deeply held and aptly humble monotheism.

The Need for Unity with Diversity

Rabbinic sources demonstrate the necessity and legitimacy of vigorous disagreement within a unified, coherent community. It is, of course, not easy to balance the twin needs for unity and diversity; each of us must discover and examine the grounds for our own beliefs and practices, stretching to see the reasons why others believe and act as they do; and each community must determine the limits of dissent that it can tolerate and still remain cohesive. Modern theories attempt to do this in a much more diversified setting than talmudic and medieval rabbis ever contemplated, one characterized not only by physical dispersion but also by widely varying forms of being Jewish. In such circumstances, it is not surprising that the theories I have considered differ significantly in the extent to which they validate the beliefs and practices of others, but the very attempt to articulate such theories bespeaks the strongly felt need to retain unity within our diversity.

According to the Talmud, just as Jews put on phylacteries (tefillin—the leather straps worn on the arm and head during daily morning prayer), so too does God. The phylacteries that Jews wear bear the verse, "Hear O Israel, the Lord is our God, the Lord is one."[70] God's phylacteries bear the verse, "Who is like Your people Israel, one nation in the world."[71] Neither unity has been sufficiently achieved. Three times each day in the *Aleinu* prayer, Jews pray that God's unity might be acknowledged by all people. The unity of the people Israel, with its vigorous diversity intact, must also be the object of our work and prayers, just as it is on the mind of God.

CHAPTER THREE

"A People Apart": A Jewish Theology of Jewish Relations to Other Peoples

R ELATIONSHIPS LINK TWO OR MORE DISTINCT PARTIES.[1] THERE-
fore, to formulate a Jewish theology of Jewish relations
to people of other religions and nations, I must first
describe the classical Jewish understanding of Jews and non-
Jews. Who is this Jewish people who would relate to others?
What constitutes its identity and what is its purpose in being a
distinct people? How does the Jewish tradition understand the
nature and status of non-Jews? In Chapter One, I discussed
some of the fundamental elements of how the Jewish tradition
understands the Jewish community, but now I extend that description with particular attention to the elements that affect
Jews' relationships to non-Jews. For reasons that I outline here,
I then propose that we deepen some of those traditional ideas
and alter others to provide the theological basis for mutually
respectful and cooperative relationships with people of other
faiths in our own time.

Jewish Identity Defined by the Jewish Covenant with God

The Hebrew Bible describes the historical roots of the Jewish
people in substantial detail, from Abraham and Sarah, to Moses
and the Exodus from Egypt, to the eventual conquest of the

Promised Land. For the Bible, though, it is not these historical events that constitute the raison d'être of the Jewish people; it is rather the theological phenomenon that the Jews are called by God to enter into a covenant with Him, with mutual promises and responsibilities. The history is not irrelevant; it is the stage on which the covenant is first made and on which it is to be carried out for all time. This is very much a covenant *within history*.[2] But it is the relationship with God that makes the historical events matter.[3]

According to the terms of the covenant, the Jews are obligated to be loyal to God and to love Him, expressing that love primarily through obedience of God's commandments. These commandments demand that Jews live out God's will in the thick of life, not just in a cloistered environment like a synagogue or monastery, and that they teach them to their children and "Recite them when you stay at home and when you are away, when you lie down and when you get up."[4] They are, in other words, to pervade each Jew's life.

In return for such love and loyalty, God is to reward the Jews with continued existence through progeny as numerous as the stars in the heaven, ownership of the Land of Israel, material well-being, and—probably the most important of all—a continued, special relationship with God. On the other hand, failure to abide by the covenant will, the Bible assures us, produce the reverse: physical debilitations, loss of the Promised Land, and detachment from God. In respect for the promises He made in the covenant, however, God will not abandon the people forever, even if they sin grievously, but will rather forgive them and return them to the Promised Land and to the blessings of progeny and well-being. God will do this also because God by nature is not only just but loving and merciful.[5] God's patience, though, is also a function of His own interest in preserving the covenant, for the People Israel were to be God's great experiment with humankind, God's "Chosen People" to be "a light of the nations," a model for all other peoples of what God really wants in His human creatures.[6] Consequently, God has a vested interest in having Israel as a Chosen People: Apparently convinced that He cannot demand model behavior from everybody, God nevertheless wants a group of people who can exemplify what living a godly way of life is all about.

God's need for a model people forces Israel's hand. They agree to the covenant amid thunder and lightning at Mount Sinai, hardly an opportunity for free, coolly reasoned, informed consent![7] The Rabbis later tell two stories about this process. According to one, God went to all the other peoples of the world and offered them His covenant, and they each refused when they found out some of its demands. Finally, as a last resort, God went to the measly People Israel, and they agreed to it without ever hearing its terms![8] That is consent, but certainly not informed consent. The other story picks up on the biblical description of the awesome setting of Mount Sinai and says that God actually held the mountain over their heads and said, "Either accept the covenant, or this will be your burial place!"[9] On that account, Israel's consent to be God's covenanted people was both uninformed and coerced. Similarly, another rabbinic source has God saying this:

> "For I am the Lord your God who brought you up out of the land of Egypt to be your God: you shall therefore be holy, for I am holy."
> ... When it says, "to be your God," it means even against your will.[10]

Clearly, then, it was not Israel's calm, voluntary choice that brought them into this special relationship, but rather the love and fear of God.

Just as the People Israel has no choice in entering the covenant, it cannot leave the relationship either. Especially after the pogroms of the Middle Ages and the Holocaust of the twentieth century, Jews have complained bitterly of God's failure to live up to His promise of protection and continuity. Some Jews, faced with these realities, have even converted to Islam or Christianity or, more recently, have rejected Judaism for secularism or have adopted an Asian religion such as Buddhism.

According to Jewish law, though, once a person is born to a Jewish mother or is converted to Judaism at age thirteen or older, he or she is Jewish for life. A Jew who converts to another religion loses all privileges of being a Jew, such as marriage, burial, and community honors, but retains all responsibilities of Jewish identity: "A Jew, even if he has sinned, is still a Jew," the Talmud says.[11]

This is because Jewish identity has never been defined by religious affirmations, although Judaism certainly has them; being Jewish has rather historically been a function of being part of the Jewish people. As I described in Chapter One, the Jews do not make up a voluntaristic community, based on people's desires or convictions; they are rather part of a corporate entity from which they cannot sever themselves, just as the heart and lungs cannot choose to leave a person's body. Some Jews may try to hide their Jewish identity, but it is still theirs.[12]

While some Jews may see this inextricable bond to the Jewish people as a burdensome trap, most Jews experience it as a great gift. No Jew need ever feel alone. "All Israel are friends," the liturgy proclaims.[13] This is perhaps most dramatically felt at weddings and funerals, which Jews are commanded to attend to help the parties involved rejoice or mourn, but it is much more pervasive than that. Jews take care of one another. This means that Jews shoulder great responsibility for fellow Jews on a daily basis. They are required to visit the sick and, if possible, to pray in the company of a quorum of ten Jews (a minyan), two examples to illustrate that Jews must support their fellow Jews in satisfying their emotional needs and in aiding each other's spiritual quests. When necessary, Jews must also support each other financially, as indicated in Chapter Six, for example. At times of persecution, Jews have had to engage in massive, expensive, and sometimes dangerous efforts to ransom captives and to relocate refugees to safe havens. Jews can rest assured knowing, though, that other Jews will look after them, too. They thus experience their bond to other Jews as not only unbreakable but beneficial—indeed, a source of great blessing.

Jewish law defines Jewish identity on genealogical grounds—specifically, either physical birth to a Jewish woman or symbolic rebirth as a Jew through the conversion rites. The substance of Jewish identity, however, is not merely national or ethnic; it is, as we have seen, highly theological and moral. Jews must retain their Jewish identity because of the awesome seriousness of their covenant with God and its goal, namely, modeling what human individuals and what a human society can and should be. Even in contemporary times, when a significant percentage of Jews do not consider themselves religious, the sense of a unique role to play in making this a better world persists as a critical factor in Jewish self-understanding.[14]

This aspiration for the moral has evoked mixed reactions among non-Jews. Some people have admired Jews for their accomplishments and moral commitment, born out of their covenantal relationship to God and their drive to reach the Promised Land, not only literally but figuratively as well.[15] Many others, however, have resented the Jews for these traits, because proclaiming that we are a Chosen People implicitly makes Jews seem haughty and holier than thou while making non-Jews feel inferior and even guilty.

This makes it imperative to point out the normalcy of the People Israel. Like all other peoples of the world, Jews have the usual goals of simply living life as it comes—with, we hope, some achievements and joy—and of carrying on the traditions of their ancestors. Richard Rubenstein, in particular, has stressed the need for reminding Jews and non-Jews of the normalcy of the Jewish people, for the medieval pogroms and the Holocaust were caused at least in part, he maintains, by the fact that Christians turned the Jewish claim to chosenness inside out, making Jews not people struggling to be more godly but the embodiment of Satan himself.[16]

Consequently, we must state openly that the Jewish people is, after all, a normal group, with the usual human needs, desires, and foibles. Despite the Holocaust, however, and despite modern secularism, the covenant idea is so deeply ingrained in the Jewish tradition that it permeates the consciousness of most Jews, even those who do not consider themselves religious. Whether consciously or subconsciously, and whether in its original, theological form or in a new, secular one, the covenant makes Jews strive to push the envelope of what human beings can *morally* and *humanly* achieve. Jews singly and collectively may fall short of being what God desires, "a kingdom of priests and a holy nation," but they judge themselves, and others judge them, by those high standards.

Idolaters and Monotheists

The other peoples of the world, whom the biblical authors and the talmudic rabbis knew, were, by and large, not monotheists, but idolaters, whether Canaanite, Greek, or Roman. The Hebrew Bible is relentlessly opposed to idolatry, prominently enshrining the prohibition against it in the Decalogue announced on Mount Sinai and repeating it as well in many other places in the Bible.[17] Moreover, according to the Torah, the reason God wants the Israelites to occupy the Land of Israel and displace the seven nations already there is precisely because of the natives' idolatry and the immorality to which it led them.[18] The Bible speaks, for example, of the sacrifice of children to Molech and of sanctified acts of adultery and incest within the Canaanite cult.[19]

The Rabbis carried this further. They devoted an entire tractate of the Mishnah and Talmud—*Avodah Zarah*—to the subject of idolatry to define it clearly and to prevent Jews from getting too close to idolatry or idolaters lest they be tempted by such practices. In some passages, the Rabbis actually made fun of idolatry, and they wrote liturgy that thanks God for enabling Jews to be part of those who spend their time in studying and practicing the Jewish tradition rather than being among those who waste their lives away following the emptiness and immorality of idolatry.[20]

Another part of the Jewish rejection of idolatry is based on theological considerations. Worshiping the sun, moon, or stars amounts to making part of reality the whole of it, taking one of God's creatures as God Himself. That error is even more egregious if one makes an idol of a human artifact, for then one reduces God to what human beings can make. Thus idolatry involves both moral and theological errors that ultimately make it impossible even to recognize God let alone to worship God properly.

To accomplish their divinely ordained task, then, Israel had to remain separate and apart from the other nations that might lead them astray: " 'You shall be holy' [means that] even as I am holy, so you too should be holy; as I am separate [the prime meaning of the Hebrew word usually translated "holy"], so you too should be separate."[21] The Torah records that fraternization with the Moabites led the Israelites to both idolatry and immorality,[22] and that early incident set the stage for the Jewish tradition's evaluation of non-Jews. Through the ages, Jews' assessment of non-Jews varied with both the character of the surrounding non-Jewish community and the conditions it created for Jewish life under its rule; but by and large, Jews saw people of other faiths as both theologically wrong and immoral. That lesson is repeated many times in the books of the Former Prophets in regard to the Canaanites and Philistines.

Later, the Rabbis suggested that Jews thank God for not making them like the Romans, for they spent their days in the emptiness and immorality of the street corners and circuses while the Jews spent their lives studying the Torah and following its precepts to do good deeds.[23] Indeed, the early morning blessings, in their traditional form, include one for *not* making us gentiles.[24]

This worry about being corrupted by the gentiles may seem remarkable, because the Torah does not portray the Israelites themselves as all that pious or moral. On the contrary, it makes clear that God's choice of Israel for this task is not based on any rational grounds. It is not because of Israel's greatness that God chose Israel for this task, for Israel is among the smallest of peoples. It is also not because of the People Israel's goodness, for they stubbornly persist in their evil ways.[25] Indeed, shortly after entering into the covenant at Mount Sinai, the people abandon God for the Golden Calf, and they sin again in not trusting God to take them into the Promised Land after ten of the twelve spies report the difficulty of the task ahead.[26] In both cases, God seriously considers destroying the people forthwith and starting over again with Moses leading some other people; but Moses, using a series of lawyerly arguments, prevails on God to retain His ties with the People Israel. Thus Israel's size, piety, and goodness are not the reasons that God chose it as His people; it is rather because of God's love for Abraham, Isaac, and Jacob; His promises to them; and His need for a model people that He agrees to continue His relationship with their descendants, no matter what. The Jewish People, though, were to be what the Moabite seer Balaam described as "a people that dwells apart, not reckoned among the nations."[27]

Nationalism and Universalism in the Traditional Concept of the Covenant

The national character of the covenant is clear-cut in both biblical and rabbinic literature. The covenant is specifically between God and the Jewish People; its terms do not apply to others:

> Now then, if you will obey Me faithfully and keep My covenant, you shall be My treasured possession among all the peoples. Indeed, all the earth is Mine, but you shall be to Me a kingdom of priests and a holy nation.[28]
>
> I the Lord am your God who has set you apart from other peoples. . . . You shall be holy to Me, for I the Lord am holy, and I have set you apart from other peoples to be Mine.[29]

> He issued His commands to Jacob,
>   His statutes and rules to Israel.
> He did not do so for any other nation;
>   of such rules they know nothing.
> Hallelujah.[30]

The Rabbis continued this theme. Probably the best indication of this is what they say with reference to the Sabbath, which is the symbol of the ongoing covenant between God and Israel and consequently, according to the Rabbis, the equivalent of all the other commandments.[31] The Torah says:

The Israelite people shall keep the sabbath, observing the sabbath throughout the ages as a covenant for all time: it shall be a sign for all time between Me and the people of Israel.[32]

On this the Rabbis commented:

"It [the Sabbath] is a sign between Me and you," that is, and not between Me and the other nations of the world.[33]

This is not simply a matter of ideology: It has a pervasive effect on practice as well. Specifically, Jewish law operates like any other legal system in assuming that its rights and obligations apply fully only to the members of the national group. The Rabbis made this explicit by asserting that non-Jews are subject to only the seven commandments given to the children of Noah—that is, prohibitions against murder, idolatry, incest, eating a limb torn from a living animal, blasphemy, and theft and the requirement to establish laws and courts.[34] Non-Jews are given certain protections and privileges in Jewish law,[35] as aliens often are in other legal systems, but they are not required to take on "the yoke of the commandments" (a rabbinic expression)[36] because that was exclusively a feature of God's covenantal relationship with the Jews.

That part of the Jewish covenantal notion should be fairly easy for Christians to understand because Christianity also conceives itself as the prime way of relating to God—indeed, as the "New Covenant" that supersedes the "Old Testament." Anyone who refuses to believe in Jesus is, according the Christian Scriptures, condemned: "No one who believes in him [Jesus] will be condemned; but whoever refuses to believe is condemned already because he has refused to believe in the name of God's only Son."[37] Indeed, despite all the progress in Catholic–Jewish relations since the Vatican issued its 1965 document *Nostra Aetate,* in a recent papal statement on the subject, the Vatican asserts that Catholicism is the only "instrument for the salvation of all humanity," that all other faiths are "gravely deficient," and that even other denominations of Christianity "suffer from defects."[38] It makes perfect sense that people of all faiths should consider their own to be best, for otherwise why would they affirm it? In contrast to the three Western religions, many Eastern religions do not claim to have an exclusive hold on the truth or the good and, therefore, permit adherents to embrace several religions simultaneously; but even followers of those religions clearly think that their chosen faith(s) is (are) the best. Minimally, people think that their own faith is best for *them,* and many would go further, claiming that their faith is best for *everyone.*

What is probably harder to communicate is the fact that for the Jewish tradition the superiority of Judaism does not mean, as it historically has for much of Christianity and apparently still does for Catholicism, that it is the *only* way in which people can fulfill God's will for mankind and be "saved" (a word that means in Christianity to be delivered from sin but in Judaism means instead liberation from the dangers and limitations of life, including rule by others). Jews are required to obey the law because they are part of God's covenant with Israel at Sinai;[39] non-Jews were never part of the Sinai covenant and, therefore, are not obligated under it.

This does not mean, though, that non-Jews are excluded from God's concern or prevented from enjoying God's favor. On the contrary, if they abide by the seven commandments given to Noah and seek to be righteous, they have done all that God wants of them. "The pious and virtuous of all nations participate in eternal bliss," the Rabbis said[40]—a sharp contrast to the eternal damnation inherited by those who reject Jesus according to some versions of Christianity.[41] Even at the prime moment of nationalistic triumph, the Exodus from Egypt, the Rabbis picture the ministering angels singing songs of praise over the destruction of the Egyptians in the Red Sea, but God rebukes them, saying, "My children lie drowned in the sea, and you sing hymns of triumph?"[42] Thus, contrary to many versions of Christian and Muslim faiths, the Jewish covenant does not entail exclusivity or triumphalism.

Moreover, the Rabbis did not seek to convert non-Jews to Judaism, and many of them maintained that the righteous among the idolaters of ancient times shall inherit a place in the world to come.[43] This, of course, has direct implications for the relationships of Judaism to truly idolatrous faiths in our time, like Hinduism. Judaism would never embrace its polytheism as a vision of the truth or its idolatry as appropriate worship. Nevertheless, idolaters remain creatures of God and must be respected as such; indeed, some of them may be among the "the righteous of the nations" (*hasidei u'mot ha-olam*).

If polytheists are to be granted that measure of respect, monotheists qualify for it even more; for monotheism is, after all, one of the core theological convictions of Judaism. Consequently, because medieval Jewish sources recognized Islam's strict monotheism, they did not classify Islam as idolatrous. Because of the Christian doctrine of the Trinity and because of the practices of some Christians to bow down to holy relics and to statues of saints, medieval Jewish sources were less sanguine about Christianity; but some among them—most especially Rabbi Menahem ben Solomon Meiri (1249–1316)—understood Christianity as monotheistic as well.[44] Clearly, Christian persecution of Jews in many times and places did little to encourage such positive evaluations of Christianity; however, even within that context some rabbis understood the monotheism at the heart of Christianity, and modern rabbis have done so with increasing regularity.[45]

It is not easy, though, to balance the firmly held belief that, as God's creatures, all people are the object of His concern and eligible for His favor with a sense of appreciation and pride in being God's covenanted people, following God's preferred way. Historically, largely depending on the particular circumstances in which Jews found themselves, the tensions involved inevitably meant that sometimes one of these tenets was emphasized to the exclusion of the other. Thus from the rabbis who endured the Hadrianic persecutions one understandably hears expressions of extreme antipathy toward non-Jews, such as that of Rabbi Akiva's student Rabbi Shimon bar Yoḥai, who, after seeing his teacher flayed by the Romans, said, "[Even] the best of gentiles should be killed." On the other hand, during the more friendly atmosphere of early Sassanid Babylon, Samuel claims that God makes no distinction between Israel and the other nations on the Day of Judgment.[46] Overall, though, Jews have tried to strike a balance between their nationalism and their universalism.

Both the tensions and the balance are probably best illustrated in the Jewish notion of Messianism. The ultimate aim, as the biblical prophet Isaiah declared, is that all people worship God so that there will be universal peace among people and in nature, even to the extent that the wolf will lie down with the lamb.[47] But Israel has a special role to play as "a light of the nations";[48] and as several biblical prophets asserted, it is Israel's God that all people will ultimately worship and Israel's Torah that they will practice.[49] Moreover, according to the Rabbis, in Messianic times Jews will be rewarded for their efforts to make God's will known by the reunion of the tribes of Israel in the Land of Israel, the rebuilding of Jerusalem, the restoration of Jewish political autonomy, and general prosperity—so much so that non-Jews will seek to convert to Judaism to take advantage of Jews' new status but will not be allowed to do so because their motive is not disinterested:

> "You brought a vine out of Egypt." As the vine is the lowliest of trees and yet rules over all the trees, so Israel is made to appear lowly in this world but will in the Hereafter inherit the world from end to end. As the vine is at first trodden under the foot but is afterwards brought upon the table of kings, so Israel is made to appear contemptible in this world ... but in the Hereafter the Lord will set Israel on high, as it is said, "Kings shall be your nursing fathers."[50]
>
> In the Hereafter the gentile peoples will come to be made proselytes but will not be accepted.[51]

Thus those who are part of God's covenant with Israel are to enjoy special privileges for the added covenantal responsibilities they have borne, but ultimately all people are to participate in the human fulfillment of Messianic times and the hereafter.

The tension between national pride and universalist convictions that is evident in the biblical and rabbinic doctrine of the covenant is also manifest in modern treatments of the subject. Early-twentieth-century Jewish thinkers Franz Rosenzweig and Martin Buber, for example, affirmed both elements of the balance, but Rosenzweig emphasized the special character of Israel and Buber stressed the universal aspirations of the covenant. In that sense, the first is a "nationalist" and the second, a "universalist." A third resolution of this tension is the theory of Mordecai Kaplan, founder of the Reconstructionist approach to Judaism, who maintained that Jews ought to think of themselves not as having been chosen, for that carries with it too many negative implications about how Jews view non-Jews. Rather Jews should see themselves as having a specific "vocation" to carry out their own history and traditions, just as every other civilization has its own special vocation.[52] This preserves the national character of the Jewish people while enabling Jews to recognize, in theory as well as in fact, the unique character and special contributions of many of the world's other nations and civilizations.

Historical, Epistemological, and Theological Groundwork for Jews' Relations to Other Religions

I would like to suggest yet another understanding of theology to establish a firm foundation for Jewish relationships with other peoples in our time. It is based on the same three considerations that argue for pluralism within the Jewish community—history, epistemology, and theology—but their application to interfaith relations requires some careful thought.

Clearly, the question of how Jews should interact with non-Jews does not arise in matters of justice, commerce, or other, general human concerns, for there what governs Jewish behavior are Jewish conceptions of God as the Creator of us all and Jewish laws insisting that all people be treated fairly.[53] Later Jewish law went further: To establish good relations between Jews and non-Jews, Jews must help the poor and the sick of all religions and aid in burying their dead and in comforting their mourners.[54] That kind of care for others is unusual even for peoples in the modern world. Moreover, the ways in which

Christians and others persecuted Jews throughout history make this high standard of civility in traditional Judaism remarkable: Jewish theology, unlike some versions of Christian and Muslim theology, did not blind its believers to the human necessity of being honest, fair, and caring toward others who believed differently.

The deeper question, then, is not practical, but theological—namely, how can and should Jews understand the truth status of other religions? How shall we understand their moral claims and practices? Are other peoples simply deluded, or may their religions contain truths and values from which Jews can themselves learn? On the other hand, if other religions do contain truths and commendable values, why should Jews remain Jewish? Answering such questions about one's own religion clearly and convincingly is absolutely critical for people of all faiths, if adherents of the different religions or of none are ever going to go beyond persecuting others, avoiding them, or, at best, merely tolerating them and advance to the point of actually understanding and appreciating others while retaining their own convictions and sense of identity.

Historical Groundwork

I apply my historical argument first to Western religions and then to Eastern faiths.

Historically, Christianity has been subject to change and redefinition at least as much as Judaism has, if not more. Within both faiths, even within the same denomination, creeds created centuries ago have continually changed, sometimes through outright amendment; sometimes through new interpretations, emphases, or applications; and sometimes through simply ignoring them. This constantly evolving nature of both Judaism and Christianity makes some of the faithful uneasy; they long for certainty and stability. Each religion, though, has retained its relevance and its dynamism only by opening itself to change.

The same is true about each faith's understanding of others. The Second Vatican Council's repudiation of blaming Jews living then or now for the death of Jesus and the recent rejection by the Evangelical Lutheran Church of America of Luther's many anti-Semitic writings are relevant cases in point. Conversely, few modern Jews dismiss other faiths out of hand as being theologically false and morally bad; on the contrary, this very chapter is but one of many attempts to create a positive Jewish understanding of other religions.[55]

At the same time, history does not undermine a religious community's ability to draw boundaries and to take a strong stand on what it believes. Even though the contemporary Jewish community is much exercised over the question of who is a Jew, for example, it has uniformly and authoritatively determined that groups like Jews for Jesus are decidedly *not* Jews. The historically evolutionary nature of both faiths should, however, help contemporary Jews and Christians get beyond the feeling that the present articulation of their faith is the only one possible for a decent person to have; on the contrary, history should teach us that people of intelligence, morality, and sensitivity most likely exist in other faiths too.[56]

Muslims affirm the importance of not only the Koran but also the oral traditions, the *hadith*. Moreover, Islam includes a variety of denominations, of which Shi'ite and Sunni are the chief divisions, but each has many subdivisions (for example, Ishma'ili). The historical record and the present reality of Islam, then, make it clear that the faith has developed in several forms.

However, Muslims—even Muslim scholars—are loathe to interpret their tradition historically. Not even the most liberal schools of Islam study the Koran with the modern historical and linguistic techniques of scholarship that many, although not all, Jews and Christians apply to their own scriptures and traditions. As a result, Muslims treat the Koran as only fundamentalist Jews and Christians see their respective Bibles—that is, as the direct and indubitable word of God. Muslim scholarship, then, frankly denies what non-Muslims would assert—namely, that Islam from its earliest stages is the product of historical influences, that the Koran itself and all later Muslim sources and practices manifest the effects of Judaism, Christianity, and the other cultures from which Muslims learned in each age. Only when Muslims acknowledge historical development in their own faith will they be open to relations with other faiths that are not exclusivist and triumphalist.

Awareness of Asian faiths should, if anything, make the point of this section—that all faiths continually develop over time— all the more compelling for devotees of all three Western faiths. Because Eastern religions differ from Judaism more extensively and obviously than the two other Western faiths do and because the Eastern religions and peoples have not had a long history of conflict with Jews, as people of the other two Western faiths have had, Jews can view Asian religions more objectively and dispassionately than they see Christianity and Islam. The same, I would imagine, is true for adherents of Christianity and Islam (except, perhaps, for those Muslims living in countries such as India, where they come into direct contact with devotees of Eastern religions). Moreover, much less is at stake in subjecting another religion to modern, critical analysis.

Acknowledging that all of the world's faiths took a little from here and a little from there in shaping what has come down to us moderns as the particular forms of contemporary religions will,.I hope, help Westerners recognize the same process of development in their own religions. That, in turn, should convince people of all religions that the present embodiment of their own faith's convictions will not likely be the way it will always be. Moreover, because even their own religion will inevitably change over time, the present form of it cannot be the only possible way for all people of intelligence and moral sensitivity to think and act.

The very awareness of historical development, then, should engender flexibility in understanding all religions, including one's own. Cognizance of the rampant borrowing among all cultures and religions should undermine exclusive claims to truth or goodness. Moreover, even if relations between people of specific faiths have not been good in the past, they *can* be reshaped in the present and future, because all religions change over time.

Epistemological Groundwork

This realization is only reinforced when one turns from historical considerations to philosophical ones. In Chapter Two, I espoused the position of epistemological relativity in contrast to absolutism on the one side and relativism and subjectivism on the other. Relativity, when applied to interfaith relations, asserts that all human beings, whatever their background or creed, suffer from the same limitations of human knowledge. Many of us have sacred texts and traditions that, for us, reveal God's nature and will—or, for nontheological traditions, ultimate reality and morality—as clearly and fully as we think possible. We all must recognize, though, that other peoples make the same claim for their sacred texts and traditions. Moreover, we have no grounds outside the different traditions to provide shared criteria to judge them; medieval Western philosophers tried to use reason to justify and compare all three Western faiths, but we now know that the rules of reason themselves vary with cultures and over generations. Therefore we must either resort to vacuous and disingenuous debates like those of the Middle Ages about whose tradition is right or we must finally confront the fact that none of us can know God's nature or will with absolute certainty.

At the same time, just as historical considerations like the interactions of nations and cultures do not make all faiths the same or spoil the significance of living by one specific faith, so too philosophical factors like the relativity of human knowledge do not undermine faith altogether. We may think that our particular understanding of God and all other religious topics is the correct one for all people, *as far as we can tell.* We may also advance arguments toward convincing others of its truth and worth and even of its preeminence over other faith claims. We must do so, however, knowing ahead of time that no human argument on these matters can be conclusive, for no person is omniscient and no human vantage point can claim inherent superiority over all others.

Moreover, we must recognize that part of the reason that the arguments for my faith seem most persuasive to me is because it is, after all, *my* faith and that of my family and my people.[57] One need not deny cognitive meaning to religion to take such a position, as A. J. Ayer, R. B. Braithwaite, and others did in the middle of the twentieth century,[58] for people of all faiths are trying to respond to objective reality as they see it. One need only be humble enough to recognize that none of us sees the world through transparent lenses; that we all view it through the lenses of our particular religion or philosophy of life and from one or another viewpoint; and that our autobiographical backgrounds inevitably do, and perhaps should, play a role in determining what we see and how we respond to it.[59]

This explains why I think that *Dominus Iesus,* the Vatican's document on interfaith relations issued on September 6, 2000, is based on a fundamental philosophical error. The document censures the spread of "religious relativism," "the mentality of indifferentism [that] leads to the belief that one religion is as good as another." Instead, although the Church has "sincere respect . . . for the religions of the world," followers of non-Christian faiths have "gravely deficient" chances for salvation; and other Christian churches have "defects," partly because they do not recognize the authority of the pope.[60]

The Vatican's mistake is to think that the only alternative to religious relativism is the kind of absolutism that the document embraces. As I indicated earlier, proponents of all religions certainly have the right to like their own religion best and even to declare that among the various religions and philosophies of the world theirs most adequately articulates what is both true and good *as far as they can tell.* What they cannot do with philosophical warrant is proclaim that they have objective grounds for preferring their faith, for the inevitable perspectivism of human knowledge means that no person has such grounds. Especially given the immense steps that the Vatican itself has taken in interfaith relations since the Second Vatican Council, it is both surprising and disappointing that the 2000 document seems to undermine all that progress. The Vatican, I suggest, can have confidence in the rightness of Catholicism for Catholics and also reach out to people of other faiths if it instead adopts the epistemological relativity that I have been explaining and advocating.

Now that I have applied epistemological relativity to both internal Jewish discussions and to external interfaith matters, I would like to describe more of why it makes sense to think of human knowledge in that way. The stance I advocate is, in philosopher Van Harvey's terminology, "soft perspectivism" rather than "hard perspectivism" or "nonperspectivism."[61] Nonperspectivists claim that we look at the world through epistemologically transparent eyeglasses, that our personal and cultural differences make no difference whatsoever in how we see the world. Hard perspectivists, on the other end of the spectrum, maintain that one's perspective so strongly affects what one sees that it inevitably makes it impossible to understand, let alone learn from, those who see the world from other viewpoints. Instead of these two extremes, we should say, as soft perspectivists do, that we each have a perspective that influences how we think and act but that our perspectives are permeable enough so that we can all understand each other and even learn from each other.

Later, Hilary Putnam and Robert Nozick articulated the same approach from the other end, emphasizing the realism involved in it, even though the real world is always perceived through a particular lens.[62] Thus, as they each point out, it is erroneous to think of knowledge as our social conventions about what is true, by which a statement is true if and only if it accords with a given society's "language game." That severs knowledge from any explicit tie to the real. On the other end of the spectrum, it is also wrong to assert "metaphysical realism"—that is, that human beings can apprehend that which is beyond all human conception or possibility to know, namely, the world as it objectively is. Such a view ignores the limitations of human knowledge, especially the fact that none of us is an objective observer of the world, that we each see the world through conceptual lenses of one sort or another. Individuals may be able to refine their own lenses as they learn more about life, and they may even be convinced that they need to exchange their present lens for a new one, but there is no escaping the necessity of viewing the world from a particular vantage point and through some lens. Instead, we should embrace what Putnam and Nozick call "conceptual realism," by which one affirms both the tie to the real and the need for a perspective to access it. As Gordon Tucker pointed out, this last theory about knowledge avoids the tyranny that both of the other theories produce (either that of the society that claims to determine the truth or that of the one person who somehow has absolute knowledge of the metaphysically real), and it opens the way for dissent, debate, and—I would add—democracy.[63]

Westerners who are used to an either–or approach to truth in both their philosophy and their religion will undoubtedly feel ill at ease with the both–and approach I am advocating. The religions of the Far East would find this approach quite compatible, for they have historically been inclusivist rather than exclusivist. That is, they have stated their convictions and practices and permitted individuals to adhere to them while simultaneously adopting other faiths. Rabbinic Judaism would also find my epistemological approach congenial, for, as discussed in Chapter Two, the Rabbis understood that texts are open to multiple interpretations and that even impressive events like the Revelation at Mount Sinai are experienced and understood differently by different people, each according to his or her abilities.

At the same time, this position does not entail that there is no such thing as knowledge and that people should, therefore, believe whatever suits them. The realism in the position I am espousing makes it possible to be right or wrong—and to debate with others about which position is correct. Thus having strong convictions about the true and the good is compatible with a pluralistic approach to people of other faiths as well as one's own; I must just acknowledge that however much I believe in what I affirm, I am not omniscient and, therefore, may be wrong. I must thus be open to discussions with people who hold other views to understand them, evaluate them, and either oppose them or learn from them.

Indeed, the only people who are philosophically ruled out of an accepting, pluralistic approach are those who maintain a brand of metaphysical realism, often coupled with fundamentalism, because such people insist that only they can be right. That cocksure stance is not only philosophically unfounded and intellectually fascist, often leading, when such people have power, to political fascism; it is also, in essence, an idolatrous worship of their own intelligence and views. For pluralism to take place, all people involved must have a much more accurate and humble understanding of their own knowledge, including the awareness that they may be wrong. At the same time, they must have the intellectual wherewithal and thoughtfulness to affirm convictions that they are prepared both to defend and to evaluate.[64] That stance, embracing epistemological relativity, soft perspectivism, and conceptual realism, has the double advantage of realistically describing human knowledge and simultaneously making pluralism and strong interfaith relations possible.

Theological Groundwork

In addition to these historical and philosophical considerations, Judaism contains some important theological tenets that can be used to lay the groundwork for a genuine appreciation of others. Many of the same sources that I reviewed in Chapter Two to justify pluralism within the Jewish community, although originally intended for that context, can be applied, with different degrees of stretching, to the interfaith context as well.

Thus, for example, the Rabbis' assertion of the uniqueness of both the body and thoughts of each individual is, of course, true for non-Jews as well as Jews. In those remarks, the plain meaning of the Rabbis' comments applies to all people without any expansion of their comments whatsoever.

On the other hand, in claiming that at Sinai God did not reveal the truth about Himself or His will completely but rather wants us to argue with each other in each generation to discern it, the Rabbis clearly were talking about the conversations among Jews based on the Torah; and so applying that comment to non-Jews takes it beyond its intended context. Even so, biblical and rabbinic sources indicate that Jews learned about theological and moral matters from their discussions with non-Jews. Thus, although Job and his friends were not Jewish,[65] the Rabbis intentionally included the Book of Job in the biblical canon, undoubtedly because they knew that Job's discussion did indeed increase our knowledge of God and His ways.

In fact, much of the Bible, and especially the Wisdom Literature (Proverbs, Job, Ecclesiastes, etc.), reflects the significant influence of the ancient cultures near whom the Jews were living.[66] Furthermore, the Talmud records a number of conversations between the Rabbis and non-Jews on theological and moral topics, including, for example, the theological questions posed by Tineius Rufus, the Roman governor of Palestine, to Rabbi Akiva.[67] In some of the talmudic conversations with heathens, the point is to demonstrate not only the superiority of Judaism but also the difficulty of the topic. Thus, in some cases, the rabbi gave the non-Jew a facile answer, but then the rabbi's students said, "You have pushed him away with a [weak] reed, but what are you going to say to us?"[68] In all these biblical and talmudic conversations with heathens, the Jews involved are stimulated by the non-Jews' questions and thoughts to real learning.

And yet there are some limitations to this line of reasoning as the basis for Jewish relations to other faiths. It may be the case that God wants us to think independently; but ultimately the Jewish tradition asserts that Judaism's Torah is God's true teaching, the one that all nations, according to the biblical Prophets, will ultimately learn.

One should note that Micah, a younger contemporary of Isaiah's, copies the latter's messianic vision but then adds a line of his own that effectively changes it: "Though all the peoples walk each in the names of its gods, we will walk in the name of the Lord our God forever and ever."[69] This is a decidedly pluralistic vision of Messianic times: Every people shall continue to follow its own god. Even so, Micah added this line *after* quoting Isaiah's vision that "the many nations shall go and say: 'Come, let us go up to the Mount of the Lord, to the House of the God of Jacob, that He may instruct us in His ways, and that we may walk in His paths.' For instruction shall come forth from Zion, the word of the Lord from Jerusalem."[70] Thus even for Micah, apparently, other gods and other visions of the good life might exist, but only Israel has the true understanding of God's will.

In sum, God may indeed want multiple conceptions of the divine, but traditional sources assign non-Jewish views to a clearly secondary status. God may like variety among His creatures, and He may hold non-Jews responsible only for what they could be expected to know (the seven Noahide Laws); but ultimately only the Jews know what is objectively correct and good. This is liberal toleration—and it should be appreciated as such—but it certainly is not a validation of others' views. In that sense, it falls short of Rabbi Simon Greenberg's criterion for genuine pluralism—namely, that "your ideas are spiritually and ethically as valid—that is, as capable of being justified, supported, and defended—as mine."[71] And, indeed, Greenberg himself may not have wanted to extend his thesis beyond disagreements among Jews.

I take a somewhat broader view. It is only natural that the Jewish sources discussed in this chapter should reflect a tension between nationalism and universalism. God is, according to Jewish belief, the God of all creatures; but at the same time, He chose the Jews to exemplify the standards He really wants for human life. This is how *Jews* understand God's will, the reason Jews commit all their energies and, indeed, their very lives to Jewish belief and practice.

Despite this nationalistic side of the Jewish tradition, however, what ultimately rings through it is the Rabbis' assertion that non-Jews fully meet God's expectations by abiding by the seven Noahide Laws and the Rabbis' statement that "The pious and virtuous of all nations participate in eternal bliss."[72] Jewish sources that speak about God wanting plural approaches to Him within the Jewish community can, therefore, apparently be applied, without too much tampering, to intercommunal relations as well. Of course, the same segments of the Jewish community that have difficulty with pluralism within the Jewish community would undoubtedly shun it in dealing with non-Jews, except on the most pragmatic of levels. For that matter, even some Jews committed to pluralism within the Jewish community need to stretch their understanding and sensitivity to apply Jewish theology to interfaith relations. Nevertheless, a firm basis for this kind of theology exists within the Jewish tradition, and so theological as well as historical and philosophical considerations can and should make Jews open to serious interfaith discussions and motivate them to participate in many interfaith activities on behalf of the general good.

Reciprocal Christian and Muslim Recognition of the Theological Validity of Judaism

If Jews are to stretch in this way, they justifiably can expect Christians and Muslims to do likewise. I personally have no doubt that Christians and Muslims *can* find the requisite sources within their own tradition to do this, *if they choose to do so.*

Historically, of course, that has certainly not been the choice of most Christians and Muslims. They have instead seen Christianity or Islam as the sole road to God. As a result, Christians and Muslims have at best tolerated the continued existence of Judaism and Jews within their midst, and Christians especially have often actively persecuted Jews for not converting to Christianity.[73]

Christians

For Christians, that has been motivated by some features of the Gospel accounts themselves. Portrayals of Pharisees as hypocrites and narrow-minded, cruel boors who care more for the letter of the law than for its spirit; the figure of Judas as a symbol of Jewish treachery; and the depiction of the Jews as having a hand in the condemnation of Jesus before Pilate, all provided ample basis for continuing Christian persecutions of Jews throughout history, including pillage, rape, and murder. Christians who want to correct Christian anti-Semitism in our day have a serious challenge, for they must confront and reinterpret texts that are at the very heart of the Christian story as articulated in Christian Scriptures and reenacted each year in Good Friday rituals.

Nevertheless, since the 1960s, there have been significant moves away from this dangerous teaching of contempt on the part of many Christians. Because the Catholic Church is by far the most populous Christian denomination and because its opening to the Jews in 1965 stimulated many other Christian groups to follow suit, I use their efforts in this regard to illustrate my point. As you will see, despite significant movement by the Catholic Church within the last thirty-six years toward mutually respectful relations between Catholics and Jews, so far the Catholic Church has stopped short of validating the Jewish experience as a mode of salvation for Jews. *Nostra Aetate*—which, as noted earlier, broke open a new, salutary spirit in Catholic–Jewish relations—recognizes Judaism as the historical root of Christianity, but it does not describe it as a distinct religion with a substance and mission of its own. The *Guidelines,* published by the Vatican in 1974 to implement *Nostra Aetate,* moved to correct this: "Christians . . . must strive to learn by what essential traits the Jews define themselves in the light of their own religious experience." Paragraphs 2 and 3 of the official Vatican *Notes* to the *Guidelines,* published in 1985, require Catholics to study Judaism in a way that is not "occasional and marginal" but rather essentially and organically integrated in catechesis, and the Judaism they are to study is not only the religion of the Bible but "the faith and religious life of the Jewish people as they are professed and practiced still today."[74]

Subsequent paragraphs of the *Notes,* however, make it clear that while Christians are to *study* Judaism as it is practiced by Jews, they are not to ascribe it divine legitimacy as a way to salvation for Jews; they are not, in other words, to assume that God continues to want Judaism to be practiced. The most distressing and exasperating section of the *Notes,* then, especially after all this time in dialogue, is the following:

7. "In virtue of the divine mission, the Church" which is to be "the all-embracing means of salvation" in which *alone* [emphasis add-

ed] "the fullness of the means of salvation can be obtained" (*Unitatis Redintegratio*, 3) "must of her nature proclaim Jesus Christ to the world" (cf. *Guidelines*, I).

This exclusivist view was just recently reaffirmed by the Vatican's document *Dominus Iesu*, written by Cardinal Ratzinger. That and earlier documents cite what Jesus affirms in John 10:16: "There shall be one flock and one shepherd."

Similarly, Jesus' famous reply to Nicodemus makes belief in Jesus the exclusive way to be saved from condemnation:

> Yes, God loved the world so much that he gave his only Son, so that everyone who believes in him may not be lost but may have eternal life. For God sent his Son into the world not to condemn the world but so that through him the world might be saved. No one who believes in him will be condemned; but whoever refuses to believe is condemned already, because he has refused to believe in the name of God's only Son.[75]

Thus Christianity and Judaism cannot be seen as two parallel ways of salvation, and the Church must witness to Christ as the Redeemer for all, "while maintaining the strictest respect for religious liberty in line with the teaching of the Second Vatican Council."[76]

I certainly understand that Christians neither can nor want to abandon the texts of their tradition, and I would not ask them to do so. In contrast to fundamentalist Protestants, however, Jews, Catholics, and nonfundamentalist Protestants are keenly aware that the *meaning* of biblical texts and the very *choice* of which texts to emphasize and which to ignore are crucially shaped by the ongoing *tradition* of each faith. Unfortunately for both communities, the verses cited from the Gospel of John and several others have for centuries determined the way Christians have thought about Judaism. After the Second Vatican Council, Jews sincerely hoped that Catholics were moving beyond the triumphalism embedded in that verse. To do so would *not* require Christians to abandon their sacred texts; it would simply necessitate that they move away from focusing on John's perception of non-Christians and instead embrace and emphasize the many other elements of Christian tradition that recognize the legitimacy—and perhaps even the special vocation and aptness—of other peoples' faiths for them.

Indeed, the end of this very section alludes to how it might be done. The Second Vatican Council's *Declaration on Religious Liberty* clearly articulated a Catholic perspective;[77] it was no less than the position of the most authoritative body in the Church. I am not sure what theological resources in Catholic tradition motivated that statement. Perhaps it was the ultimate recognition that a loving and moral God can and does understand and appreciate the various ways in which human individuals and groups reach out to Him. Whatever its basis, I would plead with Catholics that *that* statement of the Vatican Council shape the evolution of their tradition in our time so that they can move beyond the triumphalism found in John and in paragraph 7 of the *Notes*.

A related matter concerns the relationship between the Hebrew Bible and Christian scriptures. The *Guidelines* maintains that the Old Testament "retains its own perpetual value" and "has not been canceled by the later interpretation of the New Testament," but "the New Testament brings out the full meaning of the Old, while both Old and New illumine and explain each other." Similarly, the *Notes* argues for a typological interpretation of the Bible, designed "to show the unity of biblical Revelation (Old Testament and New Testament) and of the divine plan," for "the definitive meaning of the election of Israel does not become clear except in the light of the complete fulfillment (Romans 9–11), and election in Jesus Christ is still better understood with reference to the announcement and the promise (cf. Hebrews 4:1–11)."[78]

Jews relate to the Hebrew Bible in a similar way. For Jews, of course, it is the rabbinic tradition that is the fulfillment of the Hebrew Bible, not the New Testament. As Christians do with the New Testament, Jews consistently relate passages of rabbinic literature to biblical sources, and, conversely, they see biblical texts through the eyes of rabbinic interpretations of those texts. Although some medieval Jewish commentators distinguish, on occasion, between the plain meaning of a biblical passage and the rabbinic interpretation of it, until the twentieth century Jews by and large have virtually identified the meaning of the Bible with the interpretations the rabbinic tradition gave it. In an oft-repeated passage, the Rabbis maintained that "even what a learned student will say before his teacher in the future was already revealed to Moses at Sinai."[79] The continuation of the Bible in the words of the Rabbis was so fundamental an assumption among Jews that, with the exception of Spinoza, it was only in the twentieth century that Jews even considered the possibility that biblical religion might have been different from its later development in rabbinic Judaism. In fact, it is only in the last sixty years or so that Jewish scholars have applied the tools of historical analysis to the Torah. Orthodox Jews still refuse to do so.

As a result, Jews can certainly understand the linkage that Christians affirm between the Hebrew Bible and their continuing tradition based on it. We only want Christians to recognize that Christian scriptures and tradition are the continuation and fulfillment of the Hebrew Bible *for Christians*. Similarly, the four pairs of concepts that the *Notes* wants to balance in reading the Bible—promise and fulfillment, continuity and newness, singularity and universality, uniqueness and exemplary nature—are unobjectionable to Jews if it is clear that Jews and Christians apply these principles differently.[80] The "fulfillment" of the liberation and salvation of the Exodus, for example, and its "newness" are, for Christians, preeminently Jesus, whereas for Jews it is the Messianic era still to come. Until such time, the Exodus and Sinai, as understood by the rabbinic tradition, continue to govern our vision of what is and ought to be.

As part of the rapprochement between Christians and Jews in our time, then, Jews want contemporary Christians to abandon the triumphalism and chauvinism of the past, both in their relationships with Jews and in their reading of the Bible. One important manifestation of doing this would be a shift in policy on missionizing among Jews. Jews can understand Christians' desire to spread their faith, and they certainly appreciate that the *Guidelines* warned Catholics to "take care to live and spread their Christian faith while maintaining the strictest respect for religious liberty, in line with the teaching of the Second Vatican Council." However, because Jews represent less than half of 1 percent of the world's population and Catholics more than 25 percent, and because Jews lost one third of their numbers in the Holocaust and face major demographic problems due to assimilation and intermarriage, Jews hope that Catholic respect for Judaism and Jews results in a policy of renouncing conversionary efforts among Jews altogether and that that policy is adopted by all Christians.

Jews do *not* expect Christians to abandon their belief in Jesus as *their* way to salvation. Furthermore, the recognition of legitimacy that I am seeking is *mutual*. As noted, Jews have always believed that Judaism is really what God wants, that, ultimately, in the words of Isaiah 2:3, all peoples will come to Jerusalem to learn the Torah from Israel. But for millennia, Jews have understood that Jewish law is only incumbent on Jews, that indeed it is the *Jewish* way to salvation, and that righteous people in other groups can attain salvation in their specific ways. This Jew hopes that Catholics—and Christians of the other denominations as well—are increasingly coming to the same realization.

Muslims

Similar concerns apply to Muslims; but there, frankly, the work will be much harder because with very few exceptions, Muslims have not applied to the Koran and the *hadith* the same kind of historical analysis that many Jews and Christians have applied to their holy scriptures. That is, they have not seen the Koran as a product of its time, limited in its vision by the frustrations of Muhammad to convert Jews and Christians. They instead take a fundamentalist view of the text, believing it to be a direct transcription of the word of God with no possibility of human error in the understanding of the revelation or in its transcription. As a result, while Muslims have respected both Jews and Christians as People of the Book, in accordance with the text of the Koran, they have seen them as second-class citizens, indeed, as the Koran says, as sinners:

> People of the Book, now there has come to you Our Messenger [Muhammad], making clear to you many things you have been concealing of the Book, and effacing many things. . . . O you who believe! Do not take the Jews and the Christians for friends; they are friends of each other. And whoever among you takes them for a friend, then surely he is one of them; surely Allah does not guide such unjust people. . . . They are unbelievers who say, "God is the Messiah, Mary's son." . . . Say the Jews and Christians, "We are the sons of God, and His beloved ones." Say [to them]: "Why then does God chastise you for your sins? . . . Say: People of the Book, do you blame us for any other cause than that we believe in God and what has been sent down to us, and what was sent down before, and that most of you are ungodly?" Say: "Shall I tell you of a recompense with God worse than that? Whoever God has cursed, and with whom He is wroth, and made some of them apes and swine, and worshipers of idols—they are worse situated and have gone further astray from the right way. . . . They are unbelievers who say, "God is the Third of Three." No god is there but One God. . . . Believers, many are the rabbis and the monks who defraud men of their possessions and debar people from the path of Allah.[81]

Based on one of the passages just quoted, mullahs in Gaza have continually called Israelis and Jews in general "apes and swine," and that refrain has become part of the Arab press. Moreover, the Taliban arrested Christian missionaries precisely because Christians who believe in the Trinity are, according to the Koran itself, unbelievers. Muslims will have to go a long way to rid themselves of the supercessionism inherent in their sources; only then can Muslims and their governments hope to have anything but suspicious and hostile relations with the West.

A Realistic but Open Model
of the Covenant for Our Times

With these considerations as a background, I am now prepared to suggest some features of a contemporary version of each religion's covenant with God that, on the one hand, is realistic in its understanding of the past and present of all three religions and their respective communities of adherents but, on the other hand, holds out promise for better mutual relations. Such an interpretation of each of the three Western religions has, I think, the following elements.

The Role of Individuals in the Covenant

Modern versions of Judaism, Christianity, and Islam all too often ignore the mode and method of modernism and the Enlightenment philosophy that motivated it—that people exist as individuals first and as members of groups second. What was exclusively a philosophic doctrine in the seventeenth century gained political expression in this country in the eighteenth, through the Declaration of Independence, the Constitution, and the Bill of Rights; but it has taken the better part of the last two centuries for that ideology to become part of the thinking, customs, and daily life of a large number of Americans. This *has* happened, however: People are crossing group lines (whether they be racial, religious, ethnic, or whatever else) in their schooling; their jobs; their housing; and, most important, their friendships (even to the point of intergroup marriages). Whether this is good or bad, it is a fact that has a strong influence on the thinking and action of moderns living in the United States. This is somewhat less true in other Western countries, and it is not true at all in many Muslim lands. Still, a covenant concept that translates and applies the meaning and import of Judaism, Christianity, or Islam to the modern world must come to grips with the individualism of modernity.

Individualism has implications for the covenant both internally and externally—that is, within each group and in the group's relations to outsiders. Internally, it means that religious leaders must recognize that individuals raised in a given tradition will not automatically have loyalty to that tradition. People do need community and many do want to have a relationship with God, but they now increasingly feel free to shop around for the form of religious expression that is most meaningful to them. *As individuals,* they choose whether to affirm the covenant, and, if so, how.[82] Consequently religious leaders have to redouble their efforts in communicating the message of their form of the covenant if they want to retain their adherents, and religious groups have to prepare themselves religiously and socially for integrating many converts into the fold—a process for which Jews are especially unprepared, because of the traditional lack of missionizing and conversion in Judaism.

Externally, modern individualism means that both the Christian and the Jewish communities must recognize that members of each faith vary widely in their conceptions and practices: There is no stereotypical Jew or Christian, and the more that Muslim countries confront the modern West, the more the differences among Muslims in ideas and practices will become apparent. This feature of the modern religious landscape holds great promise for relationships among people of the three faiths in that there is now a much greater chance that members of each faith community can relate to those of the others as people and not as card-carrying members of a specific group. This, I hope, will make people more aware that people with patterns of belief and practice different from their own have worth too.

The Role of the Group and Its Traditions in the Covenant

However much we moderns are individuals, we also deeply need to be part of a group. The Covenant speaks directly to this need, because through being covenanted with God as a community, we are also covenanted with each other and with our ancestors and our descendants for all time. Part of the power of the Covenant idea is precisely the rootedness in a historical community that it affords.

This means that no modern concept of covenant can safely ignore the past and present traditions of the group in both belief and practice. That is, the individualism that moderns feel and live must be balanced with the social associations and commitments that we also feel and live. A modern covenant concept must contain enough of the group feeling and traditions to make it recognizably Jewish, Christian, or Muslim for the group functions of each covenant to take place.

The Role of Universal Ideals in the Covenant

Judaism, Christianity, and Islam have both particularist and universalist strains in their literature,[83] and it is important that a modern conception of covenant not lose sight of the universalism in each tradition in its efforts to accommodate the need for individualism and nationalism. The biblical and rabbinic traditions achieved a *balance* of the national and universal— and *not* by just asserting that everyone else should become Jewish; Christians and Muslims, with their supercessionist roots, must find ways to articulate a genuine universalism that is not based on everyone becoming either Christian or Muslim.

The universal aspect of the covenant has two manifestations, both of which are important to retain and to develop. Universalism in our own day involves the recognition that God can and does relate to all people. The particular way in which God relates to each group may vary, and it is inevitable that people will feel that their own way is best; but this should not produce the conclusion that other ways are necessarily bad, ineffective, or inauthentic. It may well be that God wisely entered into different forms of relationship with different peoples to fit the traditions, talents, and sensitivities of each group. It may also be that God has planned different roles for each group. Franz Rosenzweig, an early-twentieth-century Jewish thinker, suggested that Jews model what God wants and that Christians carry the message to the Gentiles; the respective numbers of the Jewish and Christian communities and their respective policies on missionizing seems to support such a view. As Seymour Siegel, a rabbi and professor of the Conservative Movement, said:

> If this suggestion were to be accepted by Jew and Christian, it would be possible to open a new era of dialogue and mutual enlightenment. Christians would not denigrate Judaism by viewing it as a vestige, an anachronism of ancient times. They would cease their missionizing activities vis-a-vis Jews. For Jews, there would be a new recognition of the importance of Christianity, of its spiritual dimension and its task to bring the word of God to the far islands.[84]

While Rosenzweig knew much less about Islam and did not paint a good picture of it, I want to affirm that the same considerations would apply to Islam: We need to get rid of supercessionism, to embrace our own faith with passion and commitment while still recognizing that intelligent, moral people reach God through other paths; therefore, we need to stop missionizing among peoples of other faiths.

The other aspect of covenantal universalism affects our hopes for the future. The biblical promise of a Messianic time when there would be universal peace, prosperity, goodness, and fulfillment; when God's teaching will be put "into people's inmost being" so that everyone will heed Him; and when, *mirabile dictu*, God shall even "reconcile fathers with sons and sons with their fathers"[85]—that biblical promise is a crucial element of the covenant concept that must be continually reinforced. This goal-directedness puts our lives in a broader context, thereby making them much more meaningful: I am not struggling for naught, because my actions can contribute to bringing about Messianic times for all humanity. No wonder this universalist element has been part of the covenant idea from the start.

The Role of God in the Covenant

The Covenant is not just the constitution of a group of people, but an agreement with God. It is the divine component of the Covenant that gives it ultimate authority, that pushes us to expand the scope of the Covenant to encompass all human beings, and that holds out plausible promise for a Messianic future. God's participation in the Covenant also provides a powerful rationale for human worth and an effective antidote to loneliness. If God, after all, seeks relations with human beings, we must be worthy of such association (at least potentially); and since every human being incorporates divine worth, each person can relate to God, even at the times when it is difficult to relate to other human beings. No interpretation of the Covenant that leaves God out can plausibly claim to be Jewish, Christian, or Muslim.

The elements of the Covenant that I just described give it its social import, and any modern view must incorporate all of them. This, of course, is easier said than done, for several of them do not sit well together. If the Covenant is to speak to the individual, how can it re-enforce group associations and traditions; and if it is to do that, how can it be open to all human beings? These are real tensions in the covenant idea, but it is good that the concept has those tensions, because they are part of life as we know it as individuals, as members of a faith community, and as part of humanity generally. May God help us reinterpret our traditions so that the nasty and chauvinistic elements in them no longer lead to suspicion, hatred, abuse of the other, and even war; let them instead do what they were intended to do: help us rise to the mutual respect and cooperation that we should have for all human beings as we each follow our own tradition's path to the holiness that God expects of us all.

In this process, we Jews will remain a people apart, committed to our mission of being a light to the nations, modeling our own understanding of God's will. In doing this, we will carry out the duties of our own covenant with God. As the Psalmist said:

> O offspring of Abraham, His servant,
> O descendants of Jacob, His chosen ones.
>
> He is the Lord our God;
> His judgments are throughout the earth.
> He is ever mindful of His covenant,
> the promise He gave for a thousand generations,
> that He made with Abraham,
> swore to Isaac,
> and confirmed in a decree for Jacob,
> for Israel, as an eternal covenant.[86]

CHAPTER FOUR

The King's Torah: Judaism and National Policy

I F JEWS MUST DETERMINE THE FOUNDATIONS AND PARAMETERS FOR their interactions with other Jews and with people of other faiths, the topics of the previous two chapters, they must also think through the ground rules for their relationships with the modern democracies in which the vast majority of today's Jews live. Recognizing that the structure defining the relationship between religion and state varies among modern nations, I argue in this chapter that even in the United States, where religion and state have legally been kept at a great distance, there is room for some forms of healthy interactions between them. Some of the same considerations and conclusions that I draw in regard to the United States apply even more easily to nations that have laws establishing a closer link between religion and state. Conversely, I also argue that in some areas the separation of religion and state is well warranted; separation in such arenas should be carefully guarded in the United States and introduced in Israel and other countries with legally established religious institutions.

The Historical Relationship of Jews to the State

If, after you have entered the land that the Lord your God has assigned to you, and taken possession of it and settled in it, you decide, "I will set a king over me, as do all the nations about me," you shall be free to set a king over yourself, one chosen by the Lord your God. Be sure to set as king over yourself one of your own people; you must not set a foreigner over you, one who is not your kinsman. Moreover, he shall not keep many horses . . . And he shall not have many wives, lest his heart go astray; nor shall he amass silver and gold to excess.

When he is seated on his royal throne, he shall have a copy of this Teaching written for him on a scroll by the levitical priests. Let it remain with him and let him read in it all his life, so that he may learn to revere the Lord his God, to observe faithfully every word of this Teaching as well as these laws. Thus he will not act haughtily toward his fellows or deviate from the Instruction to the right or to the left, to the end that he and his descendants may reign long in the midst of Israel.[1]

In these verses, the Torah describes a biblical view of religion and state. While Moses ran a theocracy, where the religious leader was also the leader of state, during the time of Samuel in the eleventh century B.C.E., the Israelites requested and were granted rule by a secular monarch.[2] Thus by the time the passage in Deuteronomy was written in the late seventh century B.C.E., the Torah's ideal state is no longer a theocracy, but rather a monarchy.

Nevertheless, religion was to have a dominant role in the biblical state, determining the criteria of eligibility for the rulers and much of the content of their decrees. Thus the king must be an Israelite and, moreover, committed to the Torah. Furthermore, he must possess and repeatedly read his own copy of the Torah so that God's laws are fresh in his mind. In the end, his own decrees may not "deviate . . . to the right or to the left" from God's Instruction (Torah). The Bible's historical accounts of Israel's and Judah's rulers in the books of Judges, 1 and 2 Samuel, and 1 and 2 Kings indicate that this ideal was not often achieved; but the biblical authors had a clear conception of the proper role of religion in government and used that theory to judge Israel's rulers.

However much contemporary American Jews are committed to Judaism, they certainly cannot apply the Torah's theory straightforwardly to American government. For one thing, the vast majority of American citizens are not Jewish. For another, the founding documents of the government of the United States proclaim both religious freedom and, as interpreted by the Supreme Court, "a wall of separation" between church and state,[3] however much that wall has been weakened or breached by recent decisions. These circumstances and legal provisions in the United States are clearly vastly different from the ones the Torah contemplated or intended.

For more than 80 percent of the nearly four-thousand-year history of the Jewish people, though, Jews have not lived under the conditions that the Torah describes. Until the creation of the modern State of Israel in 1948, Jews ruled themselves only during the First Temple period (c. 950–586 B.C.E.) and the Maccabean period (165–63 B.C.E.). In all other times and places, Jews have been a minority population living under some other group's sovereignty. Babylonians, Persians, Greeks, Romans, Muslims, and Christians have all ruled the places where significant numbers of Jews dwelled. Jews were sometimes granted the right to govern the internal matters of their own community, but they were second-class citizens at best and a persecuted minority at worst. They were routinely subjected to heavy taxes and restricted liberties, and sometimes they were forced to convert, leave, or die.

As a result of this precarious, minority status, one can readily understand why, on the one hand, the Rabbis would say, "Pray for the welfare of the government, for without respect for it people would swallow each other alive";[4] while, on the other hand, they would also say, "Love work, hate lordship, and seek no intimacy with the ruling power" and "Be on your guard against the ruling power, for they who exercise it draw no man near to them except for their own interests; appearing as friends when it is to their own advantage, they do not stand by a man in his hour of need."[5] The respect for authority with the simultaneous wariness of it, as embodied in these early rabbinic comments, shaped the attitude of Jews toward government in most times and places throughout the last two thousand years, articulated perhaps most famously by the rabbi's comment in the opening number of the musical *Fiddler on the Roof:* "May God bless and keep the czar—far away from us!"

The Enlightenment and the emancipation that followed in its wake were a breath of fresh air for Jews. For the first time since the era of the Maccabees, Jews were to be accepted as full citizens, eligible for voting, university education, government service, residence anywhere in the realm, and equal treatment in the courts. Moreover, all of these were to be a matter of moral and legal *right*, not just kind (and usually temporary) toleration. This was, indeed, a new world.

The new equal status, though, would come with some troubling consequences. These were already evident in the questions Napoleon posed to the Sanhedrin of Jewish leaders he convened in 1807. Would French Jews marry French non-Jews? In what areas would French law govern Jews, and in what areas would the rabbis insist on their own authority?[6]

The questions of intermarriage and assimilation in an open society plague American Jews to this day. Jews worry publicly about the continuity of Judaism and the Jewish people. After all, while Christians make up a full third of the world's population, Jews constitute 0.2 percent, and so defections from the Jewish people threaten its very existence. While we Jews have managed to survive persecution for all these centuries, it is unfortunately not clear that we can survive the conditions of freedom.

Arguments for Separation of Church and State

In response to these realities, some religiously and politically conservative Jews argue that a strong Christian hand in government and in society generally would ultimately be good for the Jews living in predominantly Christian lands, for it would strengthen the Jewish resolve to remain Jewish. After all, people define themselves, at least in part, by what others are doing. If everyone is (or appears) the same, nobody will have a robust sense of separate, unique identity. A strong Christian voice in government and society, then, might produce a strong

Jewish response. Those who argue this also maintain that many of the policies backed by the Christian right parallel Jewish values, and so we should support a hearty Christian presence in government for that reason as well.[7]

My own view differs substantially from that. With all of its pitfalls, the separation of church and state is, for me, one of this country's most important assets. The great experiment in pluralism that the United States embodies is, in no small measure, a product of that separation, and so I value it as an American.

My Jewish roots, too, prompt me to support the separation of church and state. The Jewish people's historical experience makes me wary of living under a government ruled by one religion. I cannot trust that such a government would, in the end, preserve my right to adhere to my own religion. That would be especially true of a fundamentalist religion, because adherents of such groups tend to be completely sure that they are right and all others are wrong. While Judaism certainly champions strong families, communities, educational institutions, and the like, Jewish methods for arriving at those stances are definitely not fundamentalist, and Jews' interpretation and application of them are not conservative either. On the contrary, most Jews consistently vote in overwhelming percentages for liberal candidates; and although Jews as a group work vigorously to improve schools, social services, and society in general, they are considerably less judgmental than fundamentalist Christians are of those who have different views or ways of life.

Finally, my philosophical background motivates me to support a strong separation of church and state. Epistemologically, I believe in the Aristotelian model for attaining social wisdom—namely, that all views should be aired in the marketplace of ideas, with none given a priori authority (a provision parallel to the "Establishment" clause of the First Amendment of the U.S. Constitution). Thus, rather than deductively basing the definition of American concepts and values on a particular religious view, I would seek to determine America's commonalities in thought and values *inductively,* testing for agreement amid the diversity of traditions and attitudes brought to the table. This approach also parallels both the method and "the sound and the fury" of each page of the Talmud, where multiple opinions must be heard and evaluated before a decision is made, and where some arguments are left standing for lack of sufficient human wisdom to make a decision.

This Aristotelian and rabbinic method of arriving at a decision is ultimately based on an acknowledgment that no human being is omniscient and that nobody has justification to claim absolute knowledge—the same epistemological humility that grounded my approach to both Jewish pluralism and interfaith relations. In light of the limitations to human knowledge, the best that we can do is to pool our views in an attempt to arrive at the best policy.

Coherence and Continuity amid Freedom and Diversity

How, though, can agreement be reached if so many disparate voices are to be heard and somehow accommodated? When using an inductive model of decision making, consensus is most probable, of course, when the people participating in the discussion come from similar backgrounds in the first place. Since they share common assumptions, they are more likely to agree on specific policies. Colonial America, in which Madison and Jefferson created their ground-breaking provisions for religious freedom, was much less diverse than modern America is, and so America's Founding Fathers could more easily be assured that tolerance of religious differences would not undermine a coherent American society.

Although consensus may be harder to achieve when the participants come from diverse backgrounds, I am convinced that agreement is possible and that, moreover, the ultimate result will most likely be all the wiser for the variety of the experiences and views that are aired while shaping it. Liberty in America need not amount to anarchy; a core set of concepts and values can still define America as a coherent society.

Some examples will make this clear. In the two major national discussions on health care—that of the President's Commission on Health Care in the early 1980s, and that of the Clinton Health Care Task Force of 1993—a remarkable degree of agreement prevailed. In reflecting on the essays produced during and for the President's Commission, Daniel Wikler, editor of the commission's report, noted this:

> It is true that each essay provides a different account of equity in access to health care and insists that rival accounts are mistaken. Yet there is one policy recommendation supported by each of these essays: Every person ought to be assured of access to some decent minimum of health care services. This conclusion cannot be said to have been "proved" by this collection of arguments, but the fact that a recommendation of universal access to (at least some) health care follows from such disparate sets of premises suggests that the recommendation is "insensitive" to choice of moral theory. Even if we do not know which moral theory is correct, then, and thus cannot provide a ground-level-up proof that all should have access to a minimum of health care, such a belief has been rendered reasonable and perhaps even compelling. In this sense, this diverse and inconsistent collection of theories of justice in health care delivery supports the consensus reached by members of the President's Commission concerning the moral obligation of our society to ensure access to health care for all its people.[8]

As a member of the Ethics Committee of the Clinton Health Care Task Force, I can report that its experience was much the same. The theoretical debates were many and, in some instances, heated. For example, in formulating the arguments for the government to guarantee universal health care, all of us agreed that the moral grounds for such a system included convictions enshrined in the nation's constitutive documents, specifically, equality, justice, and the government's duty to "provide for the general welfare." Religious members of the committee, though, wanted to include what Protestants call "our obligations of stewardship"—that is, our duty to take care of God's property, including our bodies. Even though the draft specified that the values held by all Americans would argue for universal health care and that religious Americans have yet other reasons to support the same policy, the secularists on the committee argued strenuously and heatedly to drop any and all religious language. Despite that controversy about its theoretical underpinnings, the policy advocated by both sides was the same—namely, that all Americans should be guaranteed health care.

Another example in a completely different arena will shed further light on both the strengths and pitfalls of this point. In view of a perceived failure of America's families and religious institutions to inculcate fundamental moral values, some school districts are now in the process of formulating a list of such values together with curricular approaches to teach them. Clearly, such school districts have to be careful of running afoul of America's diversity in moral perspective. Indeed, these efforts are usually associated with the right wing in American politics that advocates "character education" to teach morality rather than the "values clarification" techniques favored by the more liberal elements. Values clarification assumes that each of us has his or her own unique list of values and/or interpretation of them, thus emphasizing individual freedom; character education, however, assumes that there is a core of objective values, regardless of background. Values clarification was popular in the 1960s, 1970s, and for part of the 1980s, but, more recently, character education has taken hold. So, for example, the Character Counts! Coalition, with an advisory council that includes individuals from a variety of religious backgrounds, lists sixty-one institutions as member organizations, including such national educational groups as the American Association of School Administrators, the American Federation of Teachers, and the National Education Association. It formulated the Aspen Declaration:

1. The next generation will be the stewards of our communities, nation, and planet in extraordinarily critical times.
2. The present and future well-being of our society requires an involved, caring citizenry with good moral character.
3. People do not automatically develop good moral character; therefore, conscientious efforts must be made to help young peo-

ple develop the values and abilities necessary for moral decision making and conduct.

4. Effective character education is based on core ethical values which form the foundation of democratic society—in particular, respect, responsibility, trustworthiness, caring, justice and fairness, and civic virtue and citizenship.

5. These core ethical values transcend cultural, religious, and socio-economic differences.

6. Character education is, first and foremost, an obligation of families; it is also an important obligation of faith communities, schools, youth and other human service organizations.

7. These obligations to develop character are best achieved when these groups work in concert.

8. The character and conduct of our youth reflect the character and conduct of society; therefore, every adult has the responsibility to teach and model the core ethical values and every social institution has the responsibility to promote the development of good character.

Along with this declaration, the Josephson Institute—which coordinated the effort to formulate the Aspen Declaration and to have it approved by a wide variety of national bodies—produced a series of educational materials for children and adults to explain in greater detail the values enumerated in paragraph 4 of the document and to apply them to issues of daily living.[9]

While the liberal side of me, nurtured by my minority status as a Jew and by the feisty, argumentative nature of the Jewish tradition, worries about such sweeping statements that confidently ensure unanimity in moral viewpoint, I must admit that I have no quarrel with the six values articulated in paragraph 4 of the Aspen Declaration or with the educational materials produced by the Josephson Institute to inculcate them in a cross-cultural setting. Indeed, as I explained in Chapters Two and Three, I think that the proper moral view is relativity, not relativism. These educational developments, then, as well as the policy examples on health care I presented, illustrate that diversity need not amount to incoherence, that liberty need not produce license for lack of any unity of vision. Instead, America's wide variety of cultures and religions—Eastern as well as

Western—can all be plumbed cooperatively to produce coherent social policy.

Areas of Moral Disagreement

Sometimes, of course, religious differences make for differences in policy as well. According to Thomas Jefferson, public policy should be based on morality, but only when all religions agree on the moral course of action: "The practice of morality [is] necessary for the well-being of society. . . . The interests of society require observation of those moral principles only in which all religions agree."[10]

The most obvious example of a case in which no such agreement exists is abortion. Since the Supreme Court's decision in *Roe v. Wade* (1973), Americans have had the constitutional right to have an abortion during the first two trimesters of gestation, without any requirement to justify that decision to the doctor or government. Because America's religions differ markedly in their stance on abortion, the Supreme Court's policy appears to accord with what Thomas Jefferson himself wanted. Still, we ask, what should freedom of religion entail when a particular medical procedure like abortion is required by some religions under at least some circumstances, permitted by others, and forbidden by others?

The Jewish tradition takes an intermediate stance on abortion between that of the Catholic Church and other Right-to-Life advocates and that of secularists and feminists that it should always be a woman's own choice. According to Jewish sources, the human body belongs to God; God, therefore, can and does make demands on how we are to care for our bodies. This includes positive obligations (such as proper diet, sleep, hygiene, and exercise) and negative duties (such as refraining from harming, let alone destroying, our body).[11] Thus, contrary to secularist views, Judaism holds that a pregnant woman does not have free reign to determine the fate of her fetus, any more than any man or woman has ultimate authority over their bodies; God's rules govern how we are to treat our bodies.

On the other hand, Judaism takes a developmental view of the growth of the fetus into a human being. The Talmud classifies the embryo up to forty days of gestation as "simply water"; it becomes the "thigh of its mother" from the forty-first day until birth; and the fetus becomes a full human being only upon birth. Normally, neither men nor women have the right to amputate their own thigh; that would be injuring one's body, which belongs to God. If one's thigh turns gangrenous, though, one has not only the right but the duty to amputate the thigh in an effort to save one's life. Similarly, if the fetus threatens the life or health of the mother, she has the duty to abort the fetus, even if, as in the movie, *Steel Magnolias,* she does not want to do so. More recent rabbinic opinions also permit an abortion when the fetus is, on the basis of testing, found to be grossly malformed or afflicted with a genetic disease like Tay-Sachs. Otherwise, though, abortion is prohibited, not as an act of murder, as Roman Catholic authorities see it, but as an act of self-injury. During the first forty days of gestation, the justification for an abortion need not be as strong as in the later period; but even then abortion must have a warrant, for it is still potential life.[12]

Given that stance and the contrary positions of Catholics, on the one hand, and secularists, on the other, how should Jews—and, for that matter, all Americans—handle the issue legally? My own view, like Jefferson's, is that we should all argue for governmental noninterference. That is, when there is substantial moral agreement among Americans, the government should enact that moral standard. That clearly holds, for example, for laws against murder, theft, and even more recently accepted moral positions such as bans on smoking in public, closed places.

Where Americans of good conscience differ widely on a given issue, though, as in the case of abortion, the government should remain neutral. It is then up to the leaders of each group to explain their position on abortion to their fellow members.

As a rabbi, then, I urge Jews to refrain from abortion, except under the circumstances mandated or permitted by Jewish law, even though it is legal in the United States. This is not as unusual as it may first seem, for individuals can and do decide not to do many things that the law allows, whether out of personal preference or for religious or ideological reasons. American law allows me, for example, to gain five hundred pounds, and yet I choose not to do so for many non-legal reasons. The Jewish stance on American law on abortion is simply another such case.

Another good example of this form of reasoning, but with a different result, is the debate on assisted suicide. Some people ask for assistance in committing suicide to stop their pain. Judaism permits (or, on some readings, demands) the use of as much medication as necessary to quell pain. Other people ask for help in dying because it seems to them that nobody cares whether they live or die. To counteract the feelings of abandonment and loneliness that often produce such requests, the Jewish duty to visit the sick (*biqqur holim*) becomes all the more important in our time of broken and far-flung families. Supplying pain medication and visiting sick people are appropriate Jewish responses to a person's serious illness; assisting in a suicide is not. My rabbinic ruling stating these positions was approved overwhelmingly by the Conservative Movement's Committee on Jewish Law and Standards on March 12, 1997.[13]

Even though the Jewish position on assisted suicide is thus unambiguous, at least for Conservative Jews, that did not, in advance of the Supreme Court's ruling, automatically require us to submit *amicus curiae* briefs to the court asking it to adopt our view. Furthermore, now that the court has ruled that the Constitution does not guarantee a right to assisted suicide and that the states have the authority to govern this matter, our stance for Jews does not automatically entail strongly lobbying against state initiatives to permit rendering assistance in suicides. After all, some of our opposition to assisted suicide stems from distinctly Jewish conceptions of the value of life and of the role of God in it, and those arguments would be inappropriate grounds for court rulings or state legislation. Moreover, serious moral arguments have been adduced by two federal appellate courts and by others in favor of allowing such assistance. Thus, before I would feel impelled by my Jewish stance against assisted suicide to pursue political means to make it the law of the land, I should carefully consider whether I have sufficiently strong, nonreligious reasons in addition to my religious grounds to oppose assisted suicide.

As it happens, I do have such reasons. Specifically, requests for assistance in suicide almost never arise in a morally pure context. That requires all of the following conditions: sufficient pain medication is afforded; the patient is supported socially, psychologically, and spiritually by the presence of family and friends; and psychological depression is treated. All of those interventions must be tried before assisted suicide would ever approach being justifiable. Moreover, in an era of managed care, the *right* to assistance in committing suicide can all too easily become the *duty* to accept such assistance. These reasons—independent of religious perspectives— make me willing to lobby against initiatives permitting assisted suicide.

Jewish religious beliefs may assuredly influence my own view of any matter and, I hope, that of other Jews as well; but in the pluralistic environment that is America, we must learn to separate out those concerns from arguments that apply to all Americans, regardless of their religious affiliation or lack thereof. Although I am not happy with the number of abortions performed in this country or the reasons for many of them, I cannot formulate good, secular grounds for opposing other people's rights to have them when they decide that it is morally appropriate; hence it would be wrong for me to lobby for legislation to forbid them. In contrast, I can articulate grounds for Americans of all religious persuasions to oppose assisted suicide. Therefore, on the latter issue I am willing to take a more assertive stand in arguing for my position's adoption into law.

Justifying This Approach Philosophically and Theologically

If I have a clear position on abortion, though, why should I advocate it in public forums and among my own co-religionists but hesitate to push for its adoption as law? That reluctance comes from my views about, and my commitment to, pluralism. That conviction, in turn, is rooted in the series of historical, philosophical, and theological arguments I discussed in Chapters Two and Three.

Pluralism, of course, is never easy: If you are convinced that you are right in a given position on a matter that you consider important, your natural inclination is to fight for it in every way possible. To fail to do that, in fact, seems to question the seriousness of your own beliefs. Moreover, if you think that God requires a given stance, to fail to fight for that position makes the strength of your religious convictions suspect.

Nevertheless, further philosophical reflection along the lines I presented in previous chapters reveals that while you may be absolutely certain of the correctness of your stance, you are, after all, a human being who lacks God's omniscience. You inevitably see things from your specific perspective, and even that you can understand only in part.

Some religious leaders of Judaism and other faiths try to trump these philosophical considerations about the limits of human knowledge with the theological claim that God Himself has mandated a given doctrine or value, thus replacing human fallibility with divine infallibility. Further theological thinking, though, indicates that we can only know so much of God and His desires, for God is by nature partially hidden.

The Jewish tradition, of course, maintains that God revealed His will for us through some process and that we have the record of that Revelation in the Torah. The status of the knowledge of God's will that the Torah affords us, though, was itself a matter of debate as early as the second century, with Rabbi Akiva claiming that every letter was revealed by God to Moses, and Rabbi Ishmael maintaining that "only general rules were given at Sinai."[14] As I have described in some detail elsewhere,[15] contemporary theologians take yet a wider variety of positions on the way that Revelation happened at Sinai and continues to occur in our day. Some theologians maintain that God *spoke* in specific Hebrew words at Sinai; some, that God *inspired* Moses to write what we have; and some, that the *encounter* with God then and now stimulates human beings to write what they understand the meaning and import of that encounter to be.

Even if you believe, as Rabbi Akiva did, that God spoke in discrete words at Sinai and, furthermore, that we have a completely accurate record of those words in hand in the version of the Torah that has come down to us, to understand and apply that divine communication *human beings* must interpret it. That inevitable human component in understanding God's message immediately undermines the claim to absolute certainty that divine communication was supposed to afford us. We will always have to ask whether we understood God correctly in interpreting His words. Fundamentalism thus becomes theologically and philosophically impossible to justify.

The Rabbis of the Talmud and Midrash already understood this. As I discussed in Chapter Two, they were impressed with the Bible's difficulty of differentiating a true prophet from a false one. Even when they were convinced that a new prophecy was true, though, they ruled it out of court, for God Himself had determined that after the Torah had been given, all future legal decisions were to be made by a majority of the human court. In a famous talmudic debate, when the Rabbis refused to accept a new revelation because it did not fit within the accepted, interpretive method of knowing God's will, God laughed and said, "My children have overcome Me, my children have overcome Me," for now human beings will determine how God and God's will should be understood. In another understanding of the same Hebrew word *nitzhuni,* deriving it not from *natze'ah* (overcome) but rather from *netzah* (eternal), the last line of that talmudic passage has God saying, "My children have eternalized me, My children have eternalized Me"— presumably by making the law live in each generation's debates and decisions.

The Rabbis knew, indeed, that "just as a hammer causes numerous sparks to flash forth, so is a Scriptural verse capable of many interpretations."[16] They, therefore, insisted that one should pay more attention to the words of the interpreters than to the Torah itself, "for the Torah is shut up [cryptic and therefore ambiguous] and consists entirely of headings . . . but from the words of the Sages one can derive proper law because they explain the Torah."[17] Even those who stood at Sinai, according to the Rabbis, understood the Revelation given there through their own individual abilities and perspectives.[18] This did not prevent coherence, for there were limits to pluralism even within the Jewish community (as noted in Chapter Two), but nobody could claim to trump the human process of inquiry and discussion by invoking the decree of God. The very meaning of such a decree depends on the definition of its human interpreters.

Thus the Jewish way to know God's will is to study the Torah and its ongoing interpretations through the centuries and to engage in a discussion with others about its proper meaning and application in our time. This methodology is remarkably similar to American democratic theory. In each there is an authoritative text (the Torah or Constitution), and in each there is a deliberative process through which its meaning and application must be determined. People can and should argue vigorously for their own understandings and applications of the text and the tradition based on it, but ultimately only the group as a whole can decide. Nobody can circumvent or supersede that process by any claim to certain knowledge of what the text meant in the past and should mean now.

Furthermore, an openness to the opinions of others must apply not only to the debate about what the communal policy should be but also to the limits of when a communal policy should be adopted in the first place. Sometimes reasonable and morally sensitive people disagree, and sometimes the society is better off allowing multiple forms of both opinion and action to take place. Social coherence does not require that everyone think or do absolutely everything the same way.

On the contrary, some flexibility within the practice of the community enables it to flourish more fully. If every action is mandated by law, then people may rebel, either openly or subtly by ignoring the law or finding ways to circumvent it. Alternatively, they may become so docile that they will stop thinking for themselves, leaving the definition of all norms to others.

Pluralism not only in debate but in practice goads people to think hard about their own positions, and the variety of practices that people see in their community encourages them to rethink their own practices often. Pluralism in practice also promotes tolerance and understanding, for when you see other intelligent and morally sensitive people, especially those you know and like, doing something differently, you are hard pressed to claim that your way is the only possible way.

Openness to discussion and even tolerance of other people's practices are difficult not only on an intellectual level but on an emotional level as well. If it is hard to understand how you can passionately assert a given position on an important topic like abortion or assisted suicide and yet allow that others who disagree may be just as intelligent and morally sensitive as you are, it is even harder to live with them, witness what they do, and still like them. Here Jewish theological concepts and values can help immensely. As noted previously, Simon Greenberg pointed out that God *intends* that we be pluralistic and that we exercise every effort possible to love our neighbors sufficiently to listen to their views, to weigh those views seriously, and to learn from their explanations and actions, even as we ask them to do the same as we live by our own views. One must, like Hillel, be affable and humble and teach opinions opposed to one's own, citing them first.[19] Only then can human beings hope to arrive at policies that are informed, thoughtful, cooperative, and maybe even wise.

Bringing Religion and Nation Closer Together

I grew up in the 1950s and 1960s, when Jews roundly applauded each new brick being added by the Supreme Court to the wall of separation between church and state. The position that I take in this chapter thus represents somewhat of a change for me. Jefferson and Madison had good reason to fear the entanglement of religion in national matters. The European experience had demonstrated beyond all reasonable doubt that that is not good for either religion or the state. Moreover, the Jewish historical experience might suggest the same, for Jews have been badly burned when governments have enforced religious norms.

In America, though, we do ourselves, religion, and the nation a disservice if we think that religion should have no role in shaping national policy. No religion should have the power or right to determine national policy, because that all too easily leads to intolerance, oppression, and sometimes even bloodshed. On the other hand, if public discussion of important social issues is to reflect the nation as a whole and if it is to attain the richness and wisdom that only multiple parties with differing views can give it, each religion must enter the fray of public debate and contribute its own views.

The separation of religion and state in the United States has given us the great gift of freedom of religion, by which we regularly come into contact with people who not only think but act differently from the way we do. Americans differ not only in private matters, like beliefs and home rituals, but also in moral principles and actions that affect society as a whole. Tolerating at least some differences in moral practice is good for both individuals and the nation. Seeing a variety of moral practices encourages individuals to think hard about their own moral positions and thus stretches their understanding of, and feeling for, others. A plurality of positions on given moral issues also fosters public discussion and, I hope, good social planning based on a broad base of views.

Thus both in the shaping of opinion and in moral practice, religion should not be stuck behind a "wall of separation." It should rather be integrally involved in our attempts to achieve the American dreams of pluralism, creativity, and wisdom.

CHAPTER FIVE

Procedural Justice: Making a Fair Decision

Procedural and Substantive Justice

"**J**USTICE, JUSTICE SHALL YOU PURSUE"[1] RINGS THROUGH THE ages as one of the Torah's major principles. The biblical prophets rail against the people for their failure to achieve justice, and they issue clarion calls for reform that have shaped the conscience of Western civilization for thousands of years.

"Justice, justice shall you pursue" appears after several verses in the Torah that demand the institution of courts located in all regions where the people dwell, that prohibit bribes, and that warn against prejudice in judgment. By mixing procedural concerns (like the placement of courts in convenient places) with substantive issues (like the prohibitions against bribes and prejudice), the Torah indicates its awareness that the two are inextricably intertwined, that procedure affects substance and substance demands certain procedural rules.

No human being can always know whose cause is right, for only God is privy to the sum total of every person's actions and intentions. Nevertheless, the Torah obligates us to establish courts to dispense justice as well as we can, and it specifies procedural rules to help us do that well.

So, for example, at least two witnesses are required to establish a fact in court in order to forestall collusion.[2] To accentuate its prohibition of false testimony, the Torah includes it in the Decalogue, announced amid thunder and lightning at Mount Sinai.[3] Moreover, a 20 percent fine is levied against witnesses who knowingly lie in a civil case,[4] and full retribution is required of those who testify falsely in a criminal case.[5] A judge's acceptance of bribes is roundly condemned, "for bribes blind the clear-sighted and upset the pleas of those who are in the right."[6] Each person is to be judged for his or her own actions exclusively,[7] a principle assumed without question in modern Western societies but very much at odds with the practices of many societies in ancient, medieval, and even modern times, in which relatives were punished for the crimes of their family members.[8] The Torah insists that neither rich nor poor may be favored: "You shall not be partial in judgment: hear out low and high alike. Fear no man, for judgment is God's."[9] The alien, too, is to be treated fairly: "Decide justly between any man and a fellow Israelite or stranger."[10]

The Rabbis of the Talmud and Middle Ages added many more procedural rules to ensure impartial treatment. For example, one litigant may not be required to stand while the other is sitting, both parties to the case must wear clothing of similar quality, judges must understand the languages spoken by the people before them, and people related to each other or to the litigants may not serve as witnesses, and neither may those engaged in illegal or immoral activities.[11] Through rules such as these, procedural justice is strengthened and made a reality.

Substantive justice speaks not to the method by which a judicial decision is made, but to the character of the results of court procedures and, more broadly, of society's policies. In Plato's *Republic*, substantive justice amounts to social harmony; and that can be achieved, according to Plato, only when everyone does what his or her station in society demands. The biblical view of substantive justice is radically different, stressing the equality of all human beings and their right to equal protection of the law. Thus the Torah demands that aliens, widows, and orphans not be oppressed either in court[12] or in society generally;[13] on the contrary, they must be cared for because they have no protectors.[14] Similarly, the mistreatment of the defenseless and the failure to protect them in court were denounced by the Prophets as a sign of the decadence of the Israelite society of their time.[15] The poor are also to be treated honorably and justly,[16] and they, too, are to be cared for;[17] failure to treat the poor in that way was also part of the prophets' complaint against their society.[18] (I discuss this aspect of justice in the next chapter.)

Not only is it the downtrodden whose cause the Torah champions as part of its insistence on substantive justice but it is all members of society who must be treated justly. The Torah, therefore, includes lengthy lists of civil and criminal laws for society as a whole,[19] and the later rabbis developed this area of Jewish law extensively, beginning with the Mishnah's Order *Nezikin*.

The Torah itself, and the Rabbis even more, appreciated the fact that justice, to become a reality in people's lives, could not be left as a pious hope but must rather be translated into concrete norms. By presenting specific cases, both the biblical and the rabbinic traditions made the demands of justice clear and binding. It was not enough to require a person who finds a lost object, for example, to return it (as in Deuteronomy 22:1–3). What if not one, but several, people claim it? How shall you determine the real owner? What happens if you cannot? What should you do, on the other hand, if nobody comes forward to claim the object? Must you keep it? If so, for how long? To what extent must you go to publicize that you have it? If it requires care (for example, if it is an animal), must you spend your own money to provide that care? To what extent? May you use the object in the interim? Returning a lost object is a relatively simple demand of justice. But, as these questions demonstrate, even a straightforward requirement such as that easily becomes complicated—and the Rabbis, in fact, devoted an entire chapter of the Mishnah and Talmud to this issue (chapter 2 of *Bava Metzi'a*). Without that discussion, the Torah's imperative to return a lost object would remain imprecise and unworkable, demanding, in some understandings, too much and, in others, too little to make this aspect of justice part of an ongoing practice within Jewish communal life.

Aspiring to Be Holy: Beyond the Letter of the Law

Although the Torah and the later Jewish tradition went about as far as any society could go in translating its moral and spiritual commitments into legal terms, rabbinic authorities recognized that justice never can be captured totally in law. As a medieval Jewish phrase puts it, one can be a "scoundrel within the limits of the law" or, interpreted somewhat differently, "a scoundrel with the sanction of the Torah" (*naval b'reshut ha-Torah*).

Consequently, although the Bible as a whole depicts the substance of the law as both life giving and the source of goodness[20]—in sharp contrast to the abominable acts of the other nations[21]—the Torah in addition requires the doing of "what is right and good in the sight of the Lord."[22] The Rabbis of the Talmud take that and other verses in the Torah as the basis for declaring that people are obliged to act "beyond the letter of the law" (*lifnim m'shurat ha-din*).[23] Commenting on that biblical verse, Nahmanides (1194–c. 1270) said:

> This refers to compromise [rather than judgment according to strict law] and conduct beyond the requirements of the Law. The intent of this is that initially [in Deuteronomy 6:17] God had said that you should observe the laws and statutes that He had commanded you. Now God says that, with respect to what He has not commanded, you should likewise take heed to do the right and the good in His eyes, for He loves the good and the right. This is a great matter, for it is impossible to mention in the Torah all of a person's actions toward his neighbors and acquaintances, all of his commercial activity, and all social and political institutions. So, after God had mentioned many of them . . . He continues to say generally that one should do the right and the good in all matters through compromise and conduct beyond the requirements of the Law.[24]

Indeed, the Rabbis state that the Second Temple was destroyed because people did not acknowledge or fulfill such moral duties.[25]

Thus, while the Torah and the rabbinic tradition help make justice a reality by giving it concrete expression in law, Jewish law itself recognizes that justice sometimes demands more than the law does, that moral duties go beyond the letter of the law. Moreover, such moral duties sometimes require reshaping the law itself so that in each new age it can continue to be the best approximation of justice.

The underlying conviction that pushes Jewish law not to stop with defining justice in its procedural and substantive aspects but to insist instead that we must go beyond the letter of the law, if necessary, to achieve justice is the belief that God requires us to aspire to a moral and theological ideal. Specifically, justice in its fullest form is necessary for holiness. All Israelites are obligated to aspire to a life of holiness: "You shall be holy, for I, the Lord your God, am holy."[26] In the verses that follow this divine demand, the Torah specifies that holiness requires providing for the poor and the stranger; eschewing theft and fraud; rendering fair and impartial decisions in court; treating the blind, the deaf, and the stranger fairly; and ensuring honest weights and measures. These are all components of a society that has both procedural and substantive justice and even more—namely, generosity and caring. We are to treat each other as members of one extended family. To the degree that we can and at least in some areas, then, holiness requires that we go beyond insisting on our due and look instead at what seems to be good results for everyone concerned.

Arbitration and Mediation

That, of course, is not only hard to do; it is even hard to know what such a full sense of justice demands in every case.

That is why Nahmanides, in the passage quoted earlier, said that fulfilling the Torah's command that we "do the right and the good" also requires us to compromise with each other rather than suing each other in court. The Rabbis, in fact, suggest a host of reasons to avoid the court system whenever possible to ensure justice:[27]

1. The Time, Expense, and Bother of Taking a Case to Court. In some counties in the United States, civil cases can take up to five years to be heard. Even in places where the courts are not as badly backlogged, there are almost inevitably many, many delays, especially when the stakes are high. In fact, my son, a business litigator until he decided to become a law professor, told me that one of the conscious strategies of the system is to delay trials with motions for so long that the parties decide on their own to settle.

2. The Cumbersome Procedures of Court Trials. The many and complicated evidentiary rules of courts would dissuade people from lending money without interest, as Jewish law demands, and so the Talmud waives a number of its requirements in order "not to lock the door before [potential] borrowers."[28] In the American context, justice in civil matters was only available to the rich until small claims courts were created to make it possible for people with small claims to garner at least some measure of justice, even if they cannot avail themselves in that setting of the full array of protections and assistance to which a more lucrative case would entitle them.

3. The Possibility of Making Mistakes in the Law. If God legislated and ultimately enforces Jewish law, human judges can be understandably nervous about reaching the just decision that God demands. After all, people cannot possibly know everything, and so they may exonerate the guilty or convict the innocent. They may also award money to the party who does not deserve it. Even without this divine backdrop, it is easy to understand how judges in government courts may have doubts about how to decide a case and how to assign punishments or civil penalties. This is especially worrisome in capital cases, when mistakes cannot be remedied to any degree once the person has been executed; but the same concerns apply to those wrongly convicted for lesser offenses, when release from prison can never replace the years lost or when a judgment against a person or company may have meant bankruptcy.

4. The Desire to Avoid an Oath. Jewish law prosecutes perjury just as American law does. Removing oaths from the procedures circumvents that possibility for both parties. In the Jewish context, avoiding oaths has an additional benefit. Sometimes people swear false oaths not knowing that they are false. God, however, presumably does know. God may forgive the person, since his or her act was unintentional, but it is better not to have taken the oath in the first place.

5. The Need to Reach a Conclusion. Sometimes neither judges nor juries can decide a case, and that leaves the dispute unresolved. That is bad not only for the parties involved but also for society as a whole, because one major goal of the justice system, after all, is to bring harmony to society by deciding the matters brought to court.

6. The Desire to Produce Peace. When courts decide cases, someone wins and someone loses. That might resolve the issue for society, but it leaves the parties at loggerheads. Mediating a case, such that both parties agree to a settlement, can not only conclude the disagreement but also make it possible for them to resume their relationship.

For all these reasons, Jewish law prefers a nonjudicial forum to settle disputes. That might be arbitration, in which the parties agree to let someone hear the case and decide how it should be settled, with the understanding that, contrary to a trial, the arbitrator is not required to declare a winner and a loser but might rather split the difference in some way; or it might be mediation, by which the mediator has the power only to persuade the parties to accept a compromise. According to Maimonides:

> It is commandment to say to the litigants at the outset of a trial, "Do you want a judgment in law or a settlement by mediation?" If they want mediation, we mediate a compromise between them. Every court that constantly effects mediation is to be praised, and it is of such a court that the verse says, "Render a judgment of peace in your gates." Which judgment contains peace? Surely it is mediation.[29]

In recent years, though, arbitration has been used in oppressive ways. Some companies have required as a condition of employment that employees sign an agreement that if there is a dispute between an employee and the company, the employee will not sue the company in court but will rather take the case to an arbitration panel. Depending on the specific terms of the agreement, one or more of the following problems arise in such situations:

1. Often the company has the exclusive right to choose the arbitrator(s).
2. The employee bringing the case must pay the costs of the arbitration, and the fee of the arbiter alone typically ranges from two to four hundred dollars an hour.
3. Even employees who convince the arbiter of the justice of their case can obtain, according to many of these agreements, only a fraction of the damages they could have been awarded in a jury trial.
4. Although the agreement requires workers to arbitrate disputes, the company itself is often free to pursue any claims against employees in court, with no cap on the amount for which the company may sue.

On August 24, 2000, however, the California Supreme Court sharply limited the kinds of mandatory arbitration agreements that companies can impose on their employees. The court did not forbid such binding arbitration agreements altogether, but the court required that the deals must permit employees the chance to collect as much money as the law would allow in a jury trial, and the company must pay the costs of arbitration. Furthermore, according to the court's decision, the agreement must bind both parties.

Even with the new restrictions, George S. Howard, who represents the Employers' Group, the largest association of employers in the state of California, said that companies will still come out ahead after paying an arbitrator because "the savings in time and money are so great" when the courts are bypassed.[30]

Thus arbitration must be carefully structured to guarantee fairness, as the California case demonstrates; but, as the Jewish tradition asserts, when those precautions are taken, arbitration and mediation are still good alternatives to court trials in the pursuit of justice.

God's Justice

In Western legal systems, justice is an instrumental good, a commodity important for social peace and welfare. That motivation to achieve justice appears in Jewish texts as well, but Jewish sources add another important motive. God demands justice and makes the existence of the world depend on it because God Himself is just. In fact, He is the ultimate judge who "shows no favor and takes no bribe, but upholds the cause of the fatherless and the widow, and befriends the stranger, providing him with food and clothing."[31] As Moses proclaims in his parting poem,

> For the name of the Lord I proclaim;
> Give glory to our God!
>
> The Rock!—His deeds are perfect,
> Yea, all His ways are just;
> A faithful God, never false,
> True and upright is He.[32]

It is precisely because God is just that Abraham can call Him to account for His plan to destroy Sodom, regardless of the innocent people in it, with words that ring through the ages: "Far be it from You to do such a thing, to bring death upon the innocent as well as the guilty, so that innocent and guilty fare alike. Far be it from You! Shall not the Judge of all the earth deal justly?"[33] God's justice is also at the heart of Job's complaint,[34] and God thunders in reply, "Would you impugn My justice? / Would you condemn Me that you may be right?"[35]

Some passages in the Bible and Talmud, though, describe God as demanding or allowing unjust things, and others have God Himself acting unjustly—or at least so it seems.[36] Moreover, biblical and rabbinic literature include the doctrine of vertical retribution, according to which people both benefit and suffer from the deeds of their ancestors. That seems grossly unfair. Because I have explored these troubling aspects of God's justice elsewhere,[37] I will not repeat that discussion here. Suffice it to say that for classical Jewish literature and, indeed, for many modern Jewish theologians, even those writing after the Holocaust, God's justice may be inscrutable, but it is undeniable, a core characteristic of the Divine.

Not only does God, according to the Bible, possess justice as a defining characteristic of His being but He enforces His demands of justice on human beings. He hears the cry of those who suffer injustice and responds by punishing the perpetrators. Thus the Torah admonishes: "You shall not abuse a needy and destitute laborer, whether a fellow countryman or a stranger in one of the communities of your land. You must pay him his wages on the same day, before the sun sets, for he is needy and urgently depends on it; else he will cry to the Lord against you and you will incur guilt."[38]

From the Torah to our own day, though, Jews have been questioning God's enforcement, noting that sometimes the righteous suffer and the evil prosper (*tzaddik v'ra lo, rasha v'tov lo*).[39] That challenge has become all the more strident in our own time, with some Holocaust theologians denying God's justice altogether and others, somewhat more moderately, claiming that God failed to enforce justice during the Holocaust and, therefore, our own relationship to God must change.[40] As horrific as the Holocaust was, though, it was clearly the product of human beings, and so morally and even theologically the "free-will defense" must surely carry considerable weight. That is, human free will can be preserved only if God lets us use our powers for ill as well as for good, and so God may have allowed the Holocaust to happen but is not solely or even primarily responsible for it. That defense does not work, though, to explain why some people are born with many more intellectual, moral, aesthetic, and physical gifts than others, and why some people have strong families, schools, and enough money to live comfortably while others suffer from broken families, poor schools, and poverty. Even worse, how can we justify God in the face of, say, a three-year-old child suffering from leukemia? These are, for me, the really hard challenges to God's justice.

As I have developed elsewhere, I myself maintain that God is indeed involved in injustice as well as justice, that the fundamental principle of the oneness of God requires that we assert that. Still, while not hiding from the concrete and awesome evidence against God's justice, I nevertheless affirm that by and large God enforces the rules of justice, grounding that faith in the many times that we do indeed see that individuals and groups reap what they sow.[41] I have a much harder time wrestling with the inequalities that people inherit as their lot in life and even more problems with the child with leukemia and similar cases in which people suffer for no apparent fault of their own. It is such cases that make me resonate with the passages in the Jewish tradition in which Jews have angrily challenged God's justice and declared it inscrutable. Such people—Abraham, Job, the Rabbis, and Levi of Berdichev especially come to mind—nevertheless maintained their faith in God, His link to justice, and the importance of our own efforts to achieve justice. Indeed, while some who lived through the Holocaust lost their faith in God, others who suffered through that same awful experience came to the exactly opposite conclusion—namely, that the Holocaust proved beyond any shadow of a doubt that *human beings* could not be trusted on their own to render justice and that, therefore, we *must* turn to God for that, however many problems we have at times in understanding God's justice.

Justice and Love

One other aspect of the biblical and rabbinic concept of justice derives from its theological foundations. As I have discussed in Chapter Three, God, according to the Torah, loves the People Israel for reasons having nothing to do with its number or power, the usual marks of a nation's greatness, and God promises the Patriarchs to continue that relationship through the generations.[42] The Israelites, in turn, are to love God and "always keep His charge, His laws, His rules, and His commandments."[43] The commandments of the Torah are thus not legalistic formalisms, totally divorced from human compassion, moral values, and a spiritual relationship with God—as some Christian writings portray them. Quite the contrary, the practice of justice is an extension of love, as demonstrated by commandments calling on all Israelites to "love your fellow as yourself,"[44] to "love the stranger" (repeated thirty-six times in the Torah),[45] and to "love God."[46]

In fact, one of the primary expressions of God's love is precisely that He provides human beings with rules of justice. Very much like parents who love their children enough to take the time and energy to insist on proper behavior because they know it will ultimately be in the children's best interests, so "the Lord commanded us to observe all these laws, to revere the Lord our God, for our lasting good and for our survival, as is now the case."[47] Again, "Bear in mind that the Lord your God disciplines you just as a man disciplines his son. Therefore keep the commandments of the Lord your God: walk in His ways and revere Him."[48]

In sum, then, the Jewish tradition makes justice a concrete reality by spelling out at least most of its demands in specific laws. The Torah and the later rabbinic tradition insist, though, that we do the right and the good even when the details of the law would permit us to do otherwise. The Jewish tradition thus recognizes both that the legal framework is indispensable in making justice a reality and that the demands of justice extend beyond the law, however extensively it is defined. The Torah and the later Jewish tradition also place the demand for justice in a theological context, thereby undergirding the authority of the demand for justice and giving it a rationale: We are to be just because God requires it of us and because that is one important way in which we can imitate God's ways. These legal, moral, and theological parameters of the biblical and rabbinic concepts of justice make it an ongoing, active component of a life lived in loving covenant with God.

CHAPTER SIX

Substantive Justice: A Jewish Approach to Poverty[1]

WHILE FORMAL JUSTICE REQUIRES THAT SOCIETY'S *PROCESSES* treat everyone fairly, substantive justice looks to the *results* of social policies. Philosophers differ in their understanding of substantive justice, and politicians do likewise. On one end of the spectrum, libertarians maintain that in the just society everyone gets their due—that is, what people have is what they have earned. On the other, Marxist end of the spectrum, everyone in a just society has equal shares in society's goods, no matter what they contribute to that wealth. Most philosophers and most Western societies have opted for some position in between these two extremes. Some, like Sweden, have adopted a predominantly socialist approach, with emphasis on social equality but with some room for variation in wealth as a result of individual initiative. Others, like the United States, have instead focused on rewarding individuals for their particular skills and efforts while at the same time providing a safety net for those who lose in the capitalist game.

The Jewish tradition has taken an approach even closer to the middle of the extremes than those represented by the modified socialism of Sweden and the modified capitalism of the United States. Its legal texts assume a regulated form of capitalism, but its thick sense of community makes it advocate a much stronger safety net than the United States has ever provided, except, perhaps, during the Depression of the 1930s.

Civilized societies have confronted poverty for millennia. Some have seen it as a moral fault, and some have even imprisoned debtors who could not pay their bills. Jewish ideology, ethics, and law instead affirm that it is an obligation of both the individual and the community to care for the poor and ultimately to bring them out of poverty. Traditional sources on the subject of poverty are not merely hortatory. Many of the rules were enforced as law. Until the very recent past, in most places and times, the decrees of Jewish courts were enforced on Jews by the Jewish community itself and, under certain circumstances, by the non-Jewish host government. The way we Jews have interpreted and met our obligations to the poor has changed over the years with our shifting economic and political fortunes and the varying political, social, and economic conditions of the countries in which we lived. Nevertheless, responsibility to the poor has endured as an essential ingredient both in Jewish values and in Jewish practice.

Jews generally know that our heritage manifests great concern for the poor. Some even identify as Jews primarily through efforts to take care of the downtrodden. Equating Judaism with social action alone is a mistake, for Judaism is much richer than that; but Judaism does concentrate a large portion of its attention on the care of those in need. In this chapter I delineate what Judaism specifically requires of its adherents in this area and why, with that as a foundation, contemporary Jews will be able to draw on traditional religious ideals and instructions in making practical political decisions about minimum wage, unemployment, or welfare reform as well as personal decisions about their support of others.

Both vision and action are necessary. Without an overarching framework to justify and motivate our efforts to help the poor, we devote less time and energy to the task, carry it out less well, and ultimately lose interest in it. On the other hand, pious theories about the need to provide such aid are useless without appropriate policies and action to effectuate them. By including, then, both the theoretical framework for a Jewish approach to poverty and some specific guidelines for action to combat it, this chapter provides a structure for Jewish thought, feeling, programming, and action.

Jewish Value Concepts Relevant to Concern for the Poor

From the very outset it is important to note that there are very good reasons *not* to help the poor. These include, but are not limited to, the following:

1. The poor often do not work for a living and, therefore, do not deserve our help. This is substantive justice in its libertarian meaning.
2. It may ultimately be detrimental to the poor to offer them aid, for they may come to depend on it and never take the initiative to extricate themselves from poverty. Hence the cycle of poverty that affects so many generations of the poor.
3. Sometimes giving money to the poor actually contributes to their harmful habits and thus injures them immediately and physically. Stories of poor people who turn down offers of food or coupons that can be exchanged for only food reinforce the impression that too many poor people spend money that they beg for on alcohol or drugs.
4. When people on the streets ask for a hand-out, you never know whether they really need it. That is, the possibility of falling prey to deception is great, and nobody likes to be duped. If I am already going to give some of my money away, I at least want to be assured that it is going for a good purpose.
5. Worse, beggars on the streets might even pose a danger to you, for if they do not get what they want, they may attack you—especially if they are on drugs.
6. Even if beggars do not pose a physical threat to pedestrians or to drivers stopped at a light, they are surely bothersome. Society as a whole, and businesses in particular, have an interest in making sure that people can walk the streets without being accosted by beggars.

7. Part of the reason that pandering is bothersome is that beggars instill a sense of guilt in us, even if we earned each penny of our own resources legitimately. The vast majority of us are not rich, and we surely cannot support everyone in the world who needs help. But how can one walk past this particular person who seems so needy? Our duty to help others, coupled with sheer compassion for the plight of the truly unfortunate makes us want to give money to each and every one we pass. Pandering thus makes it hard to make good decisions about how to spend that part of our own private resources that we can devote to helping the poor.

8. Begging is inherently demeaning, and as individuals and as a society we do not want to encourage behavior that cheapens our sense of the dignity of human beings. If people need money, we should help them with education and jobs, not alms.

In light of these and other reasons to refuse to help the poor, why should we ever think of coming to their aid? One can easily think of humanitarian reasons to support the needy, but general rationales and good wishes tend to lack color and staying power. Religions do not guarantee moral action, but they can provide an ideological and social context for thinking seriously about moral issues and provide strong motivations to carry out our moral resolves. Therefore, it is helpful to plumb Jewish priorities and attachments that foster advocacy for the poor.

Two methodological points before we begin. First, whenever we examine sources from our past on this or any other matter, we must be careful to understand them *in their historical context.* The Conservative movement, in particular, is committed to that kind of sensitive, contextualized reading of traditional sources. Sometimes such a reading will surprise us—especially when Jewish sources say things radically different from what other peoples were doing in the same time and vicinity. At other times, Jews may be thinking and doing things that are virtually identical to those living around them. In either case, the historical evidence may at times convince us that current conditions require a different valuation of things altogether, and sometimes all that is needed is a new application of the underlying principles and values that we still hold today. At other times both the rationales and the specific expressions of those rationales expressed in the sources can and should apply straightforwardly. The important thing here is to note that we must first begin with an accurate understanding of the source in its historical time period before we can legitimately and sensibly decide how to apply it to our own times.

The second methodological point—also at the heart of Conservative Judaism—is that Judaism is a civilization. Therefore Jewish law cannot be correctly read as if it were isolated from all the other expressions of the Jewish tradition. On the contrary, we must see Jewish legal sources as part of the entire matrix of what it means to be Jewish. Jewish theology, moral convictions, social and economic concerns, and even, on some issues, artistic expressions may influence how we understand and apply Jewish law—and conversely. When we focus, as I do in this chapter, on Jewish law regarding the poor, then, we must be aware not only of the historical context of these sources but also of their ideological underpinnings and their practical expression within the Jewish tradition.

Precisely because of this latter point, it is important to begin this study with a description of the Jewish theological tenets that undergird Jewish discussions and laws concerning poverty.

Piqquah Nefesh: Saving or Guarding Human Life

The major Jewish concern in relation to poverty is to provide the underprivileged with enough food to sustain themselves. As I explained in Chapter One, *piqquah nefesh* is of paramount importance in the Jewish tradition, and so concern over human health and safety takes precedence in Jewish law over all but three of the biblical commandments.

Jews take it for granted that life has supreme value, but other cultures definitely do not. Stalin's Russia, Mao's China, Hitler's Germany, and the killing fields of Cambodia are stark twentieth-century examples of whole societies that valued life very little, even when their own citizens' lives were at stake. The Jewish tradition not only values Jewish lives but non-Jewish ones as well. Indeed, on Passover night we diminish the cup of joy for our Exodus because some of God's children (the Egyptians) had to be killed for the Exodus to happen, and Jewish sources on just wars (including contemporary discussions in Israel on "pure wars") are concerned about unnecessary deaths on both sides.[2] American ideology values life too—as an "unalienable right," according to the Declaration of Independence—and other Western societies have also inherited that Enlightenment value. Even so, very few cultures or religions value life as much as the Jewish tradition does—even to the point of worrying about the lives of enemies. This, then, is not only a deeply rooted value of the Jewish tradition but a distinctive one, in degree, if not in kind.

Community

Another conceptual underpinning of the Jewish value of caring for the poor is that it exemplifies and expresses our existence and character as a community. Feeding, sheltering, and clothing the poor are part of our social contract, for such activities help the community as a whole. Community is a theological value, for God makes His covenant with the whole People Israel. Community is also a moral value because many of the tradition's moral demands can only be fulfilled in community. Over the ages, care for the poor became nothing less than a defining characteristic of Jews, a manifestation of what it means to be a Jewish community. Maimonides went so far as to say, "We have never seen nor heard of an Israelite community that does not have a charity fund."[3]

The value of community is practical as well as moral and theological. It is practical because Jews cannot do the work of the world, let alone take care of specifically Jewish issues, as individuals. It is also practical because Jews, like people everywhere, need to live with others. It is theological, in that we imitate and act in partnership with God when we care for the poor.

Members of the community were legally required to contribute—the equivalent of a tax in today's society. The amount depended on the wealth of the individual, but there was no escaping this obligation. "The court may even seize his property in his presence and take from him what it is proper for that person to give. It may pawn possessions for purposes of charity, even on the eve of the Sabbath."[4] The degree to which a person was obligated to contribute to the poor became the mark of membership in a community:

> One who settles in a community for thirty days becomes obligated to contribute to the charity fund together with the other members of the community. One who settles there for three months becomes obligated to contribute to the soup kitchen. One who settles there for six months becomes obligated to contribute clothing with which the poor of the community can cover themselves. One who settles there for nine months becomes obligated to contribute to the burial fund for burying the community's poor and providing for all their needs of burial.[5]

According to Jewish law, at least two people must approach a donor to collect funds for the poor, and a minimum of three must jointly distribute the funds, to convey to all concerned that the entire community is collecting and distributing money in fulfillment of its corporate obligation.[6] In our own day, when Jews differ sharply in beliefs, practices, and customs and when we live and work among non-Jews to a much greater extent than in times past, the shared work of collecting and distributing charity is a significant mechanism through which individual Jews *become* a Jewish community.[7]

Individuals also are held responsible for helping the needy, but an individual is not normally required to shoulder the burden of financing the total needs of a petitioner; that is a collective responsibility. Only if the community will not or cannot cooperate in giving assistance is the individual liable to satisfy all of a petitioner's needs—assuming, of course, that the donor can afford the requisite aid. The rule became to help family members first, then close friends, then the poor of one's own community, and then the poor of other communities.[8] Because there are more people in need than anyone has resources to help, ongoing programs traditionally concentrate on the local poor. One is best equipped to know both the problems and the resources in one's own area, and the ties that one feels to others who are near and dear are a powerful motivation to help. Even so, the record of medieval Jewish communities that put themselves out for refugees fleeing persecution and expulsion is truly impressive. A leading scholar estimates that in 1160 in the Cairo (Fustat) Jewish community, there was one relief recipient to every four contributors.[9]

This value concept is also distinctly Jewish. As I discussed in Chapter One, American society is voluntary and thin by comparison to the organic society Judaism creates. This comes through in the different degrees to which Americans and Jews hold themselves responsible for the welfare of the destitute. Jews do not have the luxury of saying that the poor should just take care of themselves or go elsewhere and seek the aid of some other community; we ourselves are responsible for each other, whether we like it or not.

Compassion

Compassion is probably the primary motive for the many private groups that engage in poverty-relief efforts. It is clearly an important Jewish motivation too, but Judaism goes beyond the basic humanitarian feelings that all of us have as human beings. We are enjoined not so much to have sympathy but, more important, empathy, as the following biblical passage makes clear:

> You shall not subvert the rights of the stranger or the fatherless; you shall not take a widow's garment in pawn. Remember that you were a slave in Egypt and that the Lord your God redeemed you from there; therefore do I enjoin you to observe this commandment. . . . When you gather the grapes of your vineyard, do not pick it over again; that shall go to the stranger, the fatherless, and the widow. Always remember that you were a slave in the land of Egypt; therefore do I enjoin you to observe this commandment.[10]

In the ancient world, even among Jews, one way people became slaves was by falling into debt; slavery was, then, the method of last resort to regain financial solvency.[11] Consequently, the imagery in this passage from Deuteronomy is very powerful: Jews are to care for the poor because they themselves have known the slavery to which poverty subjects a person. Historical experience imposes a special responsibility on Jews because we, if anyone, should be sensitive to the indignity and, indeed, the slavery that poverty produces.

God's Commandment

For many modern Jews, the previous three motives for caring for the poor are immediately relevant: The value of human life, a sense of community, and the cultivation of empathy come more or less naturally. In the minds of most Jews until the twentieth century, though, the ultimate reason for assisting the poor was that God commanded us to do so. For many, that was enough; if God, who was all-knowing and all-wise, commanded such action, then it must be the proper thing to do. For others, the belief that God would enforce divine commandments by reward and punishment was the crucial factor. For most Jews, both aspects of this divine imperative were operative.

These motivations are not simply a description of what was but also, potentially, an exploration of what is becoming increasingly relevant to contemporary Jews—that is, the theological dimension of life. Our theological beliefs, whatever their form, affect everything we think, feel, and do, including, quintessentially, the way we treat the poor.

As historian S. D. Goitein noted, after the year 70 C.E., when "there was no longer the Temple where one could express one's gratitude toward God or seek his forgiveness by sacrifices, gifts to the poor served as substitutes. This idea, so impressively expounded in Talmudic and medieval literature, was taken literally and seriously."[12]

Jewish medieval philanthropy was not just an activity of the rich. Every Jew (even the poor themselves) contributed to the welfare of the destitute. All assets of the community were called *qodesh* (holy, or "reserved for Temple use") to convey the idea that anything contributed to the common good was in effect given to God. This language "strongly emphasized the religious character of charity and certainly was not without influence on the minds of the givers."[13]

Acknowledgment of God's Dominion over the Earth and Humanity

One consistent theme in the Bible is the fact that God is not only the Creator of the earth, but the "owner" of it.[14] Because God is the owner of all assets, He has the right to distribute them as He wills. Human beings may, at God's behest, own property, but God requires us, as the Torah's commandments indicate, to give charity from "our" resources, gained from our temporary lease on God's property. Those who refuse to provide for the poor thus effectively deny God's sovereignty, for such people dispute God's ultimate legal claim to all the earth and the right of God to demand that some of His property be redistributed to the poor. Consequently, the Rabbis deemed refusal to assist the poor nothing less than idolatry.[15]

This is especially true of the Land of Israel, where another factor is significant. God promised economic prosperity to all Israelites who live in the Land.[16] The poor and the priests, however, are deprived of that prosperity, the former through their economic circumstances and the latter by the biblical law denying them title to any part of the Land of Israel. These two groups, therefore, directly depend on God, who reserves for their sake part of the harvest that He grants the People Israel.[17] Thus the landholder, in obeying God's command to designate some of his crops and animals for the priests and the poor, is helping God fulfill His promise to the entirety of the People Israel while simultaneously recognizing God's ownership of the Land of Israel.[18]

Assisting the poor in biblical times took the form not only of direct aid but also of relief from servitude, and that too was rooted in respect for God's ownership of the world. While an Israelite could be sold into slavery to pay a debt, the master was required to set the slave free within six years, even if the debt was not totally redeemed by that time. If the slave chose to remain in servitude, he could do so, but only until the Jubilee year, when even the reluctant had to go free. Moreover, the master could not abuse the slave. The Bible specifies clearly that the rationale behind these commandments is that all Jews "are My servants, whom I freed from the land of Egypt; they may not give themselves over into [perpetual] servitude."[19] Thus care for the poor, in this case the poor enslaved to pay off their debts, is required because ultimately God owns us all, together with the world in which we live.

The Dignity of Being God's Creature

According to the Jewish tradition, the dignity of all human beings—that which raises us above the status of other animals—derives from the fact that we are created in God's own image: "And God created the man in His image, in the image of God He created him; male and female He created them."[20]

The primary way in which humanity is like God is in our abilities to understand and follow an argument for justice, to know right from wrong, and to choose the right.[21] To do these things is both the privilege and the responsibility of being created in God's image. As Jews, God has given us the Torah to help us make the right decisions, and hence study of the tradition is an aid to good practice.[22]

Even without a thorough Jewish education, though, we may not hide from the implications of being created in the divine image.[23] Thus a variety of biblical and rabbinic sources demand that we preserve not only the lives of the poor but their dignity as well.[24] So, for example, if someone injures another person, the attacker must compensate the victim for the injury itself (lost capital value), the pain involved, the medical expenses, the time lost from work, and the degradation.[25] When discussing payment for degradation, the Talmud's basis for comparison is the embarrassment involved in poverty. That is, the clear case of degradation, to which other cases can be instructively compared, is the embarrassment involved in being in need.[26]

Since poverty is an affront to the dignity inherent in us as creatures of God, all those who can are obliged to help. By the same token, the poor themselves must take care to protect their own dignity. One way of doing this is to give charity—no matter what one's economic state. "Even a poor person who lives entirely on charity must also give charity to another poor person."[27] Also, the poor who need aid are encouraged to apply to the community fund and are discouraged from door-to-door begging, because it diminishes their own dignity.[28]

Membership in God's Covenanted Community

Why should we obey God's laws—including God's laws on aiding the poor? One prominent biblical reason is that we have established a special relationship with God through the covenant. The mutual promises between God and our ancestors morally and legally bind us to the covenant's obligations beyond the sheer coercion with which God can enforce His divine will. Similarly, even though, as Job complains, God cannot be summoned to a court to answer for His failure to abide by the terms of the covenant, He is nevertheless morally bound by the promises He made to our ancestors at Sinai and earlier.

But not only does the covenant establish the rules of engagement between God and Israel but, much like a wedding document, it intends to create an eternal, personal relationship between God and the Jewish people. That personal relationship, like marriage among human beings, produces obligations even stronger than those of a promise or a contract; its duties carry the authority of love.[29] Thus honoring the dignity of the poor fulfills not just the letter but the spirit of the covenant.

Because caring for the poor is considered a covenantal obligation, Jewish sources discourage Jewish poor people from taking charity from non-Jews in public. That would entail shame for the Jewish community and *hillul hashem,* "profanation of the Divine Name."[30]

Aspirations for Holiness

Finally, and perhaps quintessentially, Judaism bids us to care for the poor in order to be holy. The Hebrew term *qadosh* denotes something set apart from the usual and mundane, something special or even God-like. Many of the biblical laws regarding poverty occur in the sections of Leviticus that scholars call the Holiness Code. Leviticus 19, in which some of the poverty provisions appear, begins: "The Lord spoke to Moses, saying: Speak to the whole Israelite community and say to them: / You shall be holy [*qadosh*], for I, the Lord your God, am holy."

What does it mean to be holy like God? In part, we are told in the Bible, it requires caring for the poor, for God does just that. God will not forget the poor, He pities and comforts them, and He cares for them;[31] conversely, in biblical legal and prophetic literature, God seeks social justice for the poor and warns against oppressing them.[32] Such biblical passages put the poverty laws in a striking, theological context: You shall care for the poor because that is part of what it means to be holy, to be like God.

The ancient Rabbis spelled it out even more clearly:

> Rabbi Hama, son of Rabbi Hanina, said: What is the meaning of the verse, "You shall walk behind the Lord your God"? ... [It means that] a person should imitate the righteous ways of the Holy One, blessed be God. Just as the Lord clothed the naked . . . so too you must supply clothes for the naked [poor]. Just as the Holy One, blessed be God, visited the sick . . . so too you should visit the sick. Just as the Holy One, blessed be God, buried the dead . . . so too you must bury the dead. Just as the Holy One, blessed be God, comforted mourners . . . so too you should comfort mourners.[33]

The very word for "charity" in Hebrew, "*tzedakah*," is a derivative of the word "*tzedek*," meaning "justice." Another derivative of that word is "*tzadik*," "a righteous person." We care for the poor because it is the just and righteous thing to do. We seek to be just and righteous ultimately because that is the holy and God-like choice. Acting for the welfare of the poor is thus perceived as a way of imitating and finding God.

Jewish Poverty Programs

Biblical Provisions for the Poor

The Bible treats the support of the poor primarily in two sections: parts of the Holiness Code, especially Leviticus 19 and

25, and sections of the laws of Deuteronomy, especially chapters 14, 15, and 23 to 26.

Ongoing biblical aid took several forms. Farmers were to leave for the poor the corners of the fields (*pe'ah*), sheaves or fruit forgotten while harvesting (*shekhihah*), the stalks that by chance fall aside from the edge of the farmer's sickle (*leket*), grapes separated from their clusters (*peret*), and defective clusters of grapes or olives (*olelot*). During the sabbatical year (*shevi'it*), when fields were to lie fallow, the poor had first rights to the sabbatical fruits. In addition, during the third and sixth years of the sabbatical cycle, a tithe of all of one's crops was to be designated for the poor (*ma'aser oni,* "the tithe of the poor"). During the sabbatical year, everyone had an open privilege to eat their fill from a neighboring vineyard or field. The first tithe (*ma'aser rishon*), given yearly to the Levites, was also a form of aid to the poor, because the Levites had no other income.[34] Finally, the Bible provides that every fifty years, during the Jubilee year, all land reverts to its original owners; this was intended to prevent permanent impoverishment.[35]

In addition to these agricultural gifts, several other provisions of biblical law helped prevent poverty. Specifically, workers were to be paid promptly,[36] and those who had money were to extend loans to their fellow Israelites in need without usury.[37] In the sabbatical year, debts were to be canceled altogether; despite that, Israelites were not to "harbor the base thought" of refusing to loan money to needy Israelites when the sabbatical year was near.[38] Clothing taken as a pledge for a loan had to be returned each evening for use by the poor person at night. When collecting such a pledge, the creditor had to stand outside the poor person's home, thus reinforcing that person's abiding dignity despite his or her poverty.[39] It was the duty of the judge to protect the rights of the downtrodden, although not at the price of fairness.[40]

It is not at all surprising that biblical provisions for the poor focus primarily on agricultural gifts, for most Jews of that time earned their living through farming. A monetary economy was not well established until later times.

What is surprising is that there is any provision for the poor at all. No other ancient law code stipulates gifts for the poor based on each year's crops, as the Torah does.[41] Until modern times, in fact, most law codes make the assumption that poor people are not simply unfortunate but that their poverty is caused by some moral fault of theirs, and they, therefore, do not deserve to be helped. On the contrary, in many legal systems the poor were to be punished. In England and the United States, for example, debtors' prisons were common until the nineteenth century; and even when they were theoretically abandoned at that time, imprisonment on other charges, such as concealment of assets or vagrancy, continued some of the substance of the idea that debtors should be imprisoned for their wrongdoing.[42] Thus the biblical laws proclaiming that the poor are not to be blamed but rather helped are truly unprecedented and innovative, and they can be explained only on the basis of the Israelites' theological convictions described in the previous section.

Rabbinic Poverty Law

By the time of the Talmud, Jews had become involved in commerce and trades, and so rabbinic law provided for the urban as well as for the rural poor. This law included a number of curative and preventive measures.

CURATIVE MEASURES

Forms of Assistance   There were three rabbinic forms of relief: the soup kitchen (*tamhui*), medical attention (*rippui*), and the charity fund (*kuppah*).

The Mishnah establishes the requirement that each community have a soup kitchen for the daily dietary needs of the poor. It also prescribes that a traveling poor person be given no less than a loaf of bread; if he or she stays overnight, the townspeople must supply enough food for a night's lodging; and if the stay includes a Sabbath, the locals must give the traveler three meals.[43] In the Middle Ages, synagogues were the site of daily food distribution to the local and traveling poor. This system was gradually superseded by three other forms of aid that included dietary assistance: reception of poor travelers in the homes of the rich, provision for vagrants in communal hostelries or inns, and aid offered by benevolent societies for strangers and the resident poor.[44]

Although there was no formal institution to give medical care to the poor, physicians gave of their services freely. The Talmud approvingly notes the example of Abba the bleeder, who

> placed a box outside his office where his fees were to be deposited. Whoever had money put it in, but those who had none could come in without feeling embarrassed. When he saw a person who was in no position to pay, he would offer him some money, saying to him, "Go, strengthen yourself (with food after the bleeding operation)."[45]

There are similar examples among medieval Jewish physicians, and the ethic must have been quite powerful because it is not until the nineteenth century that a rabbi rules that the communal court should force physicians to give free services to the poor if they do not do so voluntarily.[46] Moreover, the obligation to heal the poor devolves on the community as well as the physician. The sick, in fact, enjoy priority over other indigent persons in their claim to private or public assistance, and they may not refuse medical aid out of pride or a sense of communal responsibility.[47]

The most substantial form of assistance to the poor required by Jewish law is the charity fund. Eligibility for its beneficence is generally limited to the resident poor, rather than to passersthrough.[48] It is clearly defined in other regards as well:

> Whoever possesses two hundred zuz [that is, enough money to support himself for a full year, from one harvest season to the next] may not collect gleanings, forgotten sheaves, [crops from] the corners of the fields, or poor man's tithe. If he possesses two hundred zuz less one dinar [that is, 199 zuz], even if one thousand [householders each] give him [one dinar] all at the same time, this person may collect [produce designated for the poor]. If he possesses two hun-

dred zuz [that he cannot freely use because the money serves as] collateral for a creditor or for his wife's marriage contract, this person may collect [produce designated for the poor]. They may compel him to sell neither his house nor the tools [of his trade so that he might acquire through his sale two hundred zuz in cash].[49]

Along with food, the community authorities arranged for shelter. Jewish communities commonly fulfilled this obligation through a compulsory hospitality rotation, wherein the townspeople were required to take turns providing lodging for guests.[50] The charity fund also provided clothing, although food for the starving took precedence over clothing for the naked.[51]

The Hierarchy of Recipients   Jewish law provides that, as a general rule, women are to be aided before men—assuming that there is not enough for both—because "it is not unusual for a man to go begging, but it is unusual for a woman to do so."[52] This assumed gender differentiation is probably based on, or combined with, fear for the physical safety of a begging woman.

As noted earlier, family members (especially women) are to be aided first, then close friends, then the poor of one's own community, and then the poor of other communities.[53] Redeeming captives (*pidyon shevu'im*), though, takes precedence over helping any other Jew in need, because those in captivity, even more than the homeless and destitute, are in danger of sexual violation and, ultimately, of losing their lives:

> There are those who say that the commandment to [build and support] a synagogue takes precedence over the commandment to give charity [*tzedakah*] to the poor, but the commandment to give money to the youth to learn Torah or to the sick among the poor takes precedence over the commandment to build and support a synagogue.[54]
>
> One must feed the hungry before one clothes the naked [since starvation is taken to be a more direct threat to the person's life than exposure]. If a man and a woman came to ask for food, we put the woman before the man [because the man can beg with less danger to himself]; similarly, if a man and woman came to ask for clothing, and similarly, if a male orphan and a female orphan came to ask for funds to be married, we put the woman before the man.[55]

Redeeming captives takes precedence over sustaining the poor and clothing them [since the captive's life is always in direct and immediate danger], and there is no commandment more important than redeeming captives. Therefore, the community may change the use of any money it collected for communal needs for the sake of redeeming captives. Even if they collected it for the sake of building a synagogue, and even if they bought the wood and stones and designated them for building the synagogue, such that it is forbidden to sell them for another commanded purpose, it is nevertheless permitted to sell them for the sake of redeeming captives. But if they built it already, they should not sell it. . . . Every moment that one delays redeeming captives where it is possible to do so quickly, one is like a person who sheds blood.[56]

Because Jews were prime targets for kidnappers, Jewish communities had to establish limits on how much they would spend so as not to encourage future kidnaping of Jews, but they routinely erred on the side of redeeming the current captives at too high a price despite the implications of doing that for the future.

Jewish law required Jews to support the non-Jewish poor as well "for the sake of peace."[57] Remember that until the twentieth century most Jews lived in societies that were corporately organized, in which each ethnic or religious group within a nation had responsibility for dealing with its own internal affairs. Moreover, under Muslims and Christians, Jews were generally second-class citizens who had as little contact with non-Jews as possible. That Jewish law should require Jews to give charity to non-Jews at all—even if it is only for the political motive of maintaining peace—is, therefore, remarkable.

The Extent of Assistance   On the basis of Deuteronomy 15:8— "you must open your hand [to the poor person] and lend him sufficient for whatever he needs"—the Rabbis ruled that those managing the community's charity fund must take cognizance of the standard of living poor people enjoyed before falling into poverty. The fund must then afford whatever they need to regain their dignity—even if that means providing a horse and herald.[58] This does *not* mean, though, that the community was obligated to restore the poor to their former wealth.[59] Instead, the officers who distributed the funds had to differentiate between the *legitimate* call to sustain a poor person's honor and an *illegitimate* demand on the part of the poor to live lavishly at the community's expense.

Another factor obviously plays a role in how much aid the poor receive, namely, the funds available. Throughout history, most Jewish communities were themselves poor. Consequently, few poor people, if any, were provided with "a horse to ride upon and a slave to run before him," or the equivalent. Indeed, the limited resources of Jewish communities made it especially imperative that they balance the individual needs of each poor person with due regard for their obligation to aid *all* the needy.[60] No wonder the Talmud says that the distribution of charitable funds is more onerous than the collection![61]

The hierarchy of needs embedded in the sources, then, is as follows:

1. Redemption from captivity—especially for women—because captives are at risk of loss of life and physical violation.
2. Medical care for people who need it—because even those who maintain that building and supporting a synagogue take precedence over normal charity to individuals nevertheless give precedence to providing for the sick among the poor over establishing and maintaining a synagogue. Life and health take precedence over all other communal priorities, in accordance with the value of *piqquah nefesh.*
3. Food for those without it.
4. Clothing and housing. Starvation is seen as more of a risk to a person's life than clothing or housing, at least in the Middle Eastern countries where the *tannaitic* and *amoraic* sources were written. During winter in America's northern states, though, clothing and housing is urgent, sometimes even more so than food.
5. Dowries and other necessities for indigent brides.
6. Whatever is necessary to sustain a person's dignity.

Despite the economic limitations of the Jewish communities of the past, over time Jews have done remarkably well in affording medical attention, food, clothing, shelter, and marital mates for their indigent members. In the worst times, the quantities of bread and wheat "did not provide more than mere subsistence at starvation level,"[62] but Jewish communities consistently tried to afford their poor better than that. In fact, Lancelot Addison, describing the Jews of Barbary in the seventeenth century, felt the need to dispel the belief prevalent at the time that "the Jews have no beggars." He attributes this error to the "regular and commendable" methods by which the Jews supplied the needs of their poor and "much concealed their poverty."[63] Claude Montefiore was reflecting on Jewish historical experience when he correctly said, "The Talmudic ascription of charity to Israel, as a mark and token of his race, is not exaggerated or undeserved."[64] These comments are especially noteworthy in light of the fact that, until the middle of the twentieth century, in most cases it was the poor helping the destitute. That our ancestors did this should be a source of pride for us—and a source of a keen sense of duty as well.

PREVENTIVE MEASURES   Jewish family law is one mechanism by which the classical Rabbis sought to prevent poverty. According to Jewish law, fathers are obligated to teach their sons not only the Torah but also a trade. A father may delegate this responsibility to a teacher who is paid for taking the boy as an apprentice, but the father remained responsible to make sure that the son acquired a remunerative skill.[65] As Rabbi Judah put it, failure to do that is effectively teaching your son to steal.[66]

Jewish law requires Jewish communities to supply indigent young women with a dowry. Historically that ensured that there would be few unmarried women and thus, they hoped, few women who would need to go begging.[67]

The Rabbis also used their power over the marketplace to prevent poverty. They imposed a profit limit of one sixth for merchants selling foodstuffs and other commodities essential to human life (for example, clothing and rent). Concessions to the market may have undermined the effectiveness of this law at times. We see that in the provisions in Jewish law allowing merchants to include in the base price, for purposes of this law, not only the price at which they bought an item but also their costs in selling it and reasonable payment for their time and effort. Moreover, vendors were always permitted to sell at the current market price, even if it was considerably more than one sixth over the base. Nevertheless, the Rabbis' intent in establishing the regulation was clearly to ensure that the necessities of life would be available to everyone. The one-sixth profit margin provided an incentive for businesspeople to produce and sell basic necessities while keeping the price of those commodities within reach of at least most of the population.[68]

Rabbinic law also seeks to prevent poverty through making loans easily available to the poor. The Bible demands that Jews lend money interest free to a needy fellow Jew. To ensure obedience of that command, the Rabbis actually altered the court's procedural rules "so as not to lock a door in front of potential borrowers."[69]

Another important way to prevent poverty is to provide job opportunities for all. Historically, the extended family, as the basic social unit within the community, took primary responsibility for affording employment to those of its members who were out of work or unskilled; but if that failed, the community as a whole became responsible. This obligation was often not easy to fulfill. One historian estimates that between the fifteenth and eighteenth centuries approximately 20 percent of the Jewish community were unemployed or paupers.[70] In trying first to secure employment for these people, the Jewish community was helping the poor help themselves, the highest form of charity on Maimonides' famous list:

> The highest merit in giving charity is attained by the person who comes to the aid of another in bad circumstances before he reaches the stage of actual poverty. Such aid may be in the form of a substantial gift presented in an honorable manner, or a loan, or the forming of a partnership with him for the transaction of some busi-

ness enterprise, or assistance in obtaining some employment for him, so that he will not be forced to seek charity from his fellow men. Concerning this Scripture says, "You shall strengthen him," that is, you shall assist him so that he does not fall.[71]

In our own day, Richard Rubenstein has argued vigorously that this traditional demand to find employment for those able and willing to work will become harder and harder to meet. He claims that contemporary unemployment is a chronic condition fed by massive overpopulation, which itself is the product of the high value placed on human manipulation of the environment. This, in turn, is rooted in the biblical perception that human beings, following God's instructions to Adam, are to rule nature. Rubenstein thinks that sociopolitical triage, in which whole nations and entire segments of nations (especially the poor and unemployed) are deprived of food, shelter, medical attention, and other necessities, will increasingly become the way rich nations solve the problem of too many people in the world and too few resources.[72] Whether or not he is correct in measuring the extent of poverty and unemployment or in tracing our attitudinal problems back to the Torah, he is certainly right in underscoring the contemporary urgency of the traditional Jewish demand to provide employment.[73]

The Responsibilities of the Poor

If, according to Jewish law, donors and distributors have obligations, so do the poor. The goal of Jewish charity is to help the poor become self-supporting. This objective is based on the assumption that the poor will work diligently to earn themselves out of poverty to avoid the disgrace inherent in begging.[74] Jewish law does not require the poor to sell their homes or tools, nor does it force them to sell their fields at a substantial loss. Poor people are, however, obligated to work and to sell off any of their luxurious possessions in a good-faith effort to become independent of public assistance.[75] Moreover, as I noted, Jewish law requires even the poor to give charity, and it presumes that people will strive heartily to avoid the embarrassment of being on the dole.

The law could make this assumption in part because respect for labor runs deep within the Jewish tradition. In sharp contrast to many in the ancient world—including the Greek philosophers—Jews were not to disdain labor or the working classes but were rather to "love work and hate lordship."[76] Jews certainly were not permitted to wage war or engage in robbery or piracy to earn a living, as many other peoples did. It was also forbidden to simply rely on God to provide:

> A person should not say, "I will eat and drink and see prosperity without troubling myself since Heaven will have compassion upon me." To teach this Scripture says, "You have blessed the work of his hands," demonstrating that a man should toil with both his hands and then the Holy One, blessed be God, will grant divine blessing.[77]

The ideal for a human being, according to the Rabbis, is "Torah with gainful employment"—that is, knowledge and continuing study of the tradition combined with constructive work.[78] People should work not only for their own livelihood, but also for the inherent dignity of labor and the ongoing effects of work on generations to come. A popular story recounts that the Emperor Hadrian was walking near Tiberias when he saw an old man breaking up the soil to plant trees.

> Hadrian said to him, "Old man, if you had worked earlier, there would be no need for you to work so late in life." He replied, "I have toiled both early and late, and what was pleasing to the Master of Heaven God has done with me." Hadrian asked him how old he was, and the answer was one hundred. He then exclaimed, "You are a hundred years old, and you stand there breaking up the soil to plant trees! Do you expect to eat of their fruit?" He replied, "If I am worthy, I will eat; but if not [and I die], as my fathers labored for me, so I labor for my children.[79]

In addition to these moral, theological, and historical dimensions of labor, the Rabbis were sensitive to its psychological effects: "Great is work, for it honors the workers."[80] They thus did not see work as a human punishment inherited from Adam in the Garden of Eden; instead they saw it as our path to respect and self-worth. The Rabbis' esteem for the value of work was so great that at one point they interpret God's sweeping commandment, "Choose life," to mean "acquire a handicraft"[81]—a terse, but forceful expression of the connection of life itself to work.

This work ethic in the Jewish tradition is a strong factor in explaining why Jewish sources do not express the worry, as American writers and lawmakers do, that providing too much in welfare will serve as a disincentive for the poor to become self-sustaining. Another factor, of course, is that those on welfare in Jewish communities were not richly provided for, and so there was little to recommend staying on the dole. But in addition to that negative motivation to become self-sustaining, the positive value of work and the dignity that accompanies it have historically motivated Jews to get off welfare.

People taken into captivity against their will were not, of course, expected to fulfill the responsibility to earn a living to warrant the community's funds. Even so, the following paragraph from an important medieval code of Jewish law, the *Shulchan Arukh,* indicates that the heavy duty to redeem captives applies only when their captivity was involuntary; those Jews who sell themselves into slavery to repay a debt can expect only limited aid from the Jewish community:

> He who sold himself to a non-Jew or borrowed money from them, and they took him captive for his debt, if it happens once or twice, we redeem him, but the third time we do not redeem him. . . . But if they sought to kill him, we redeem him even if it is after many times.[82]

Respect for the Poor

When a poor person requests a job, a loan, or outright aid, the Jewish tradition insists that the dignity of the person asking be preserved. The Torah, as I mentioned, demands that creditors not enter the homes of those from whom they are collecting pledges,[83] and the Rabbis take this further. One must remember, they say, that "God stands together with the poor person at the door, and one should therefore consider Whom one is confronting."[84] Yose ben Johanan of Jerusalem, one of the earliest rabbinic authorities, went further still, saying "Let the poor be members of your household."[85]

Even if you cannot help a beggar, rabbinic law insists that you preserve the person's sense of dignity by speaking kindly with him or her. You may certainly not yell at beggars or even pass them by as if they are not worth notice, for "God . . . will not despise / a contrite and crushed heart,"[86] such as that of the poor person. Thus, as Maimonides asserts and repeats, "Woe onto him who embarrasses a poor person—woe onto him!"[87]

Translating from Then to Now[88]

In a variety of ways, our contemporary situation presents a new set of challenges and circumstances that did not exist when most Jewish laws and customs of charity distribution were established. Poverty itself is undergoing a significant but not necessarily positive change.[89] In the United States, it is spreading. Increasing numbers of previously stable families find themselves among the newly poor.[90] Not only are the numbers rising but people from formerly "protected" geographic and economic backgrounds are in jeopardy. From 1975 to 1994, the largest increase in poverty for children under age six was not in urban or rural areas, but in suburbia. Today, "poor" is defined as a single person with an annual income of less than $7,740 or a family of four earning less than $15,600.[91] Since the 1960s many of these people received benefits—such as housing subsidies, food stamps, Aid to Families with Dependent Children, and direct cash payments—that enabled them to achieve a minimal standard of living; but in the 1996 Welfare Reform Act, Congress put many of these programs in jeopardy.

Increasingly today, we speak also of the "working poor." As a result of rising costs and lower-paying jobs, an increasing number of families are at, or perilously near, the poverty line *even though at least one member of the family is employed.* Frequently, the working poor are becoming further impoverished rather than getting ahead. Many observers foresee a rise in unemployment, whether temporary or extended, among workers with formerly steady jobs, especially those who are unskilled or semiskilled.[92] There will be, then, in the near future, increasing competition among these different subgroups of "the poor" for the decreasing available governmental support and lower-wage jobs.

In addition, some Americans have developed a culture of poverty, in which it is acceptable or even honorable to be poor for generation after generation within a family. Rabbinic communal mechanisms to provide for the poor (soup kitchens, charity funds) presumed that poverty was largely a temporary, circumstantial occurrence in the life of an individual that could and would be alleviated through small-scale, local efforts. Although documents from the Cairo Geniza (synagogue storeroom) indicate that some medieval Jews remained on the dole throughout their lives,[93] the strong push of the Jewish tradition was for people to try to become self-sufficient. It never portrayed dependence on communal funds as a respectable form of living, let alone one to be asserted with self-righteousness.

Who is responsible to provide for the poor? Today, we try to accomplish that task through massive and far-reaching social and governmental institutions. Thus the respective obligations of the individual, the Jewish community, and the government to aid the poor in various ways need to be reevaluated and adjusted. Do our taxes, or a portion of them, fulfill part of our religious obligations to provide for the poor? If so, do we now have a religious as well as a civic duty to get involved in government to ensure that the funds are equitably, honestly, and wisely apportioned?

The answer to both questions is yes. Some of the poverty provisions in the Torah's laws are, after all, nothing less than taxes on a person's income. Because a percentage of taxes in the United States is used for aiding the poor, parallel to the use of some biblical taxes, one can legitimately argue that at least part of the duty to care for the poor is fulfilled through paying current taxes. At the same time, American social policy specifically presumes that the safety net for the poor will *not* be created by government alone; private charity must also play a significant role in this effort. Tax provisions permitting deductions for charity make this intention explicit. Jews, therefore, can fulfill only a part of their obligations to the poor through their taxes; they must, in addition, contribute some of their income to the charities of their choice. And, indeed, it is a mark of pride for Jews to be among the most generous segments of the general population, an ethic that all Jews should adopt and foster through their own giving.

Jews qua Jews certainly do not have the right to determine government policy; the First Amendment precludes that any religion be established to that extent. We do, however, have not only the right but also the duty—both Jewish and American duties—to get involved in the public discussion of public policy on poverty. To that discussion we may and should bring our specifically Jewish perceptions and values. As I argued in Chapter Four, the First Amendment stipulates that no religion may be established as the only body to determine government policy; but all of the religions are free to exercise their religious convictions, not just in their homes and houses of worship but in public discussion as well. Indeed, the wisdom of American policy depends on the widest possible discussion of important issues such as these, and so the duty to bring our Jewish concepts and values regarding poverty to the American marketplace of ideas is a Jewish obligation as well as an American one.

It is toward that end that the Rabbinical Assembly passed the following resolution in response to the concerns created by the limitations on poverty relief imposed by the Welfare Reform Act of 1996:

RESOLUTION ON WELFARE REFORM

WHEREAS JUDAISM MANDATES RESPECT, COMPASSION AND CONSIDERATION FOR THOSE IN FINANCIAL NEED;

WHEREAS MAIMONIDES TEACHES THAT THE GREATEST VALUE IN GIVING *TZEDAKAH* IS TO HELP PEOPLE HELP THEMSELVES;

WHEREAS THE DECLARED INTENT OF THE NEW WELFARE LEGISLATION IS TO
MOVE PEOPLE FROM PUBLIC ASSISTANCE TO WORK AND INDEPENDENCE;
THEREFORE BE IT RESOLVED THAT THE MEMBERSHIP OF THE RABBINICAL
ASSEMBLY URGE THE PRESIDENT, HIS ADMINISTRATION AND CONGRESS TO
CONTINUE TO EVALUATE THE CURRENT WELFARE LAW TO INSURE THAT THE
SAFETY NET STILL EXISTS FOR THE POOREST AMERICANS; AND
BE IT FURTHER RESOLVED THAT THE MEMBERSHIP OF THE RABBINICAL
ASSEMBLY URGE THE PRESIDENT TO APPOINT A BIPARTISAN COMMISSION TO
INVESTIGATE THE COSTS OF SUCH EFFORTS, AND TO PRIORITIZE DIFFERENT
WAYS OF FUNDING SUCH PROGRAMS; AND
BE IT FURTHER RESOLVED THAT THE RABBINICAL ASSEMBLY SALUTE
RELIGIOUS AND NONSECTARIAN GROUPS WHO DO SO MUCH TO EASE THE
BURDEN OF THE POOR WHILE GOVERNMENT CONTINUES TO CUT BACK ITS
ASSISTANCE TO THE MOST VULNERABLE MEMBERS OF AMERICAN SOCIETY.[94]

Jewish law's preference for the poor near-at-hand over those far away is much harder to define and justify in a world of instant communications. Within the North American Jewish community, some of the most pressing and costly needs concern Jews in places as distant as Israel and the former Soviet Bloc countries. Both morally and strategically, Western powers must be concerned with third world poverty. We may still have primary responsibility for the poor who are near and dear, but it is not as simple to apply that criterion as it was when people knew little of conditions far away from home. "To increase learning is to increase heartache," as Ecclesiastes 1:18 says.

The level of assistance that we expect to provide the poor has also changed substantially. Except for making the indigent downright rich, Jewish law specifies virtually no limit on what a community should afford poor people to retain the dignity of their former social and economic status. That is an impossible standard to maintain in modern times, as it undoubtedly was in centuries past too.

Even if the amount of aid envisioned by Jewish sources is an ideal that few communities can attain, the priorities set by Jewish law and values as to which needs we should meet first are as valid today as they were in times past. Specifically, we must seek first to save life and health, in part by providing medicine and in part by supplying food, clothing, and shelter. We must then seek to provide the skills and tools to enable people to become self-sufficient. Our methods for accomplishing these ends will surely differ in many respects from those used in former eras, but even the classical *tamhui* (soup kitchen) is alive and well as a project in many Jewish communities today through organizations such as Jewish Family Service, Sova, and Mazon.

Many of the details described in the law for collection and distribution of aid are out of place in the modern world. Designating three people to decide how to distribute the community's charitable resources, as Jewish law does, seems blatantly autocratic to us; thirty is even too small a number for the boards of directors of many of our larger charitable organizations, to say nothing of governmental agencies. Moreover, delivery of the aid is much more efficiently and honorably done through the mail or through direct deposits in bank accounts rather than by delegations traveling door to door. This is a laudable development, very much in keeping with Maimonides' ladder of charity that prefers gifts given and received anonymously over those for which the giver and/or the recipient know the identity of the other.

Jewish law gives the court legal power to force people to give an amount commensurate with their income and the community's needs, and it also assigns the court legal authority to seize the property of those who renege on a pledge. However tempting these measures may be to modern fund-raisers, Jewish communal officials no longer have such power. Government agents do have that power, of course, and collecting and distributing aid for the poor through governmental agencies is the rough equivalent of the power granted Jewish courts in pre-Enlightenment times.

Despite these differences between earlier eras and our own in the circumstances of poverty and the remedies for alleviating it, Jewish sources and the concepts and values embedded in them can have a significant impact on the way we think about poverty in our own time and on the ways we respond to it. The methods we use to prevent or alleviate poverty may be different, but the imperative to guarantee both the survival and the dignity of the impoverished—derived as it is from the fundamental concepts and values discussed in the first section of this chapter—remains just as strong now as it was in the past.

Insights from the Tradition for Contemporary Thought and Action

The Jewish tradition cannot accurately be used to support any particular ideological stance—conservative, moderate, liberal, or anything else—in responding to the problem of poverty. Nevertheless, some guidelines clearly emerge from Jewish concepts and law.

In light of God's image embedded in each of us, we must determine the recipients of aid, the donors, the methods of collection and distribution, the programs of prevention, and all other related factors in this area by asking: What is the most practical and efficient way of caring for the poor while preserving the dignity and economic viability of all concerned? God responds to Cain's question, "Am I my brother's keeper?" with the resounding "What have you done? Hark, your brother's blood cries out to Me from the ground!"[95] In responding to what is often life-threatening poverty, we must fulfill our God-given responsibility for each other by effectively and honorably providing for the immediate needs of the poor while simultaneously helping them support themselves—all in a context of respect and dignity.

Because the best type of aid by far is prevention of poverty in the first place, the clear mandate of the Jewish tradition is to support governmental and private programs of education in general and job training in particular. These programs pay multiple dividends, keeping whole groups of the population from a life of unemployment, degradation, and often crime and enabling them to become productive and dignified members of society. This priority begins first with the biblical responsibility of Jewish parents and, by extension, the community to teach children a form of gainful employment, and it puts into practice the top rung of Maimonides' hierarchy of charity.

If assistance is necessary, for both practical and moral reasons it is better to proffer employment, a loan, or investment capital to poor people than to give money as a dole. A loan or investment has the potential for making the poor person self-supporting, thus eliminating the drain on the community's resources. It also preserves the dignity of the poor person now and, if the venture succeeds, for the long term.

Even so, a poor person seeking aid from an individual cannot be denied enough for immediate sustenance. However we may react to being confronted by street beggars, Jewish law requires that we give something to those who ask—or, if we cannot, that we at least treat them kindly.[96] Jewish law intends, though, that we provide *food, clothing, and shelter* for the hungry; we need not give beggars money when we have good evidence that it will not be used for that purpose. Most commonly, this occurs when the people asking are clearly inebriated or under the influence of drugs and when the money would in all likelihood be used to feed their habit. Indeed, to give them money under those circumstances would be "placing a stumbling block before the blind," a violation of Leviticus 19:14 as the Rabbis interpreted it.[97] To avoid this problem, some people keep on their person a ready supply of food coupons redeemable at restaurants or supermarkets so that they can be sure that their contribution to a beggar will indeed be used for a legitimate purpose. Others maintain that giving people even such a specified voucher encourages them to continue on the dole and that the morally responsible thing to do is to direct them (or help them get to) a communally run program that will provide for their basic needs while simultaneously taking steps to help them become self-supporting.

In the end, confronting beggars is emotionally very difficult, no matter what you do. Even if you think that you should not give them anything for one or another of the reasons mentioned in this chapter, you clearly may not just pass by but must rather notice these people in recognition of their basic humanity. If you have neither the time nor the information to help beggars reach a responsible agency, it is probably best to give them something. Even though such people may be deceiving you and even though you may even be contributing to a bad habit of panhandling, it is better to take those risks than to pass by someone who is truly in need. On the other hand, nobody is obliged by Jewish law to supply people who ask for help with large sums of money; a small donation is all that is called for. Anything more than that undermines our concern to dissuade people from begging on the streets; we want them instead to get help from the public and private agencies created to supply assistance with continuity and with the professional expertise to assess and respond to people's actual needs.

Similarly, on a communal level, immediate sustenance should be available for the truly destitute with few, if any, questions asked. As noted, kitchens or food pantries run by Jewish Family Service agencies, Mazon, and Sova do this now on an ongoing basis. Similarly, Los Angeles Jewish Aids Services, for example, sponsors a soup kitchen for Jewish AIDS patients and their families (Project Chicken Soup), and there are undoubtedly other local programs of this sort. Mickey Weiss, may his memory be blessed, a Los Angeles produce distributor, began what became a nationwide effort to get produce distributors to donate their leftover fruits and vegetables each day to local soup kitchens, and some caterers donate their leftover food to them as well. Good samaritan laws in many states now protect such benefactors from law suits as long as the donors take reasonable care to protect the donated food from contamination. In addition, some synagogues and Jewish Family Service agencies collect money for the needy before Passover (*ma'ot hittim*) and/ or on Purim (*matanot le'evyonim*).

Jews should support as many of these efforts as possible with contributions of food, money, and time. Instead of, or in addition to, running a soup kitchen or a food pantry, communal agencies may provide food for the hungry through giving them food stamps or other supermarket vouchers. In the end, Jewish law holds us responsible for ensuring that our combined public and private efforts supply food to the hungry in adequate quantities and with sufficient regularity to meet their nutritional needs, just as these needs were met in the soup kitchens of yore.

Jewish communities of the past made arrangements of different sorts for housing the poor. Since the 1980s, severe cutbacks in U.S. government support for mental health facilities and for housing programs for the poor have forced thousands of people to live on America's streets. From a Jewish perspective, this is simply intolerable; it is, indeed, a national disgrace. Housing must be provided for the homeless, preferably on an ongoing basis but at least on nights with cold or inclement weather. If poor people have housing of their own, they should be permitted to retain it even while getting public assistance to pay for their rent and food. Welfare programs should also allow the poor to retain their tools of employment, since the ultimate social goal of these programs is to help people become self-sufficient.

One important way to prevent poverty is through education. In this world that increasingly requires skills in communication and technology, teenagers who drop out of school all too often find out that unskilled jobs are few and low paying. Major efforts, then, must be devoted to keeping teenagers in school and to improving the education students obtain there. In addition to the many other good reasons we want our children to be well educated, education must be seen as an important tool to avoid poverty.

One clear deterrent to remaining in school is teenage pregnancy, for pregnancy usually means that one or both of the parents will not finish high school. This simply perpetuates the cycle of poverty among the economically disadvantaged. Teenage sex education for boys and girls must be seen as a significant vehicle for extricating whole segments of the population from poverty. Recent statistics indicate that we have made some headway on this front, as the rate of teenage pregnancy has declined somewhat[98] and as school programs and even billboard signs announce messages like "Fatherhood is forever." These are crucial steps toward preventing poverty in the future.

Collectors and distributors of public assistance have the responsibility to act honestly, discreetly, and wisely in their sacred tasks. This includes striking a delicate balance between ensuring that those asking for aid are truly in need and simultaneously preserving their privacy and honor as much as possible. Because it is often difficult for private citizens to know whether a given person is in need without unduly invading that person's privacy and since individuals rarely have the time or ability to carry out such investigations in the first place, most people probably find it best to contribute their funds to agencies that have the personnel, expertise, and time to carry out these functions efficiently and discreetly. This also preserves the anonymity between giver and recipient that Jewish law prefers. In the end, then, individual Jews should contribute only a very small proportion of their charitable dollars to individual beggars and should instead focus their donations to established agencies for education, social services, and poverty relief.

And, as noted, the poor have duties of their own. They must responsibly manage whatever resources they have and, if at all possible, work to secure training and employment that will extricate them from poverty. That is, the ideal of making the poor self-sufficient is an ideal not only for donors but for recipients as well. Those who cannot work or find employment must try to contribute to the community in some other ways. Communal officials have the right and duty to ensure that people receiving aid are living up to these responsibilities, but they must do so tactfully and respectfully.

An Ongoing Challenge

While "there will never cease to be needy ones in your land," we are not permitted to sit back and apathetically let that situation persist. Hence Deuteronomy 15:11 continues: "which is why I command you: open your hand to the poor and needy kinsman in your land." Judaism has accepted the continuous nature of the problem of poverty but it is anything but fatalistic about it. On the contrary, in both theory and practice Jews have assumed throughout history that it is within our ability to provide for the poor and that it is our sacred task to do so.[99]

In this, all of the Jewish convictions described in the first section of this chapter play a role, but perhaps the fundamental, underlying principle is the dignity of the human being created in the image of God. Fulfilling the duty to care for the poor makes it possible for a fellow human being and perhaps a fellow Jew to escape the slavery of poverty and live as a respected member of the community, thereby gaining the status of free individuals that we all need and deserve. Preventing poverty and honorably assisting the poor are nothing short of holy activities. In making these aims our priority, we act as human beings should and imitate no less an exemplar than God:

> If your kinsman, being in straits, comes under your authority . . . let him live by your side as your kinsman. . . . I the Lord am your God who brought you out from the land of the Egyptians to be their slaves no more, who broke the bars of your yoke and made you walk erect.[100]

CHAPTER SEVEN

"A Time for War and a Time for Peace": The Ethics of War and International Intervention

A season is set for everything, a time for every
    experience under heaven:
A time for being born and a time for dying,
A time for planting and a time for uprooting the planted;
A time for slaying and a time for healing,
A time for tearing down and a time for building up;
. . .
A time for ripping and a time for sewing,
A time for silence and a time for speaking;
A time for loving and a time for hating;
A time for war and a time for peace.[1]

Although the Rabbis who shaped the Jewish tradition had trouble with some parts of the biblical Book of Ecclesiastes, these famous words from that book aptly articulate the fact that Judaism is not pacifistic. While Judaism abhors war and yearns for a Messianic world in which war will cease, it recognizes that our world is unfortunately not Messianic. It provides guidelines for determining when it is indeed a time for war and when it is not, and it establishes rules for the just conduct of wars—all the time seeking to avoid war and to work for peace. It recognizes that sometimes justice requires even violence, not only in personal self-defense but in the military action of a nation.

The issue of this chapter, the morality of war generally and intervention in another country specifically, is not one that Jews have faced very often in history. Jews enjoyed judicial autonomy in many periods and places, and consequently Jewish sources on the whole gamut of civil and criminal legal concerns abound. It is only in three relatively short periods of Jewish history, though, that Jews also held political and military autonomy— namely, from the time of Moses to the destruction of the First Temple (c. 1300–586 B.C.E.), during the Maccabean period (168–63 B.C.E.), and since the establishment of the modern State of Israel in 1948. It is only in these periods that Jews directly confronted the realities of power and the agonizing decisions of determining when to use it.

Jews, of course, have been part of other people's armies, and in democratic countries they have even fought for the right to serve. Asser Levy, for example, insisted on the privilege of personally doing his military duty in the colony of New Amsterdam and refused to pay a tax in lieu thereof.[2] But then the decisions of when and how to fight were in other people's hands. The brief periods of Jewish political autonomy provided even less of a basis for the development of a doctrine on political and economic intervention.

Nevertheless, the biblical and Maccabean experiences with war produced precedents and legal decisions that were interpreted and applied throughout the ages. Even if Jews were not in a position to decide when to initiate a war, they had to study the sources on that subject simply as part of their general obligation to study the tradition. Moreover, they had to be ready for that Messianic eventuality of the return of their political autonomy, and more immediately they had to be able to understand what they should do if they were conscripted in the armies of the countries in which they lived. The contemporary realities of the State of Israel, of course, have generated new sources on the issues of war based, unfortunately, on a surfeit of experience with it. Consequently, although Jews have not faced the issues involved in military and political power very often in their history, they do have resources within their tradition that can guide them in such decisions.

These sources become ever more important as Jews assume their contemporary roles as full participants in the decisions of democratic countries like the United States and as rulers of a country of their own. Israeli Jews have found themselves involved in preemptive military actions not only in Lebanon, where they were originally responding to attacks against their northern settlements, but also against the nuclear reactor in Iraq, where there was no immediate threat.

Jews in the United States are not solely responsible for its policies, but as active and articulate citizens they certainly have not been spared in recent decades from the realities and perplexities of intervention. In some settings, like Chile and Granada, their role has been largely one of evaluating their government's actions after the fact; in others, like Libya and Iraq, the situation is festering and ongoing. In yet other cases, like Afghanistan, the question was first how best to respond to the intervention of the Soviet Union and then how to help shape America's own intervention and its aftermath. And then, of course, there was Vietnam, where many American Jews faced complex political and economic questions as well as the immediate, personal decision of whether to serve in the armed forces. The complexities of intervention have thus indeed played a significant role in the lives of modern American Jews, continue to affect us now, and promise to do so ever more in the future.

In this chapter, then, I first examine Jewish sources on peace and on nonmilitary forms of intervention to right a wrong. I then turn to Jewish sources on war and to military intervention in another country. On what grounds, if ever, is intervention justified? Who determines that the criteria have been met? What moral obligations arise in the process of intervention? What factors mitigate against it even when it would be morally justifiable?

Jews looking to Jewish sources for guidance in these matters should not expect clear, indubitable answers to all of their questions, for such answers are available only in much less complicated affairs. They can legitimately expect, however, a point of view emerging from the tradition that expresses its values and applies them in some concrete ways. That point of view may not determine a univocal answer to all situations, but it should enrich the moral thinking of Jews and contribute to the ongoing American discussion of these issues shaped, in part, by the multifaceted viewpoints of America's religious traditions.

Political and Economic Intervention

We begin with the value of peace. Every major prayer in Jewish liturgy concludes with the plea for peace, including the grace after meals, the *Amidah,* the priestly blessing, and the *Kaddish.*[3] Rabbi Roland Gittelsohn notes that "not one single Jewish festival or holiday celebrates the waging or the winning of a war! Not one!"[4] (Hanukkah, as the name indicates, celebrates the rededication of the Temple, not the war that preceded it.) From the time that Isaiah revealed his vision of a future when even the wolf shall lie down with the lamb,[5] peace has been a cornerstone of Jewish Messianism. "Great is peace," said the Rabbis, "for all blessings are contained in it. . . . Great is peace, for God's name is peace."[6] In light of this background, the question of this chapter is: When may the pervasive value of peace be superseded to permit or even demand hostile actions against another country as a matter of justice?

Contemporary history offers many examples of political and economic interference in the affairs of one nation by another. Even in the few periods of history in which Jews have had political autonomy, however, the Jewish state was small and hardly in a position to affect another in these indirect ways. Consequently, it should not be surprising that Jewish sources on this are sparse.

The *Sifrei Devarim,* the earliest rabbinic interpretation of Deuteronomy, does include one comment on this issue, and it is rather surprising. The Torah says, "When you approach a town to attack it, you shall offer it terms of peace."[7] Commenting on the introductory clause of that verse, the Rabbis said:

" 'To attack it'—and not to make it suffer starvation or thirst and not to make it die the death of sicknesses."[8]

On the one hand, this source articulates a manifestly moral stance for our age on the ethics of using chemical warfare to contaminate the food and water supply, to spoil the environment, or to inflict illness as a means of waging a war. On the other, this source seems to require that the only legitimate form of intervention is military. Cutting off the food or water supply of an enemy is clearly a step short of killing them outright, especially since it provides an extended opportunity for the enemy to change its mind and sue for peace, and so one would expect that that would be preferable to direct attack. This source, though, apparently prefers the latter to the former, perhaps to avoid making the deaths of the enemy soldiers any more agonizing than they need be.

This source never made it into the later codes of Jewish law, however, and so its authority is questionable. Moreover, in Jewish law, as in other legal systems, killing or injuring a person is always treated more seriously than damaging his or her property, and so one would presume that nonmilitary intervention would generally be considered preferable to military forms. The grounds for political or economic intervention are not spelled out in the tradition, undoubtedly because the opportunity never arose; only the rationales for waging war are discussed. Consequently, one must extend by analogy the justifications for military intervention to political and economic forms. No thorough analysis of that sort has yet been produced. As a result, the only guidance in the Jewish tradition in regard to political and economic interference is that, as a general rule, it is preferable to military means.

Obligatory and Discretionary Wars

The Bible describes many wars, but the primary biblical source on the *laws* of war is Chapter 20 of Deuteronomy. There Moses speaks to the Israelites who are about to enter the Promised Land and who are fully aware that taking possession of it would inevitably involve them in war. In God's name he says that "when you take the field against your enemies," you shall have no fear because God is with you. He describes the exhortation of the priest before battle and several categories of people who were to be exempted from military service. A new bridegroom was one such person. Then Moses announces that "when you approach a town to attack it, you shall offer it terms of peace." He describes what the Israelites are to do if the offer is accepted and how they are to conduct the battle if it is not. A remarkable passage at the end of this chapter prohibits cutting down fruit-bearing trees for purposes of building siege works, and that becomes the basis for much of Jewish law on ecology.

Rabbinic commentaries on this biblical chapter center around a passage in the talmudic tractate *Sotah*. In discussing the biblical exemptions from military service, the Mishnah states:

> To what does that apply? To discretionary wars, but in wars commanded by the Torah (*milhamot mitzvah*) all go forth, even a bridegroom from his chamber and a bride from her canopy. Rabbi Judah says: To what do those verses apply? To wars commanded by the Torah (*milhamot mitzvah*), but in obligatory wars (*milhamot hovah*) all go forth, even a bridegroom from his chamber and a bride from her canopy.[9]

This Mishnah speaks of three categories of wars: discretionary wars (*milhamot reshut*), commanded wars (*milhamot mitzvah*), and obligatory wars (*milhamot hovah*). Unfortunately, it neither defines these categories nor applies them to specific circumstances. The plain meaning of the Mishnah seems to be that Rabbi Judah and the Sages (usually understood to be the majority of the Rabbis) disagreed about exemptions from commanded wars.

The Babylonian Talmud, however, as understood both by Rashi in his commentary to the Talmud and by Maimonides in his *Commentary to the Mishnah*, asserts that Rabbi Judah and the Sages do not disagree about the definition or the scope of the basic categories but rather about a peripheral issue. The Sages and Rabbi Judah agree that the biblical exemptions apply only to discretionary wars and not to wars commanded by

God. Furthermore, they agree that the wars waged by the kings of the House of David for the purpose of territorial expansion were discretionary, and that the wars waged by Joshua for the conquest of the land of Canaan were required by God.

The Talmud introduces a new category of war, however, and claims that Rabbi Judah and the Sages disagreed about that. The category consists of wars "to diminish the heathens so that they shall not march against them."[10] According to the Talmud, because such wars are not specifically commanded by God in the Bible, Rabbi Judah and the Sages agreed that the biblical exemptions apply, but they refer to such preemptive strikes in different terminology because they disagreed on their status in other matters. The Rabbis included such wars in the general category of discretionary wars because they are not specifically mandated by God in Scripture.

Rabbi Judah thought that even though that is the case, preemptive strikes of the sort described nevertheless fulfill a commandment because they are necessary for self-defense. In other words, even though the Torah does not *specifically* require such wars, it *indirectly* commands that we engage in them as part of the general biblical obligation to defend yourself based on Exodus 22:1, which exonerates a householder who kills a burglar.[11] Rabbi Judah, therefore, described wars of self-defense as "commanded wars" (*milhamot mitzvah*) and invented a new term, "obligatory wars" (*milhamot hovah*), to mark wars that are specifically required by God in the Torah, such as the conquest of Canaan.

The practical result of this disagreement, according to the Talmud, is based on a general principle, according to which a person who is engaged in the performance of any commandment is exempt from the fulfillment of other commandments during that period. For Rabbi Judah, since preemptive wars constitute a commanded act, soldiers engaged in them may take advantage of this exemption; for the Rabbis, though, such wars are discretionary, and thus soldiers engaged in them are still obliged to fulfill all other commandments.

In sum, the conceptual structure of the Mishnah and its talmudic commentary distinguishes two, and perhaps three, types of war: specifically commanded wars, including the wars against the seven Canaanite nations[12] and the war against Amalek;[13] discretionary wars, including the wars of King David to expand the borders of Israelite territory; and, for Rabbi Judah, indirectly commanded wars, including preemptive wars for purposes of "diminishing the heathen so that they will not march against them [the Israelites]." For the Rabbis, the last of these is simply another example of discretionary wars, but for Rabbi Judah they constitute a separate category of "commanded" wars.

Defensive Wars

There are two other aspects of the talmudic discussion of war that are relevant here. One appears in the tractate *Eruvin*. There the Talmud says:

> Rav Judah stated in the name of Rav: "If foreigners besieged Israelite towns, it is not permitted to sally forth against them or to desecrate the Sabbath in any other way on their account," and a Tannaitic source teaches the same thing. This, however, applies only where they came for the sake of money matters, but if they came with the intention of taking lives the people are permitted to sally forth against them with their weapons and to desecrate the Sabbath on their account. Where the attack, however, was made on a town that was close to a frontier [the loss of which would constitute a strategic danger to other parts of the country], even though they did not come with any intention of taking lives but merely to plunder straw or hay, the people are permitted to sally forth against them with their weapons and to desecrate the Sabbath on their account.[14]

This establishes a justification for engaging in a category of war not mentioned before—that is, defensive war. While one may have expected that such wars would be justifiable if any military activity whatsoever is justifiable, it is interesting that there is no explicit, biblical justification for engaging in defensive wars.

The Rabbis do establish a duty for *each individual* to defend himself or herself from attack on the basis of Exodus 22:1; as the Talmud puts it, "if someone comes to kill you, get up early in the morning to kill him first."[15] Because each individual has both the right and the obligation of self-defense, one might reasonably infer that the community does likewise.

Rabbi J. David Bleich, however, pointed out that there are significant problems in justifying defensive wars in that way because of the restrictions placed on the individual's right of self-defense.[16] Even if we take note of the legal obligation that each Jew has to intervene to stop a pursuer (rodef) from killing another person,[17] we cannot, according to Rabbi Bleich, find grounds from such instances of individual action to justify defensive wars fought by the community as a whole.

Bleich gives three reasons for his claim. (1) Since the obligation to stop the pursuer does not apply when that would endanger one's own life,[18] that law, if applied to communal wars, would not justify conscription—that is, coercion to endanger one's life in defending others. (2) Moreover, the law of pursuit may be invoked only in the face of imminent danger to life,[19] but the Talmud sanctions defensive wars against border settlements even when the marauding forces seek only "straw or hay." Therefore, additional sanction is necessary to justify a defensive war to ward off aggression when danger to life is not imminent. (3) And finally, under the laws of self-defense and pursuit, the intended victim, and even more so a third party, may stop an attacker only if innocent bystanders will not simultaneously be killed, for, as the Talmud says, "How do you know that your blood is redder than the blood of your fellow?"[20] Because wars, including defensive wars, inevitably involve casualties among noncombatants, engaging in them requires justification beyond that extended to an individual to defend himself or herself or to a third party to defend an intended victim.

All of the sources that Bleich cites in restricting the rights of self-defense and of intervention against a pursuer, however, are medieval. The Talmud itself does not limit these rights in that way. Indeed, despite the cogent grounds that Bleich raises to distinguish the cases, the Talmud, in the passage from *Eruvin* cited above, clearly establishes the right and the duty to engage in defensive wars. It does not connect the right and duty of communal self-defense with individual self-defense or intervention against a pursuer, and it does not consider Bleich's arguments as an impediment against establishing both the right and the duty of communal self-defense.

The standard codes follow the talmudic lead and actually expand on it. Thus Maimonides broadened the conditions under which it is permissible to construe the enemy's action as hostile to permit desecrating the Sabbath in communal self-defense, and he added the command to aid fellow Israelites caught in a war—including even the right to desecrate the Sabbath in returning home after successful action against the enemy:

> If foreigners besieged Israelite towns, if they came for monetary reasons, it is not permitted to desecrate the Sabbath on their account, and we do not make war against them [on the Sabbath]. In a city near the border, however, even if they came only for straw or hay, we sally forth against them with weapons and desecrate the Sabbath because of them. In any location, if they came with the intention of taking lives, or if they established the lines for war, or if they simply besieged us, we sally forth against them with weapons and desecrate the Sabbath because of them. It is a commandment incumbent on all Israelites who can to go out and come to the aid of their fellow Jews caught in a siege and to save them from the hand of foreigners on the Sabbath, and it is forbidden to wait until the Sabbath is over. And when they save their brothers, they may return with their weapons to their residences on the Sabbath; [this permission is given] so that they will not be deterred [from aiding fellow Jews] in the future.[21]

Yosef Karo, in the Shulchan Arukh, went yet further. He proclaimed that we sally forth against the enemy on the Sabbath when they come with the intention of taking lives "or even when they simply sally forth against the Israelites with weapons." That is, we assume that if they have weapons, they intend to take lives. He also noted that "There is an opinion that in our times, even when the foreigners come only for monetary gain, we sally forth against them on the Sabbath, for if the Jews (do not) let the non-Jews despoil and plunder their possessions, they will kill the Jews."[22]

In sum, even though the Talmud and codes do not directly connect communal self-defense to the duty of either defending oneself or intervening on behalf of another, and even though one might argue that the latter duties do not establish the former, the Talmud has no question that a community must defend itself—and even desecrate the Sabbath in the process. The codes not only endorse that duty but expand on it. Moreover, when communal self-defense is at stake, these sources do not insist on the procedures required for engaging in other types of war, to which I now turn.

Procedures for Waging War

The other aspect of rabbinic law relevant to these deliberations concerns the procedure for engaging in war. The Talmud's requirements for initiating military activity make the distinctions among commanded wars, discretionary wars, and defensive wars crucial.

A discretionary war may not be initiated on the Sabbath or within three days before it, but a commanded war may be.[23] Moreover, there are several stipulations of the Mishnah and the Talmud[24] that together require discretionary wars to be initiated by a king and approved by both the Great Sanhedrin and by God, the latter determined by consulting the *urim ve'tumim,* the breastplate worn by the High Priest. The initiative of the king and the approval of the Sanhedrin are not required for wars that God has expressly commanded, but, according to Maimonides, the approval of the High Priest's breastplate is. Even that is not required for defensive wars, however, since the Talmud and the subsequent discussions of it make no mention of such a requirement and since the duty to engage in defensive wars is articulated in the Babylonian Talmud by Rabbi Judah in the name of Rav, both of whom lived at a time in which the breastplate no longer existed.[25]

In modern times one may be sufficiently flexible in interpreting these requirements to substitute the Jewish governing authority, whatever its form, for the king and Sanhedrin,[26] but we certainly have no substitute for the approval of God through the High Priest's breastplate—especially in light of the mystery surrounding its operation when it did exist. Consequently, since the destruction of the Second Temple in 70 C.E., Jews who abide by these requirements (even with some degree of flexibility) may wage defensive wars exclusively. Thus the categorization of wars as commanded, discretionary, or defensive is crucial for those who want to guide and justify their actions by invoking Jewish law.

Preemptive Wars for Defense

Although later commentators discuss these talmudic laws, the *locus classicus* of most medieval and modern treatments of them is Maimonides's compilation in his law code, the *Mishneh Torah*. Although Maimonides is known for his thoroughness and his faithfulness to the talmudic text, his summary is rather surprising on several counts. He said:

> The king may first wage only a commanded war (*milhemet mitzvah*). What is "a commanded war?" It is the war against the Seven Nations [of Canaan], the war against Amalek, and a war to deliver Israel from an enemy who has attacked them (*she-ba aleihem*). Thereafter he may wage a discretionary war (*milhemet reshut*), which is a war against other people in order to enlarge the borders of Israel and to enhance his greatness and prestige.[27]

Maimonides's formulation completely neglects the preemptive war "to diminish the heathens so that they shall not march against them," as the Talmud put it. This omission led later commentators in the Middle Ages and in the modern period to take a wide variety of positions on the morality of engaging in preemptive wars. Here is a summary of positions, ranging from the most restrictive position to the most permissive:[28]

1. If the enemy has actually been engaged in the taking of Jewish lives, then war is sanctioned as discretionary, requiring the initiative of a king and the approval of a Sanhedrin and

God through the High Priest's breastplate. This implausible reading would mean that even defensive wars of this nature would be illicit in our day if the approval requirements are taken literally. Only defensive wars within the boundaries of the Land of Israel would be obligatory and thus sanctioned without such approvals.[29]

2. Military response to a war of attrition, in which "they kill people of Israel intermittently but do not engage in open battle," is permitted as a discretionary war.[30]

3. Preemptive military action is permitted as a discretionary war against those "nations that wage war against Israel"—that is, those with whom a state of belligerence already exists.[31]

4. Preemptive wars are discretionary when there is cogent reason "to fear lest [Israel's enemies] attack or when it is known that they are preparing themselves for attack" that is, in response to a military buildup or when it is known that the enemy is otherwise actively engaged in preparations for attack.[32]

5. A preemptive strike is a legitimate form of discretionary war when directed against a potential aggressor to prevent the enemy from developing a military capability.[33]

6. Military hostilities directed against any foreign power are justified as a form of discretionary war when designed to demonstrate military superiority to instill fear in potential aggressors.[34]

7. Military intervention is justified *as a commanded war* to defend Jews against even potential aggression, "even when there is only a suspicion that they may attack us." The dispute between Rabbi Judah and the Sages in regard to the proper categorization of war "to diminish the heathens" is limited solely to the issue of whether the Bible's groups of exemptions apply to such a war; but they agree, on this reading, that preemptive war is obligatory and thus free of the approval requirements of discretionary wars "even when there is only a suspicion that they may attack us."[35]

These positions clearly range over a wide spectrum, but note that they all justify preemptive wars for defensive purposes only.

Revenge is not countenanced as a motive for a preemptive strike, and neither is intervention to secure the rights of people in another nation. The talmudic, medieval, and modern positions that we have been considering until now may vary widely in their assessment of what constitutes a threat to personal and national security, but it is that which is the motive for any preemptive military action. Initiating a war is justified only to save lives, not to punish an enemy or even to promote the welfare of the citizens of another realm.

Consequently, it should not be surprising that Jewish law as it has developed in medieval and modern times makes several prudent requirements of those charged with deciding whether to engage in war, especially a preemptive attack. War is permitted only when the anticipation is that the lives preserved by waging a defensive war are likely to be greater in number than those lost through the war itself. The medicine must not cause more harm than the illness. Similarly, war is permitted only when there is sound military reason to assume that Israel will be victorious, for otherwise war would be tantamount to suicide, which is forbidden.[36] Thus Y. Gershuni argues that the medieval author of *Sefer Ha-Hinukh* and Nahmanides required consultation of the priestly breastplate for a commanded war, not to question the command but to determine the chances of success: If it is unlikely that the Israelites will succeed, they must not engage in the war, despite the standing command of God.[37] Even the justification of self-defense must be invoked with reason and military knowledge for it to be a sufficient sanction for war.

Military Intervention for Other Reasons

In addition to cases of self-defense, there are two other situations in which an argument for military intervention *might* be made on the basis of Jewish sources.

The first is really an extension of the self-defense argument. Jews live in almost every nation on earth, and for at least two millennia they have helped each other stay alive in the face of religious and political persecution. The command to redeem captives is, unfortunately, a familiar demand made on Jews, one they have often fulfilled at considerable cost and risk to themselves. After the Holocaust, that commitment has been coupled with a renewed realization that violation of human rights is often a prelude to physical extermination. As Professor David Sidorsky put it,

> For traditional diplomacy, it has been axiomatic that national security is the primary goal of any country's foreign policy. It is recognized that support of human rights in a foreign country may be an intrinsic and legitimate national interest, particularly when there is evidence of a connection between acts of internal repression and external aggression. Thus, it is clear in retrospect that the Nazi German government's violation of human rights of its own citizens provided an early warning signal, which was tragically ignored, of its designs for expansion and aggression.[38]

Thus both as an extension of their duty to intervene to save their fellow Jews and as a response to warnings of much worse to come, Jews might find it legitimate to intervene militarily in countries that egregiously violate the security or rights of other Jews. Precedent and prudence demand that all sorts of nonmilitary action be tried first, but Jews may see military operations as a legitimate, ultimate option.

There have not been many opportunities to test this, but the State of Israel did act according to these principles in regard to the captives at Entebbe. The United States tried similar action for its captives in Iran in 1979. Both countries engaged in military intervention in those cases not to change the ongoing government of the country in question but simply to extricate their own citizens. In addition, the State of Israel, sometimes with the help of the United States, has engaged in various forms of secret and open nonmilitary intervention to free Ethiopian Jews and Jews from the former Soviet Union.

Michael Wyshogrod, an Orthodox professor of philosophy, argued that in the face of "abnormal evil" Jews should condone intervention even if Jews are not involved. In such cases, of course, the rationale of redeeming Jewish captives is not available, and even the justification of self-defense can be invoked only by extension. Normally, Wyschogrod explained, concern for international peace requires that states not intervene in each other's affairs:

> Because they [states] are sovereign and because there is no law (I exclude, of course, the natural law or the law of God) that is capable of mediating conflicts among states, the only hope for peace among states is scrupulous determination on the part of sovereign states to respect the sovereignty of other such states by not violating their territory or otherwise meddling in their internal affairs.[39]

Some situations, however, demand intervention, and Wyschogrod's list of examples includes cases where Jews were not involved:

> From time to time, evils appear on the world scene which are in a class unto themselves. These are instances of large-scale, premeditated murder of large numbers of human beings in systematic ways. Among cases of this abnormal evil, in our century, would be the extermination of the Armenians by the Turks in World War I, the Soviet Gulag System, the Holocaust of World War II, and the recent regimes in Uganda and Cambodia. . . . You may have noticed that I have not provided you with a very clear definition of this class of abnormal evil. I have not done so because I am not able to do so. Certainly, numbers of victims have something to do with it. So does the degree of cruelty involved. And there are other factors. But basically it comes down to recognizing one when you see one. . . . When dealing with normal evil, noninterference, at least in the military sense, ought to be the rule. But when the situation reaches the level of abnormal evil, this principle of noninterference cannot remain absolute. . . . We are commanded: "Do not stand by idly at the blood of your brother" (Leviticus 19:16). There comes a point when military intervention is justified and the religious community has a duty to speak clearly when that point is reached.[40]

There is one other provision in Jewish law for military intervention. As I turn to it, keep in mind that these materials are *highly* theoretical. I frankly doubt that any Jewish regime would or should act on them.

The Bible zealously establishes a strict monotheism for Israel, and it claims that God was dispossessing the seven Canaanite nations because they engaged in idolatry and other "abhorrent things."[41] Extending this thesis through a rather implausible interpretation of Genesis 2:16, the Rabbis deduced six laws that, they claimed, had been given to Adam, and Genesis 9:4 provided another, for a total of "seven laws given to the children of Noah." The first six laws forbid murder, incest and adultery, idolatry, blasphemy, theft, and tearing and eating a limb from a living animal and the seventh requires that a government be instituted to enforce these laws and provide for the general order of society.[42] If a non-Jew fails to follow these laws, he is subject to capital punishment.[43] Maimonides summarized the law this way:

> We kill any non-Jew who is under our power if he does not accept the commandments enjoined upon the children of Noah. Moses, our Teacher, bequeathed the Torah and commandments only to Israel, as Scripture says, "An inheritance for the congregation of Jacob,"[44] and to anyone from the other nations of the world who wants to convert, as Scripture says, "for you as for the stranger [convert]."[45] But if anyone [of the other nations] did not want [to accept the Torah and commandments,] we do not force him to do so. Moses, our teacher, similarly commanded at God's bidding to force all inhabitants of the world to accept the laws enjoined upon the children of Noah, and anyone who does not accept them shall be killed.[46]

This does not justify holy wars, much as it might seem to do so. Later on Maimonides himself specified that the death penalty can be imposed only after a trial, albeit with modified evidentiary and procedural rules,[47] and thus it is unlikely that the Noahide rules provide any basis for *military* intervention. Several sources in the tradition specifically deny that Jews have the right, much less the duty, to impose the seven Noahide Laws militarily outside the Land of Israel; they apply only to non-Jews living in a Jewish state.[48] Moreover, one must remember that even if Maimonides' dictum provides a rationale for military action, if the offenders make peace and accept the seven commandments, then, according to Maimonides himself, one must not kill a single person.[49] Thus it is doubtful that Jewish law would condone military intervention to enforce the seven Noahide Laws.

Deterrents to Military Intervention

Even though Judaism permits war under certain circumstances and requires it under others, one must read these sources in the light of four factors that make Jews reticent to engage in war even when Jewish law declares it legitimate.

First, as noted earlier, there have been only relatively brief periods in which Jews had the power to wage war—namely, from Moses to the destruction of the First Temple, during the Maccabean period, and since the creation of the modern State of Israel. At all other times, Jews were often the victims of war, but not its initiators. As a result, waging war is not a significant part of the long-term Jewish historical memory and did not become an ideal filled with honor and glory, as it did in other cultures. Jewish heroes historically have predominantly been scholars, not generals. This has changed among some Jews in our own time in reaction to the Holocaust and the need for Israel to maintain military readiness, but the value system persists. Jews do not look for excuses to wage war; on the contrary, they fight only when they have no other choice.

A second important contextual feature is the inherent respect in the Jewish tradition for government. There are clearly good governments and bad ones, and Judaism developed rich source materials on the ethics and methods of protest.[50] Ultimately, though, the Jewish tradition recognized the importance of effective government. Even when Jews were suffering under Roman persecutions during the first two centuries C.E., Rabbi Hanina could say, "Pray for the welfare of the government, for were it not for the fear of it men would swallow each other alive."[51] This too would make Jews think twice before contemplating military intervention to change the policies of a government or to overthrow it.

Third, there is longstanding concern within Judaism about the inherently dehumanizing effects of war. Beginning with Deuteronomy 20 and extending through much of rabbinic literature, the Jewish tradition established rules to preserve as much moral sensitivity as possible in the essentially immoral context of war.[52] The modern Israeli army reflects its Jewish roots in spelling out these ethics of war to every soldier in training. So, for example, no guilt is incurred if noncombatants are inadvertently hurt or killed in the process of a generally defensive action, however regrettable that would be; but locations in which noncombatants would be the principal target may not be struck. Similarly, destruction of property to an extent unnecessary for defense is prohibited.

These rules are hard to apply in the contemporary conditions of war, when bombers traverse significant distances in seconds, when armies often hide their armaments in civilian areas, and when much of the action against Israel has been guerilla warfare; but these rules do remain part of the Jewish military conscience. This is poignantly illustrated in former Prime Minister David Ben Gurion's doctrine of "purity of arms" and in the soul-searching record of soldiers' conversations after the Six Day War asking whether and how one can preserve the distinction between combatants and noncombatants in modern warfare.[53] In recent years many Israelis have also openly worried about the negative characterological effects of raising two entire generations under wartime conditions.

And finally, the strong emphasis within Judaism on the importance of peace, discussed earlier, also serves to slake the thirst for war. This is especially so in our own time, because of the possibility of nuclear escalation. Rabbi Mordecai Kaplan, founder of the Reconstructionist movement within Judaism, claimed that the standard *political* sanctions for war, based on the tenet that national states should be independent and sovereign, is meaningless in an interdependent, nuclear age. We must, therefore, modify our idea of national sovereignty so that we no longer sanction the right of national states to engage in "competition for national aggrandizement, in imperialist adventures for the acquisition of territory or of spheres of influence, for markets and raw materials, and in many economic and military activities during peace times, all of which are bound to lead to conflicts of interest between national states and ultimately to end up in war."

Similarly, according to Kaplan, we can no longer tolerate the *philosophic* acquiescence to war as it appears in the philosophies of Plato, Hobbes, Locke, Hegel, and others who asserted that human beings are by nature bellicose. Rather, we must re-embrace the fundamental tenets of the three Western religions that human beings are created in God's image and that God owns the world, thus contradicting both the assertion that people must inevitably engage in war and that national sovereignty is paramount. In a world in which war can lead to universal annihilation, humanity must no longer merely pray and hope for peace; it must transform the world's entire pattern of political and economic organization to, effectively, "wage peace."[54]

Sentiments such as these have not engendered a significant pacifist movement in contemporary Judaism; Jews are generally prepared to go to war if attacked. There is indeed a pacifistic strand in talmudic literature, but it never became the dominant Jewish position.[55] Because of the impact of the Holocaust and the model of the strong, Israeli fighter, one doubts that contemporary Jews in any number would adopt absolute pacifism. Nevertheless, the traditional reticence to go to war continues, and it serves as another deterrent to military intervention in another country.

From Theory to Practice

These deterrents to military action underscore that it is only with reluctance that the Jewish tradition justifies war and, in our time, almost exclusively for self-defense. Some sources, however, legitimate even preemptive wars for that purpose. How would that viewpoint apply to some instances of intervention in recent decades?

As one might expect, in some cases the application is straightforward while in others it is murkier. In the latter cases, even scholars who have the same Jewish perspective on the general issue of preemptive war may disagree as to whether a given preemptive action is legitimate. They would agree, though, in many instances, and where they differ they would at least share the same universe of discourse so that they could argue intelligently about how to apply their shared values to the case at hand.

Let me begin with some of the clearer cases. From the perspective of the Jewish value system, Israel's preemptive strike against Egypt's air force on the first morning of the Six Day War was a justifiable act of self-defense in view of Egyptian leaders' bellicose words and actions in the weeks before that. In light of the incessant rocket and terrorist attacks against Israel's northern settlements, one could probably make the same case for the initial stages of Israel's 1982 incursion into Lebanon, although probably not for the remainder of that affair. The Entebbe raid was similarly justifiable; citizens of Israel and other travelers on its aircraft had been kidnaped. With the hindsight of the Persian Gulf War of the early 1990s, many who formerly opposed Israel's strike against the Iraqi nuclear reactor in 1981 are now thankful that Israel took that action. Even without that additional piece of information, though, the attack then was probably justifiable "to diminish the heathens so that they shall not march against them," given the continual, overt hostility of Iraq toward Israel. After the bombing of Pan Am flight 103 over Scotland, America's strike against Libya was also probably justifiable, although the terrorist provocation for it, while likely in view of Libya's past behavior, was not as publicly verifiable at the time. Similarly, in light of the bombing of its military post in Lebanon and its ship in Yemen and, ultimately, the destruction of the World Trade Center and the Pentagon, all of these preemptive and responsive actions were, it seems to me, legitimately taken in the name of self-defense.

American action in Chile, Grenada, Vietnam, El Salvador, and Nicaragua and the Israeli bombing of Beirut are, from a Jewish point of view, much less defensible. The intervention in Chile in 1976 was at least restricted to nonmilitary means. Even so, its morality from a Jewish point of view is doubtful in light of the fact that the regime, Communist though it was, did not immediately endanger the United States and, given its own internal weakness, probably would not have posed much of a threat in the long term either. A stronger case could be made for the legitimacy of the Bay of Pigs invasion in 1962 because of the direct Russian involvement in Cuba and its proximity to our shores.

The Grenada invasion was justified by the Reagan administration in part as a move to save American medical students there from captivity. If they were indeed threatened by the Communist government there and if no peaceful action could extricate them, the action would be justifiable, but the record is anything but clear on either of those points.

Vietnam, El Salvador, and Nicaragua are even more unclear. In each case, the American government claimed that military intervention was necessary to save the country from Communism. Vietnam raised major questions about whether that type of intervention works; that is important not only for practical but also for moral reasons, because one of the Jewish criteria in determining the legitimacy of going to war is the likelihood of its success. Even if success could be ensured, one wonders whether preemptive military action in those areas was or is justifiable as a means of defense of the United States. It is, after all, stretching the concept of defense against a clear and direct threat rather far.

Similarly, the Israelis in 1982 probably had justification to invade southern Lebanon to remove the guerilla bases there, but the march to Beirut and the lengthy occupation that followed cannot be justified on grounds of defense. Indeed, had the Israelis left soon after incapacitating the Palestinian Liberation Organization in southern Lebanon, the Amal militia there would undoubtedly have continued to see the Israelis as their liberators and may have provided an important defensive buffer for Israel.

Others may evaluate some of these military actions differently. If they share the Jewish point of view, however, they would assert that even when preemptive military action is justifiable as a matter of defense, it is so only after serious efforts are first made to accomplish the same ends peacefully. The reaction of the Israeli government to the clashes between Israelis and Palestinians that began in September 2000, and the American military actions against terrorists after the September 11, 2001, attacks on the Pentagon and World Trade Center, while not involving a preemptive action, have again demonstrated some fundamental Jewish principles: the duty of self-defense, the effort to confine death and injury to as few casualties as possible on both sides, and the demand to pursue peace. Some analysts have argued that the intifada proves that the Palestinians want not only a Palestinian state but the destruction of Israel, and others claim that only an Israel that routinely demonstrates its military might can deter Arabs from killing, destruction, and terrorism. Even in the midst of the clashes, though, 63 percent of Israelis, according to one poll, wanted their government to return to the table to negotiate peace with the Palestinians.[56]

"Seek peace and pursue it," said the Psalmist.[57] The Rabbis, noting the duplication of the verbs, enjoined us to work for peace not only for ourselves but for others as well—a fitting end and counterpoint to a discussion on the morality of intervention:

> The Law does not order you to run after or pursue the other commandments, but only to fulfill them on the appropriate occasion. But peace you must seek in your own place and pursue it even to another place as well.[58]

CHAPTER EIGHT

Communal Forgiveness

T HIS CHAPTER IS AN EMOTIONAL MINE FIELD. IT WILL INEVITABLY offend many readers; parts of it even offend me at times. I apologize in advance for the distress and indignation it will cause. It is certainly not my goal to raise people's hackles; by nature, I continually try to avoid that. But this chapter raises intricate philosophical complexities.

In view of these problems, discretion would have dictated that I omit this topic altogether. I nevertheless feel the need to present the topic of *forgiveness*, because the Jewish community has already faced this issue in a number of ways, and the future promises to confront us with it with yet greater variety and intensity.

The Issue

Since 1973, I have been part of the Priest–Rabbi Dialogue sponsored by the Los Angeles Archdiocese and the Board of Rabbis of Southern California. Through the years we have produced brief readings to be read before the Lenten Reproaches in all Catholic churches in the Los Angeles area to eliminate the original, anti-Semitic intention of the readings and apply them instead to the individual, Catholic parishioner who is hearing them. In addition, we have together written papers explaining our commonalities and differences on the subjects of covenant, kingdom, salvation/redemption, and the Sabbath/Lord's Day. Another local Catholic–Jewish committee, consisting of clergy and laypeople, has produced joint papers on abortion, caring for the dying person, the single-parent family, the nuclear reality, allocation of health care, and chemical dependency. All of these have been published with the agreement of the Catholic cardinal and the Board of Rabbis.[1]

After this long history of dialogue, the priests in the Priest–Rabbi Dialogue finally felt sufficiently secure in their relationships with us rabbis to raise one of the questions that certainly was in the back of all of our minds. It is no secret—to them as well as to us—that the Catholic Church historically has been anything but exemplary in its relationship with Jews. Recent Catholic statements, including a number from the Vatican and Pope John Paul II himself, have moved in the direction of apologizing for past wrongs and condemning any current manifestations of anti-Semitism. The Church has established official relations with the State of Israel, and even the most wary of Jews must acknowledge that it has made some radical changes in both word and deed since the Second Vatican Council promulgated *Nostra Aetate* in 1965.

The question that the priests were now asking us is this: With full recognition that the history of Catholic treatment of Jews has been bleak and that as recently as World War II officials of the Catholic Church were often obsequious to the Nazis, what would it take to put that history behind us? That is, what would it mean for the Catholic Church to warrant forgiveness and for the Jewish community to give it? Whether either community would *want* to engage in this process is, of course, another matter, but what would it mean to do so in the first place? How, in general, can groups engage in remorse, apology, and forgiveness—acts that we normally associate with individuals?

In our case, there is a further complication. The present generation of Jews is, by and large, not the one that was wronged. Conversely, the present generation of Catholics, while not totally free of anti-Semitism, is not responsible for perpetrating the atrocities for which we most often blame the Church. Can descendants act in any meaningful way in matters of regret and forgiveness on behalf of their ancestors?

One might seek to soften this philosophical question by noting that past wrongs continue to affect us now. So, for example, while the primary brunt of the Crusades, the Inquisition, and other Catholic acts of anti-Semitism was surely borne by Jews of those times, contemporary Jews still suffer from the results of those acts. Our dispersion, our secondary political status in many countries, continued acts of anti-Semitism seen by the perpetrators (even if wrongly) as sanctioned by the Church, and our small number itself are all effects of past offenses. Jewish wariness of Catholics in our time is, in no small measure, a function of having been burned—literally and figuratively—and of smarting still from the effects.

Jews of previous generations suffered much more than we do, though, and the conceptually more difficult question relates to them. Thus this chapter concentrates on the question of whether contemporary members of a community can grant forgiveness for the sins foisted on its previous generations. If so, under what conditions should it do so? If not, how should contemporary members of these communities deal with past misdeeds?

Similar questions have arisen in other contexts. The Evangelical Lutheran Church of America, for example, in 1996 repudiated the anti-Semitic remarks of Luther himself and has sought forgiveness for the oppression of Jews that they inspired. They have even established a commission to develop a wholly new Lutheran theology about Jews and Judaism. Germans have sought forgiveness for the horrors of the Holocaust, and they have backed up that effort with the payment of reparations over many decades. Current Americans have been asked by Native Americans and by Japanese–American citizens interned during World War II for official apologies and for reparations. Similarly, current Australians are being asked by Australian Aborigines to apologize for, and seek to repair the damage of, the government policy dating from 1910 until 1971 of taking children with mixed blood from Aborigines' families and placing them with white foster families in an attempt to integrate them racially into the white Australian population through breeding with whites over generations. In May 2000, some two hundred thousand people marched across Sydney Harbor Bridge calling for reconciliation with the Aborigines, "the largest demonstration in the country's history."[2]

In this chapter, I use my experience with the Catholic priests of the Los Angeles Priest–Rabbi Dialogue as the primary example of the issues involved, but later in the chapter I apply some of the points to Protestant Christians and to Germans. Because this is a book specifically on *Jewish* social ethics, I will not deal directly with the cases of Native Americans and Australian Aborigines, but the same principles would apply.

First, then, I briefly survey Jewish sources on communal forgiveness and the aspects of individual forgiveness relevant to that. Jewish tradition demands that we be most forthcoming in pardoning individuals who have wronged us, but its reaction to groups who have wronged Jews is anything but forgiving. With this as a background, I ask the philosophical questions listed earlier concerning, first, the notion of group regret and forgiveness and, second, the issue of descendants regretting and forgiving on behalf of their ancestors. After developing a secondary sense of forgiveness that can accommodate the realities of current Catholic–Jewish relations, I briefly explore why we might be interested in considering this in the first place—that is, what the Catholic Church has done since 1965 to warrant our considering this issue anew now—and, on the other hand, why we might still refuse to offer even a secondary form of forgiveness.

This preliminary outline should alert the reader that my interest in this chapter is *not* to argue for or against forgiving the Catholic Church, Protestants, or Germans; it is rather to explore what such an act would mean. In the end, in other words, this is not a discussion of Jewish public policy but of philosophy.

God's Forgiveness of Individual Jews and the People Israel

The Jewish tradition is confident that God will forgive both individual Israelites and the People Israel as a whole. In the Torah, God Himself proclaims that He "forgives iniquity, transgression, and sin," and the Rabbis maintained that God's forgiveness exceeds His wrath five hundred fold.[3]

There are several reasons why God forgives. God is by nature a loving Father who, like any good parent, punishes transgression when necessary to correct our ways but who always hopes that we will return to Him so that He can instead forgive.[4] After the Flood, God made a covenant with all children of Noah—and, indeed, with all living creatures—not to destroy the world again, however angry He becomes.[5] Furthermore, as an expression of His special love for Israel, He has made a distinct covenant with Israel that obligates Him to forgive and sustain it even after fiercely punishing it for multiple and egregious transgression.[6] God remembers the merit of the Patriarchs; the relationship He had with them, and the promises He made them prompt Him to forgive their descendants.[7] Because failure to forgive Israel may lead others to underestimate the extent of God's power and goodness, God forgives Israel also to preserve and enhance His own reputation among the nations.[8]

God forgives, however, only when human beings sincerely seek to make amends in both mind and deed. It is not enough to hope and pray for pardon or to perform the rituals associated with it (animal sacrifices, weeping, fasting, rending one's clothes, donning sackcloth and ashes, etc.); people must humble themselves, acknowledge their wrongs, and resolve to depart from sin.[9] Moreover, inner contrition must be followed by the outward acts of ceasing to do evil and then, in its place, doing good.[10]

Human Forgiveness of Individuals

God's forgiveness, however extensive, only encompasses the sins a person commits directly against Him; injuries to another human being are not forgiven, according to the Rabbis, until the victim has personally forgiven the perpetrator—hence the custom of seeking forgiveness from those one may have wronged in the days before the Day of Atonement, without which proper atonement to God cannot be made.[11]

The search for forgiveness and restoration of bonds with God and people, while the focus of the High Holy Day season, is not restricted to it. Judaism sees forgiveness as a critical part of ongoing human interactions, and it provides a specific way to accomplish it.[12] Here I note those parts of the tradition dealing with individuals' forgiveness of each other that form the background for Judaism's understanding of communal forgiveness.

If one has physically injured another, Jewish law maintains that payment of compensatory sums is not sufficient; the assailant must also ask the victim's forgiveness.[13] It is not only the injury that must be repaired, but the relationship.

This imposes a reciprocal obligation on the wronged party: He or she, when asked for forgiveness, must forgive. Injured parties who refuse to do so even when asked three times in the presence of others are, in turn, deemed to have sinned.[14] They are called cruel and are not regarded as descendants of Abraham; for ever since Abraham forgave Abimelech, forgiveness has been a distinguishing mark of Abraham's descendants, a special gift God bestowed upon them.[15] Such people also cannot expect divine forgiveness for their own sins: "All who act mercifully [forgivingly] toward their fellow creatures will be treated mercifully by Heaven, and all who do not act mercifully toward their fellow creatures will not be treated mercifully by Heaven."[16] Moreover, they have failed to imitate God, for just as God is forgiving, so we are supposed to be.[17]

This does not mean that people who have been wronged are supposed to squelch their feelings of anger. The Torah prohibits retaliatory action: "You shall not take vengeance or bear a grudge against your countrymen. Love your fellow as yourself." Nevertheless, in the verse immediately before that one, it sanctions, and even commands, that people express their feelings of outrage after being wronged: "You shall not hate your kinsfolk in your heart. Reprove your kinsman but incur no guilt because of him."[18] According to rabbinic interpretation, this even justified students criticizing their teachers, and the rebuke could be repeated even one hundred times over—although another rabbinic dictum urges us to admonish only those who will listen. There was a dispute among the Rabbis about whether the censure could take the form of physically striking the offender, but all agreed that it could not include public embarrassment.[19] Biblical and rabbinic law did, however, stipulate in considerable detail the ingredients of a just punishment and/or compensation for the range of human transgressions of one person toward another.

It also stipulated the rules under which a community as a whole could punish its members. The communal court would impose these punishments. One of the clearest expressions of communal distaste for an act was the penalty of excommunication, for then the very essence of the punishment was that the community was saying that a particular person was no longer fit to live with us—at least until he or she abided by the dictates of the court.

Once culprits paid the penalty, however, Jewish law requires that the community take them back into the community wholly. "When the parties to a suit are standing before you," Judah, the son of Tabbai said, "you should regard them both as guilty; but when they have departed from you, you should regard them as innocent, for they have accepted the verdict."[20] Unlike American law, under which a felon continues to suffer disabilities and embarrassment for the rest of his or her life, Jewish law demands that the community's forgiveness be complete—even to the point of not mentioning the crime any longer.[21]

In sum, while wrongs are to be redressed and the emotions accompanying them assuaged, the ultimate goal is to mend human ties through forgiveness and reconciliation. As Hillel said: "Be among the disciples of Aaron, loving peace and pursuing peace, loving your fellow creatures and bringing them close to the Torah."[22]

God's Forgiveness of Nations

The Bible spares nothing in describing the fierce punishments for disobedience that God has in store for Israel. Because of the covenantal promises God made Israel, because of God's promises to and the merit of the Patriarchs, and because of God's concern for His own reputation, however, God will not destroy Israel utterly. Twice in the Torah—after the Israelites make the Golden Calf and after the Israelite spies bring a negative report of the Land of Israel—God wants to start over with a new people and Moses must persuade Him not to do that. In the end, though, God promises in the Torah never to destroy Israel completely. Jeremiah articulates God's resultant policy:

> But you, have no fear,
> My servant Jacob
> —declares the Lord —
> For I am with you.
> I will make an end of all the nations
> Among which I have banished you,
> But I will not make an end of you!
> I will not leave you unpunished,
> But I will chastise you in measure.[23]

When the Bible speaks of nations other than Israel, however, the tone changes drastically. What rings in the mind of every traditional Jew on this subject is God's words concerning Amalek:

> Remember what Amalek did to you on your journey, after you left Egypt—how, undeterred by fear of God, he surprised you on the march, when you were famished and weary, and cut down all the stragglers in your rear. Therefore, when the Lord your God grants you safety from all your enemies around you, in the land that the Lord your God is giving you as a hereditary portion, you shall blot out the memory of Amalek from under heaven. Do not forget![24]

The rabbinic tradition understands this literally and, one must say, enthusiastically: " 'Remember' means by word, 'Do not forget' means in the heart, for it is forbidden to forget to despise and hate him."[25] In the account of this in the Book of

Exodus, it is not only Israel who is not supposed to forget: God Himself "will be at war with Amalek throughout the ages."[26]

In rabbinic and medieval literature, Amalek became the symbol of all oppressors of Israel, and that might account for the particular vilification of Amalek in the Jewish tradition. It is not only Amalek, however, for whom God rules out repentance and reconciliation. Already in God's promises to Abram, Egypt is to be punished, and the nations of Canaan are to be driven out of their homeland for their sins. "You must doom them to destruction," the Israelites are later told; "grant them no terms and give them no quarter."[27] Destroying Amalek and the seven Canaanite nations becomes, in fact, a clearly commanded war, one that, in later Jewish law, requires no consultation of the *urim ve'tumim* (the High Priest's oracular breastplate) and no confirmation by the Sanhedrin.[28] The tradition is so determined to avenge these wrongs that, particularly in the stories of Midian and Amalek, it raises difficult moral questions in ignoring the difference between soldiers and civilians.[29]

One might explain these cases as part of the tradition's attempt to make a strong case for Israel's right to the land inhabited by others, but the Bible's disdain for other nations does not stop there. It often excoriates non-Canaanite nations other than Amalek for the wrongs they have committed and warns them of the punishment to follow.[30] In these accounts, little, if any, mention is made of the possibility of repentance. The talmudic legend at the beginning of the tractate *Avodah Zarah* carries this further: It mocks other nations to the point of asserting that they could not even fulfill one "easy" commandment.[31]

One important exception to this harsh attitude toward other nations, of course, is the Book of Jonah, wherein the entire story centers on the turning of the people of Nineveh away from their sins and, therefore, the forgiveness God extends to them. This is one clear case in which God is willing to forgive not only individuals but nations, and not only Israel but others. The Rabbis probably chose this book for reading on the Day of Atonement (Yom Kippur) for its assurance that repentance can procure God's mercy, but it is striking that the example of repentance is specifically a nation, and a non-Jewish one at that.

One is tempted to think that God refuses to forgive nations that attack Israel, but when a nation's sins are moral, sometimes God forgives (as in the case of Nineveh) and sometimes not (as in the case of the Canaanite nations). The Book of Jonah states clearly that God's judgment against the inhabitants of Nineveh was because "their wickedness has come before Me," and the king's exhortation to his subjects is, "Let everyone turn back from his evil ways and from the injustice of which he is guilty."[32] One must remember, though, that Nineveh was the capital of Assyria, which had destroyed the Northern Kingdom of Israel and had besieged Jerusalem. Indeed, in the Bible itself Zephaniah and Nahum prophesy its destruction.[33] The case of Nineveh thus does not provide us with clear guidelines as to when God forgives nations and when not. Moreover, while the Torah treats Amalek, Ammon, and Moab harshly, it states that "You shall not abhor an Egyptian, for you were a stranger in his land"— even though Egypt never expressed regret for enslaving Israel.[34] Thus there are instances in which God has forgiven not only moral sins, but national ones, and other cases when God has rejected even the possibility of such forgiveness, with no clear indication of why some nations are treated in one way and some in another.

Human Versus Divine Forgiveness of Nations

There are other problems in trying to apply the example of Jonah to contemporary relations with the Catholic Church— or with any other group of people. The Book of Jonah, after all, speaks of God's forgiveness of a nation, while I am talking about what forgiveness extended by *us human beings* would look like.

This distinction has several implications. First, God presumably knows a nation's sins and can punish or forgive, as He chooses. The People Israel, in contrast, may know full well the brunt of another nation's disdain and wrath, but historically

Jews seldom have been able to respond in kind. Are contemporary Jews, then, even in a position to forgive? Must one be the equal or the superior of the culprit for one's forgiveness to make any sense, or can one also forgive those whom one could not choose to punish? Of course, if those who have power over you force you to engage in some expression of forgiveness, one could say that forgiveness has not occurred, since the act was coerced and, on your part, insincere; but what if the culprit honestly means to apologize? Can you forgive in the full sense of the word when your only choice is to withhold forgiveness?

Another way in which the distinction between God and human beings affects forgiveness is in the identity of the party extending forgiveness. There are, of course, many philosophical problems inherent in justifying belief in the existence of God and in identifying the nature of God. If one believes in the existence of a personal God, however, one presumably understands what it would mean for God to forgive, basing one's conception largely on what it means for a person to forgive. What, though, does it mean for the People Israel to forgive? It has been centuries since a Sanhedrin could speak in the name of the Jewish People. Who, then, would have the right even to consider the question of whether to forgive the Catholic Church, let alone extend such forgiveness?

The Proper Parties for Forgiveness and Regret

This problem is exacerbated by the lapse of time between ourselves and the abuses inflicted on our ancestors. If we decide that it does make sense for an underling to forgive a powerful superior, a Jewish communal court at the time of an atrocity might have forgiven the perpetrators for the ravages inflicted on the members of that specific community, but what legal or moral standing do we modern Jews have to do that? Only the victims of the Crusades and Inquisition, it seems, had that right during their lifetimes. If we were to forgive their oppressors now, it would seem to be adding insult to injury.

A corollary to this issue of time is the converse of the matter just discussed. Not only does it seem that the present Jewish community cannot rightfully forgive the sins of the past, but it seems that the present Catholic community cannot meaningfully regret the errors of their ancestors to justify such forgiveness.

Martin Golding identified three types of regret.[35]

1. *Intellectual regret:* in which the regret arises from a recognition of having misjudged the facts as they were or from a miscalculation of the future (for example, "I regret having bet on the third horse").
2. *Moral regret:* which arises out of a recognition that one has done something wrong (for example "I regret having lied").
3. *Other-oriented regret:* which one feels (and expresses) because one has wronged someone else ("I regret—I am sorry for—having stolen from you").

When one injures or otherwise wrongs someone else, one has put oneself *in debt* to that party, creating in that person *justified resentment*. Outside parties might have, in contrast, *justified indignation*. Only other-oriented regret, together with adequate steps to make amends, constitute grounds for victims to give up their resentment and grant forgiveness.

Forgiveness does *not* entail that either the perpetrator or the victim forgets the wrongdoing. On the contrary, part of the moral regeneration required in justifying forgiveness is that the culprit recognizes the violation, vows to do otherwise, and remembers the incident and the vow later on, when the same situation arises again. The victim also remembers the hurt but manages to put it in its place in a longer perspective of the relationship (or the lack of one) so that resentment is no longer a factor in dealing with the wrongdoer.

What forgiveness accomplishes, then, is not the expunging of the memory of the injury (even though sometimes that is wished), but rather the removal of a continuing justification for resentment so that relations between the parties can return to an even keel. That, in fact, is the reason it is sought in the first place. Depending on the previous relations of the parties, the culprit might want more than this minimum: He or she might want the victim to resume a positive attitude toward the perpetrator, not just a neutral one. Forgiveness, though, is the first step in reinstituting neutral relations so that positive ones might later develop.

This analysis helps define both sides of the problem. As an outside party to the injury, the current Jewish community can have only justified indignation at past atrocities, not justified resentment. It, therefore, cannot remove the victims' resentment. Only the victims themselves can do that, and they are no longer alive. Conversely, the contemporary Catholic Church cannot have appropriate regret for acts committed centuries ago since it did not do them.

Along these lines, Golding points out that if the victim is no longer alive, the most a regretful perpetrator can do is to remove the justified indignation of outside parties through appropriate amends. Those parties cannot extend forgiveness, however, because that "would be to confuse indignation and resentment and to overlook the rather dependent or secondary character of the role that outside parties have in interpersonal forgiveness situations."[36]

The Possibility of Forgiveness
As Part of an Ontological Reality

Although that articulates the problem, it also points to the solution. Golding's analysis holds for the vast majority of cases, in which the victim and the outside party on the one hand, and the perpetrator and the one seeking forgiveness on the other, are *separate* parties, however closely related. Then the current actors cannot perform the roles that the perpetrator and victim alone can. Ours, however, is not the usual situation. What makes the request for forgiveness on the part of contemporary Catholics *philosophically meaningful* is that they see themselves as the current embodiment of the Church that extends back to the Apostle Peter, and they see us contemporary Jews—as we see ourselves—as the current embodiment of the People Israel that extends back to the Exodus, if not to the Patriarchs and Matriarchs. Therefore, it is *the same* party who committed the wrong that is now seeking forgiveness, and it is *the same* party who suffered the wrong who is being asked to forgive.

Since all inhabitants of modern, Western democracies normally think of themselves in Enlightenment terms as independent individuals, it is appropriate to remind ourselves of the description I gave in Chapter One of how much that differs from the way the Jewish tradition understands us. My participation in the People Israel, in the eyes of the tradition, is not simply a voluntary act, which I can retract at will. It is rather part of my very being, which no act on my part can change. Even if I convert to another religion, I continue to bear the obligations of being a Jew.[37] That is why Hillel's comment, "If I am here, then everyone is here,"[38] is not just metaphorical (or egotistical!): We are all part of the same ontological entity, the Jewish people, and that entity is present in every one of us.[39]

Religious Jews have felt this ontological tie to the People Israel—past, present, and future—throughout time. It is probably part of what led the tradition to define Jewish identity in biological terms.[40] Even secular Jews in our postmodern age, I would argue, feel much the same. They may not accept the religious underpinnings of Jewish identity, but few would deny their Jewishness, and many would take umbrage at any offense against Jews. Sometimes, when the attack against Jews is extreme, as it was before and during the Six Day War, these Jews come out of the woodwork, as it were, to defend the people of whom they still feel a part.

The Christian reality is more complex because, as discussed in Chapter One, Christianity places much more emphasis on the individual, who alone is saved or damned. Still, in Christian theology every Christian is part of the body of Christ, however that is understood; that would give contemporary Christians a metaphysical tie to Christians in the past. Christian concepts of the universal church and the body of Christ do not translate into the kinds of specific duties that Jews have to each other as part of *Kelal Yisrael,* the community of Israel; in that sense, the metaphysical bond of contemporary Christians with those of the past and even with other Christians in our own time is not nearly as strong as the Jewish communal bond. Still, Christianity asserts a metaphysical connection among all Christians, past, present, and future. Moreover, even if that is not part of the consciousness of particular Christians, most Christians feel at least a historical tie to their co-religionists in the past. Their understanding and practice of the faith may differ from that of their ancestors, but they identify with people like Augustine and Aquinas, Luther and Calvin. In these metaphysical and historical aspects of self-identity, then, Christians are very much like Jews.

The trick, of course, is that, even with this ontological perspective in mind, contemporary Catholics and Jews are not the perpetrators and the victims themselves, respectively, but only extensions of them. As a result, even though we are, in the eyes of both our traditions, metaphysically and historically related to our ancestors, our regret and forgiveness cannot be nearly as forceful as if the Church had asked forgiveness immediately after perpetrating the atrocities (or, better yet, had taken steps to prevent them in the first place!).

This is, in other words, a *secondary* sense of regret and forgiveness that I am developing here, one that we might call "reconciliation" or "acceptance." In this form, the regret and forgiveness are not extended by the parties themselves. On the other hand, the people involved are not, in Golding's terms, strictly "outside" parties either. It is rather extensions of the groups involved in the original acts who are now called on to decide whether to engage in the process of forgiveness, and that, it seems to me, is a meaningful extension of our primary notions of regret and forgiveness. As such, it is logically appropriate for the contemporary Church to seek forgiveness and for the current Jewish community to consider whether to grant it.

This, of course, does *not* mean that contemporary Jews *should* extend the hand of forgiveness to Catholics. That is a matter of judgment that we have yet to consider. My argument so far has been only that the request is *logically meaningful,* for it is the party that committed the act (or, at least, an extension of that party) who is asking for forgiveness, and the party that suffered the act (or, at least, an extension of that party) who is being asked.

There is, though, one other problem in imagining how Jews might forgive Catholics for past offenses: Presumably the Vatican would represent Catholics, but who would represent Jews? The State of Israel? the presidents of major American Jewish organizations? the World Jewish Congress? Clearly, no one body—even the State of Israel—speaks for world Jewry as the Vatican does for Catholics. As a result, Jewish reconciliation with Catholics, if deemed appropriate, will more likely take place on the interpersonal and local levels first—that is, through friendships and joint activities of individual Jews and Catholics and through united, local initiatives to tackle common problems. If and when trust builds, national Jewish organizations in North America and elsewhere may, at some point, acknowledge progress in Catholic–Jewish relations through resolutions of reconciliation. Because of Jewish disorganization, this process will not be as neat as we might like it, but the lack of a single, worldwide Jewish representative does not make reconciliation logically or practically impossible.

One feature of forgiveness—both the primary forgiveness of the victim toward the culprit, and the extended kind of forgiveness that I have been describing—should be made clear at this point. We have already seen that forgiveness does not expunge memory of the event; it also does not eliminate moral culpability. In ancient times, people could literally "wipe clean" (*kapper*) their sins through animal sacrifices. God may still do that (perhaps now motivated by prayer, repentance, and good deeds, as the High Holy Day liturgy maintains), but human beings do not. When one human being forgives another, the victim agrees to engage in present and future relationships with the perpetrator *despite* the wrong committed; the act itself continues to be considered wrong by the victim—and, if the process of repentance works, by the perpetrator too. If one member of a couple cheats on the other, for example, the latter may agree to forgive the former and be reconciled to him or her, but neither party condones the adultery. Similarly here, if Jews decide to forgive

Catholics or Germans (the cases are clearly different), neither the memory nor the moral culpability of the abuses is at stake; the question is only whether to be reconciled despite the past wrongs.

An Argument against Forgiveness
Granted by Descendants

In an article titled "Why I Won't Go to Germany," Cynthia Ozick argues against something like the secondary kind of forgiveness that I have been describing. She says that Jews from America and elsewhere who go to Germany to explore reconciliation with the Germans permit the Germans to hide from the fullness of their sin. Germans must, she says, repent for their actions in the absence of Jews—"the absence of Jews in contemporary Germany being precisely the point." Current Jews—especially those from abroad—only becloud the issue when they go to such meetings because they permit the Germans to believe that we have the right or power to act in the victims' stead.

> This principle of surrogacy is conceived in profound error. Who will dare to suggest that any living Jew can offer reconciliation—or even simple human presence—on behalf of the murdered? . . . Americans [who visit Germany to explore reconciliation] are confusing the question by abetting the tragic and degrading falsehood of human interchangeability.[41]

What should happen instead, according to Ozick, is that Germans of goodwill should deal with the German national conscience on their own:

> The German task is, after all, a kind of "liberation" (of conscience into history), or emancipation, and the only genuine emancipation—as we know from many other national, social, and cultural contexts—is auto-emancipation. . . . Patriotism . . . is something you do for yourself, by yourself, out of obligation to the moral improvement of your country . . . it is, above all, a dream of self-transformation.[42]

It is, of course, true that no living Jew can morally represent any victim of the Holocaust or, for that matter, of any past persecution. It is also true that much of the process of *teshuvah,* whether individual or national, is the act of recognizing the sin and admitting it—both of which only the sinner can do. I differ with Ozick, however, on two counts. First, as Jewish sources specify, repentance cannot be achieved by the sinner alone. After recognizing the sin, admitting guilt for it, and expressing remorse, the offender must seek forgiveness from the wronged parties, who play a critical role in this process. Since that is the teaching of our own tradition as well as the psychological reality, we must surely understand that German or Catholic repentance cannot be limited to the acts of the Germans or the Church alone. At some point, they will need evidence of reacceptance by someone.

Second, contemporary Jews, it seems to me, are not totally incapable of performing that task. The problem, of course, is that the parties who would be in the best position to offer forgiveness—the victims themselves—no longer can. Ozick thinks that the Germans should just have to live with the inability to make full repentance and the guilt and shame this incurs; it is simply, in her view, part of the gravity of their crime and its just punishment. I agree that only the victims can offer *full* forgiveness, but, based on the corporate reasoning I have been advancing, it seems to me that the descendants can offer some lesser form of it.

Moreover, one might argue that we should. After all, by and large, in the case of the Germans, we are no longer talking about those who perpetrated or even acquiesced to the crime, and this is all the more true for the past persecution our people has suffered at the hands of Catholics and Protestants. Furthermore, by and large, the vast majority of Jews living today are not the ones who were directly abused by any of those parties. Therefore, although we cannot forgive what our ancestors suffered, contemporary members of the Jewish community can, in the name of the community, judge whether current members of the German, Protestant, or Catholic communities have done their best to prevent future conduct of that sort and whether we should consequently extend to them the hand of acceptance and perhaps even friendship. This would not be forgiveness in its pristine form; that, only the victims can give. It would, however, be a lesser form of forgiveness—reconciliation or acceptance—which would enable the communities involved to get beyond the negatives of the past and build a better future.

Precedents for Reconciliation

It is interesting that the Talmud anticipated a form of extended forgiveness somewhat similar to what I am proposing. It raises the question of what a person should do if the victim of his or her act has died before forgiveness can be sought. It prescribes that the perpetrator should bring ten people to the victim's grave and say before them: "I have sinned to the Lord, God of Israel, and to So-and-so, for thus I have done to him." Furthermore, if the perpetrator owes the victim money, says the Talmud, he or she must pay it to the victim's heirs. If the offender does not know whether the victim had any heirs, he or she must leave the money in the hands of the court and go through the process of admission described above.[43]

Here, as in our case, the aggrieved party, the one who alone can offer forgiveness in the full sense of the word, can no longer even be asked, let alone decide whether to do so. Even so, the perpetrator *can* achieve a secondary form of forgiveness by making public amends at the deceased person's grave, provided that he or she first repairs the damage itself for the heirs. The community and the heirs, in other words, are taken to be extensions of the deceased party—sufficiently, at any rate, to receive the regret and grant the forgiveness.

Our case, of course, is different from the Talmud's in that it is not the perpetrator who is asking for forgiveness; in the relationships between Jews and contemporary Catholics, Protestants, or Germans, neither the perpetrators of past atrocities nor the victims are alive. This makes the case both stronger and weaker: stronger, in that the vast majority of living Catholics, Protestants, and Germans did not commit the crimes and so bear none of the guilt that would obstruct a repair in relations; but weaker, in that current Jews did not suffer the violence and thus cannot offer full forgiveness. Nevertheless, the Talmud's case does provide a precedent for stretching the concept of forgiveness to include secondary, extended forms of it when one or both parties are no longer alive.

Moreover, there is at least one case in which a nation forgave another nation. Specifically, after World War II, the United States, through the Marshall Plan and other allocations, spent considerable sums of money to rebuild not only allies like France and the Netherlands, but also West Germany and Japan, the defeated enemies. The purpose of doing so was not to seek reconciliation with those countries but rather to rebuild them so that they would not fall prey to Communism, and hence the language used to convince the American people to adopt and to implement this program was not that of altruism but of pragmatic value. Nevertheless, Americans did not see this as a crass political act; in fact, Marshall Plan aid was even offered to the Soviet Union and the countries of Eastern Europe. In the minds of most Americans, this was rather an attempt to undo the damage of the war and to help Europe and Japan get back on their feet. This was a clear—and costly—example of reconciliation in deed, if not in word.[44]

Whether to Forgive

The Factors Against

While contemporary Jews *can* take steps toward reconciliation, it is not necessarily what we *ought* to do. That depends on the degree to which we think the repentance is real. Here I would suggest that we use the same criteria for judging nations that the Jewish tradition applied to individuals, as described in Chapter Five—specifically, evidence that the perpetrator recognizes the act as a violation, admits guilt for the act, has remorse, exerts efforts to seek forgiveness and compensate the victims to the extent that it is possible, and takes steps to ensure that the act will not happen again.[45] In that way, our policy for dealing with the repentance of nations will not be based on the general biblical response to national violation, but rather the lesson of the Book of Jonah, as solitary as it is. We will thus be shaping our tradition in the way it always has been shaped—by the conscious or unconscious choice of some parts of the tradition over others for purposes of emphasis and development.[46]

Returning now to the specific example of the Catholic Church, we need to ask why we hesitate to engage in this process of improving relations. Why are we wary?

Part of the reason is that the Church continues to do things that aggravate us. The pope's meetings with Kurt Waldheim and the delay in removing the Carmelite monastery at Auschwitz minimally indicate that the Church does not recognize the depth of Jews' sensitivity to Holocaust issues and, at the other end of the spectrum, make some Jews doubt the sincerity of the Church in making amends on this issue. The elevation of Edith Stein to sainthood puts salt in the wounds of Jews who regret that she converted from Judaism to Catholicism, and declaring Pope Pius IX and Pope Pius XII saints—two popes with questionable if not downright negative relationships to Jews and Judaism— exacerbates matters yet further. The Vatican statement *Dominus Iesus,* discussed in Chapter Three, also gives Jews pause: What does all the interfaith dialogue instigated by the Church mean if it still believes that all other faiths are "defective"?

Another part of Jewish misgivings is the reticence of the Church to admit it was wrong in the past. It has certainly condemned anti-Semitism in the strongest of terms, but it has never said in an official document that the Church itself was guilty of it, that the Inquisition and the Crusades were wrong, and that the Church's behavior during World War II was less than ideal. Even Pope John Paul II, who has gone further than any other Catholic prelate in advancing the rapprochement of the Church with Jews, will say only that individual Catholics of the past have erred, not that the Church itself did so. One gets the sneaking suspicion that the Church's condemnation of anti-Semitism is directed to the current and future Church; that in itself is good, but repentance also requires admission of guilt for the past.

Then, of course, there is the long history of persecution. Even if the Church were openly to admit its past sins, the pain those sins caused does not go away easily. In this situation as in all others, readiness to forgive is, in part, a function of the extent of damage done. The Germans have been quite forthcoming in admitting guilt for the Holocaust and in expressing remorse in both word and deed; and yet many Jews, like Ozick, would never even step foot in Germany, let alone condone resuming relations with the Germans, due to the enormity of the violence they committed against us. The Catholic Church may have had a hand in the Holocaust in permitting and fostering anti-Semitism for so long as well as in what it did or failed to do during World War II, but even its sharpest critics would not compare its abuse of Jews to that of the Nazis. Nevertheless, it was considerable, and our people's memory of it makes forgiveness—or even steps toward it—difficult. The most nagging issue, however, is that we have no right to forgive that which was done to our ancestors. That, of course, is true, and, as I have argued, this feeling is magnified by our deeply ingrained, post-Enlightenment individualism. Nevertheless, if we see ourselves as the tradition sees us, as part of the extended corporate entity known as the Jewish people, then we, as its present members, do have the right (indeed, the responsibility) to act on behalf of the group—present, past, and future—in this issue as in all others. Neither the Church's present amends nor our forgiveness would be nearly as meaningful as those of the perpetrators and victims; and we may, in the end, choose not to forgive. But it is logically and morally possible and it does carry meaning for present and future relations.

The Factors For

What, though, has the Church done to warrant that we even consider extending this lesser form of forgiveness? Launched by *Nostra Aetate* in 1965, the Vatican has engaged in a number of efforts to repair relations with Jews. Its Commission for Religious Relations with the Jews has produced two additional official Vatican documents to amplify the themes of *Nostra Aetate* and put its commitments into practice; these are *Guidelines and Suggestions for Implementing the Conciliar Declaration "Nostra Aetate"* (December 1974) and *Notes on the Correct Way to Present Jews and Judaism in Preaching and Catechesis in the Roman Catholic Church* (June 1985). These documents did not address all Jewish concerns to our satisfaction, but they went a long way. And the Vatican's subsequent diplomatic recognition of the State of Israel and the pope's visit there and to the synagogue in Rome have taken this Catholic effort yet further.[47]

The Second Vatican Council itself admonished Catholics not to hold Jews responsible for Jesus' death, and it condemned anti-Semitism in the strongest of terms. "Jews should not be presented as rejected or accursed by God, as if this followed from the Holy Scriptures," it said, and the council "decries hatred, persecutions, and displays of anti-Semitism, directed against Jews at any time and by anyone."

Aside from acting to remove the negative in this way, the Church also has tried to create ideological and institutional structures to build positive ties between Catholics and Jews. Catholics must, according to *Guideline and Suggestions,* recognize that the Old Testament "retains its own perpetual value" and "has not been canceled by the later interpretation of the New Testament." Christians, of course, still maintain that "the New Testament brings out the full meaning of the Old, while both the Old and the New illumine each other," but we Jews would make the same claim for rabbinic literature's relationship to the Hebrew Bible. To counteract the general impression of Christians that Judaism was only a prelude to Christianity, *Guidelines and Suggestions* proclaims that "Christians . . . must strive to learn by what essential traits the Jews define themselves in the light of their own religious experience." Catholics are to study not only the religion of the Bible, but "the faith and religious life of the Jewish people as they are professed and practiced still today."

The Church has been ambivalent, as one can understand, in trying to balance its mission "to proclaim Jesus Christ to the world" and at the same time to maintain "the strictest respect for religious liberty in line with the teaching of the Second Vatican Council," and it has not yet openly abandoned missionizing among Jews. The fact, though, that *both* of these commitments were published in this language in adjoining paragraphs in *Notes on the Correct Way* indicates that the Church on the highest levels at least sees this as a problem with which it must grapple.

Even though both *Nostra Aetate* and the *Guidelines and Suggestions* omitted any mention of the State of Israel, *Notes on the Correct Way* includes two paragraphs on the Land and State of Israel—to my knowledge, the first time such references have appeared in official Vatican documents of doctrine. The document points to the unbroken attachment in both memory and hope that Jews have had with the Land of Israel as the land of their forefathers and bids Catholics "understand this religious attachment which finds its roots in biblical tradition, without however making their own particular religious interpretation of this relationship." Instead, "the existence of the State of Israel and its political options should be envisaged not in a perspective which is in itself religious, but in their reference to the common principles of international law."

One can hear all kinds of hesitation here, and one frankly wonders what the simple meaning of some of this phraseology is. What is clear, though, is that in this document and in its subsequent diplomatic recognition of the State of Israel, the Vatican has deemed that it must acknowledge the special religious tie of Jews to the State of Israel if it wants to build better relations with us.

Given the sharp changes in policy these documents express, one would expect that it would take some time to implement them and that the degree of activity along these lines would vary by region. That, indeed, has happened. The pattern seems to be that in this matter, as in all others, what the Church does depends on local conditions and on the priorities of the local leadership. The Polish cardinal of Krakow, for example, whose family hid Jews during World War II, held a conference in Krakow in April 1988 of rabbis and other Jewish leaders from around the world (including some from Poland) to expose all of the seminary professors in his region to living Judaism and Jews so that they would make their charges sensitive to the sentiments expressed in these Vatican documents. The cardinal of Warsaw, on the other hand, refused to participate. By 1996, though, the Polish Church entered into an agreement with the American Jewish Committee to sponsor a Jewish professor of theology to teach in Catholic seminaries and universities in Warsaw, Krakow, and Lublin, while a Polish Catholic seminary professor would teach in a number of American Jewish seminaries. This exchange has taken place annually. As early as 1973, Cardinal Manning of Los Angeles, generally a conservative, appointed a priest with the specific portfolio of stimulating Catholic–Jewish dialogue and joint action. The cardinal's participation in the Second Vatican Council and the large Jewish population in Los Angeles were undoubtedly factors in this, but clearly his own values played a role too, because he could have put all of this on the back burner. On the other hand, in Sao Paulo, Brazil, the initiative for Catholic–Jewish dialogue and joint action has come from the local rabbinic leadership.

At this point, then, the effect of the Vatican documents depends not only on the actions of the Vatican itself but also on local conditions, and it will take time to see how much the Church can and will translate the contents and intentions of these documents into concrete results. Still, one must, in fairness, note that the Church has not buried *Nostra Aetate;* indeed, in some areas of the world the extent to which steps have been taken to reflect its principles has been remarkable.

Beyond all this, there is a practical point that must not be forgotten. For better or for worse, the Roman Catholic Church represents more than half of Christendom and is the largest single religion in the world.[48] It is, therefore, undoubtedly in the best interests of Jews to foster good relations with the contemporary Church. "Good relations" does not mean that we suppress our memories of past wrongs or our anger at present ones, but it does mean coming to some understanding that we are going to get along *despite* past atrocities.

In his book *The Periodic Table*, Primo Levi, a chemist by profession, describes contacts he had after World War II with Dr. Muller, the German in charge of the chemical laboratory in which Levi worked as a Jewish prisoner during the war. Muller had arranged for him to have a second shave each week and a new pair of shoes, and so he was not a stereotypical, unabashed Nazi; if anything, he seemed surprised at the vile treatment of the prisoners. At the same time, he was a member of the Nazi Party and did work to further its war efforts. After the war, Muller worked for a chemical company in Germany that supplied resin for the Italian varnish company where Levi worked. Coincidentally, it was the selfsame Muller who wrote on behalf of his company in response to a complaint about a shipment of defective resin to Levi's company, and it was Levi who received Muller's letter. In subsequent correspondence, Levi identified himself to Muller and sent him his book describing the horrors of his experiences during the war. When Muller wrote to Levi after some time, he was neither completely repentant nor completely defensive; he was somewhere in between. He did, however, seek to meet with Levi to "overcome the past." Levi writes:

> I did not feel capable of representing the dead of Auschwitz, nor did it seem to me sensible to see in Muller the representative of the butchers. . . .

> [I]f this story were invented, I would have been able to introduce only two kinds of letters: a humble, warm, Christian letter, from a redeemed German; a ribald, proud, glacial letter from an obdurate Nazi. Now this story is not invented, and reality is always more complex than invention: less kempt, cruder, less rounded out. It rarely lies on one level. . . . The Muller character . . . [was] neither infamous nor a hero: after filtering off the rhetoric and the lies in good or bad faith, there remained a typically gray human specimen, one of the not so few one-eyed men in the kingdom of the blind. . . .

> I made a draft: I thanked him for having taken me into the lab; I declared myself ready to forgive my enemies, and perhaps even to

love them, but only when they showed certain signs of repentance, that is, when they ceased being enemies. In the opposite case, that of the enemy who remains an enemy, who perseveres in his desire to inflict suffering, it is certain that one must not forgive him: one can try to salvage him, one can (one must!) discuss with him, but it is our duty to judge him, not to forgive him.[49]

The relationship between contemporary Jews and Catholics bears some striking resemblances to Levi's situation, but it is different in at least one important way. Like Levi, contemporary Jews are reticent to assume the moral burden of judging whether or not to forgive the perpetrators of past atrocities—or their descendants. Like Muller, the Catholic Church has recognized the immorality of some of its previous actions and the errors of some of its adherents and officials, but it has not renounced them or atoned for them in words or deeds quite as forthrightly as Jews would have hoped. The record, instead, is mixed, as most human records are. Muller, however, died before Levi had to face the prospect of meeting him face-to-face; Catholics, in contrast, are still very much alive, and Jews must decide how to deal with them as honestly and productively as possible.

The Bottom Line

Shall we forgive? That is a matter the Jewish community must still discuss. It depends, in large measure, on continued evidence of a Catholic desire to repent. A positive Jewish response to this will probably not take place in one single moment, and it will not be universally offered by Jews. Forgiveness will rather be achieved little by little, through joint word and action, just as personal forgiveness usually is. Over a period of time we will test the degree of the Church's appropriate regret and get used to working with each other in a series of cooperative ventures. Ultimately, we may apply the tradition's eagerness for forgiveness among individuals to the Catholic community as a whole. Whether we will remains to be seen. This chapter has demonstrated, though, that, at least in a secondary form of forgiveness, it is logically possible for us to do so.

If we do decide that reconciliation is warranted, our efforts to seek better relations with Catholics would be motivated not only by such practical factors but also by ideological commitments. Our tradition has not spared its contempt for nations that have attacked Israel, but it has also praised those who have sought to repair relationships. It knows quite well that sometimes human beings wrong others, and it goes to great lengths to specify what justice demands in such circumstances. But it also prescribes that we not only accept evidence of remorse in other individuals and groups but actively seek to achieve a world of peace.

> If a person has been injured, then even if the wrongdoer has not asked his forgiveness, the injured party must nevertheless ask God to show the wrongdoer compassion, even as Abraham prayed to God for Avimelech (Genesis 20:17) and Job prayed for his friends. Rabban Gamliel said: Let this be a sign to you, that whenever you are compassionate, the Compassionate One will have compassion upon you.[50]

Notes

The following abbreviations are used in the notes to the text:

B. = Babylonian Talmud (edited by Ravina and Rav Ashi in c. 500 C.E.)

J. = Jerusalem (Palestinian) Talmud (editor unknown, c. 400 C.E.)

M. = Mishnah (edited by Rabbi Judah ha Nasi [Judah the Prince], president of the Sandedrin in c. 200 C.E.)

M.T. = Maimonides' *Mishneh Torah* (completed in 1177)

S.A. = *Shulchan Arukh* (completed in 1565 by Yosef Karo, a Spanish [Sephardic] Jew, with glosses by Moses Isserles that indicate differences in German and eastern European [Ashkenazic] Jewish practice)

T. = Tosefta (edited by Rabbi Hiyya and Rabbi Oshaiya in c. 200 C.E.)

Modern works are referred to by author (or editor) and publication date. Full bibliographical information can be found in the Bibliography.

NOTES TO CHAPTER ONE

1. Scheer (1988).
2. Deuteronomy 6:18.
3. Leviticus 23:42–43.
4. Genesis 2:1–3 and Exodus 20:11 tie the Sabbath to Creation, whereas Deuteronomy 5:15 ties it to the Exodus.
5. Genesis 1:27.
6. Genesis 5:1–2.
7. Genesis 9:6.
8. Deuteronomy 21:22–23.
9. Throughout the book I use "Rabbis" (with a capital "R") to refer to the classical Rabbis of the Mishnah, Talmud, and Midrash, and I use "rabbis" (with

a lower-case "r") to refer to rabbis from medieval and modern times. In adherence to standard English form, though, the adjectival form, "rabbinic," is spelled with a lower-case "r" in all instances.

10. M. *Avot* (*Ethics of the Fathers*) 3:18. The quote is from Genesis 9:6.

11. See Genesis 1:26–27; 3:1–7, 22–24.

12. See Genesis 2:18–24, Numbers 12:1–16, and Deuteronomy 22:13–19. Note also that *ha-middaber* (the speaker) is a synonym for the human being (compared to animals) in medieval Jewish philosophy.

13. Maimonides, *Guide for the Perplexed,* part I, chap. 1.

14. See Deuteronomy 6:5 and Leviticus 19:18, 33–34. Note that the traditional prayer book juxtaposes the paragraph just before the *Shema,* which speaks of God's love for us, with the first paragraph of the *Shema,* which commands us to love God.

15. Consider the prayer in the traditional early morning weekday service "*Elohai neshamah she-natata bi*": "My God, the soul (or life-breath) which you have imparted to me is pure. You created it, You formed it, You breathed it into me; You guard it within me." Harlow (1985), 8–11. Similarly, the Rabbis describe the human being as part divine and part animal, the latter consisting of the material aspects of the individual and the former consisting of that which we share with God; see *Sifrei Devarim,* par. 306; 132a. Or consider this rabbinic statement in Genesis *Rabbah* 8:11: "In four respects man resembles the creatures above, and in four respects the creatures below. Like the animals he eats and drinks, propagates his species, relieves himself, and dies. Like the ministering angels he stands erect, speaks, possesses intellect, and sees [in front of him and not on the side like an animal]."

16. Genesis 6:10.

17. M. *Sanhedrin* 4:5.

18. Rabbi Bunam, cited by Buber (1948), 2:249–250. Compare Genesis 18:27.

19. Genesis *Rabbah* 24:7.

20. J. *Eruvin* 5:1. Epstein (1969), 182, n. 19 (on Exodus 18:12), suggests that this is a scribal error, that because the previous aphorisms in this section of the Talmud refer to welcoming scholars, here too the Talmud meant to say that one who welcomes a scholar is like one who welcomes the Divine Presence. He may well be right contextually, but the version quoted states an important broader lesson that expresses the divine image in every person, regardless of his or her level of scholarship. Along the same lines, Shammai, who was not known for his friendliness and who in the immediately previous phrase warns us to "say little and do much," nevertheless admonishes, "Greet every person with a cheerful face" (*Avot* [*Ethics of the Fathers*] 1:15), undoubtedly in recognition of the divine image in each of us.

21. For a thorough discussion of this blessing and concept in the Jewish tradition, see Astor (1985).

22. J. *Terumah* 7:20 and Genesis *Rabbah* 94:9.

23. J. *Terumah* 47a.

24. Dorff (1998a), 291–299. See also Schochet (1973).

25. B. *Berachot* 61a.

26. *Avot de-Rabbi Natan* 16; compare B. *Sanhedrin* 91b.

27. B. *Berachot* 61b.

28. *Avot de-Rabbi Natan* 16.

29. Genesis *Rabbah* 9:7.

30. B. *Avodah Zarah* 5a.

31. Deuteronomy 6:5.

32. *Sifrei Devarim* par. 32.

33. See, for example, B. *Sukkot* 52a.

34. B. *Kiddushin* 30b. For other recipes, see B. *Berachot* 5a; B. *Avodah Zarah* 5b; and, most remarkably, B. *Hagigah* 16a: "If a man sees that his evil impulse is gaining mastery over him, let him go to a place where he is unknown, put on black clothes [as a sign of mourning to sober him, or as a way of hiding his identity], and do what his heart desires; but let him not profane God's Name publicly." This source clearly does not presume that the man will successfully hide his misdeed from God, who knows all, but at least he will not flaunt his sin before his community, thereby disgracing his neighbors and defaming God, whose commandments he is publicly violating.

35. The classical statement of the Jewish conception of *teshuvah* is M.T. *Law of Return,* esp. chaps. 1 and 2. For a contemporary restatement of that concept, see Dorff 1998b.

36. Romans 7:21–8:4, 8:10, 13.

37. 1 Corinthians 7:9.

38. This general theory about the body's lusts and marriage can be found in 1 Corinthians 7, which also includes the ban against divorce. The prohibition of contraceptives is still affirmed by the Catholic Church but not by many Protestant churches.

39. Most of the Founding Fathers were deists, believing in a creative force in nature but not a personal God with a will. Their use of "the Creator" in place of "God" in the Declaration of Independence, which I quote here, is thus not accidental. Even if they had said "God," their conception of God makes God tantamount to Nature.

40. Acts 2:44–47.

41. See, for example, Rauschenbusch (1978) and Hopkins (1982).

42. See, for example, Turner (1994), Gutierrez (1973), McCann (1981), Boff (1997), and Cone (1997).

43. Declaration of Independence.

44. Deuteronomy 11:26–28

45. The Gettysburg Address was delivered on November 19, 1863. In Ken Burns's documentary *The Civil War* (1990), it was noted that Lincoln's emphasis was on the word "people": "of the *people,* by the *people,* and for the *people.*"

46. For a fuller delineation and explanation of the various rationales the Bible provides for abiding by its laws, see Dorff (1989).

47. This was certainly the practice of all governments in the pre-Enlightenment world, and the political theories of pre-Enlightenment societies supported that practice. Christianity is one possible exception here, but even that is not clear. On the one hand, it focuses on the salvation of the individual, regardless of his or her social affiliation, and that would seem to lend at least some support to thinking of people as individuals rather than as members of groups that they cannot ignore or leave. On the other hand, though, based on a passage in the New Testament (Matthew 22:21) in which Christians are told to "give back to Caesar what

belongs to Caesar, and to God what belongs to God," Christians in practice have made a sharp dichotomy between the City of God and the City of Man, as St. Augustine (354–430 C.E.) put it, reserving individualistic thinking for the City of God and ruling earthly societies in accordance with the corporate theories prevalent before the Enlightenment.

48. M.T. *Laws of Repentance* 3:4. Compare B. *Rosh Hashanah* 17a.

49. B. *Shabbat* 54b. Along with Jeremiah (31:29–30) and Ezekiel (18:20–32), this offends our sense of justice, but that is only because we are so used to thinking in individualistic terms.

50. Konvitz (1980), 143, 150, and compare chap. 5 generally. Hillel's words are in B. *Sukkot* 53a.

51. Compare T. *Avodah Zarah* 8:4, B. *Sanhedrin* 56a, *Seder Olam* chap. 5, Genesis *Rabbah* 16:6, 34:8, Canticles *Rabbah* 1:16, and M.T. *Laws of Kings* 9:1. For a thorough description and discussion of this doctrine, see Novak (1983).

52. Numbers 15:15–16; compare, for example, Exodus 12:49, 22:20; Leviticus 24:22; Numbers 9:14, 15:29; and Deuteronomy 24:14–15. According to the Talmud's count (B. *Bava Metzi'a* 59b), the demand to treat the stranger on a par with the citizen appears thirty-six times in the Torah. A stranger had recourse to Israelite courts: Exodus 22:21, 23:9 and Deuteronomy 24:17, 27:19. One must even "love" the stranger and treat him as a citizen: Leviticus 19:33–34; compare Deuteronomy 10:18.

53. B. *Gittin* 5:8–9; *Mekhilta de-Rabbi Yishmael, pisha* 15; B. *Gittin* 61a; B. *Bava Metzi'a* 70b; B. *Bava Batra* 113a; Maimonides, *Commentary to the Mishnah, Kelim* 12:7; and M.T. *Laws of Sale* 18:1. Compare *Jewish Encyclopedia*, s.v. "gentile," and *Encyclopedia Judaica*, s.v. "gentile."

54. On not missionizing, see B. *Yevamot* 47a–b; J. *Kiddushin* 4:1 (65b); M.T. *Laws of Forbidden Intercourse* 13:14–14:5; and S. A. *Yoreh De'ah* 268:2. Compare *Encyclopedia Judaica*, s.v. "proselytes." That Jews were to be an example to other nations, see, for example, Isaiah 2:2–4, 11:10, 42:1–4, 49:6; Genesis *Rabbah* 43:7; and Leviticus *Rabbah* 6:5.

55. T. *Sanhedrin* 13:2, B. *Bava Batra* 10b, and M.T. *Laws of Repentance* 3:5. According to Samuel, on the Day of Judgment there is no distinction between Jew and Gentile; J. *Rosh Hashanah* 1:3 (57a).

56. See, for example, Deuteronomy 24:10–22; compare also Exodus 22:21–26; 23:6; Leviticus 25:25–55; and Deuteronomy 15:7–11. Biblical law condoned slavery to pay debts, but it restricted the length and conditions of servitude; see Exodus 21:2–11, 20–21, 26–27 and Deuteronomy 15:12–18, 23:16–17. For one poignant example of Jewish provision for the poor in the Middle Ages, see Goitein (1971), 2:139–142, 128. See also Chapter Six herein.

57. Leviticus 19:14. Compare Astor (1985).

58. See, for example, Kirschenbaum (1970), Lamm (1971), chaps. 10, 11, and Konvitz (1972).

59. B. *Eruvin* 13b. But see its correlative in B. *Sotah* 47b.

60. Konvitz (1980), chap. 1, esp. 33–41, emphasized this point.

61. Deuteronomy 17:18–20, 2 Samuel 11–12, and 1 Kings 21. Compare also the talmudic story of the confrontation between Simeon ben Shetah and King Alexander Yannai in B. *Sanhedrin* 19a–b.

62. Deuteronomy 17:18–20.

63. M. *Avot (Ethics of the Fathers)* 4:10.

64. So claims Konvitz (1980), 53–55; the quotation is from p. 55.

65. For rabbinic sources and further discussion on these points, see Dorff (1978) and Dorff (1996a), chap. 3, sect. C. For a specific example of this, see Dorff (1997).

66. Exodus 19:6.

67. The Pharisees, the title given to some of the leading interpreters of the Jewish tradition in the last two centuries B.C.E. and the first century C.E., came from the lower elements of the socioeconomic ladder and hence were keenly aware of the challenge to God's justice posed by good people who suffer, as I describe in the next paragraph. In contrast, the Sadducees, their contemporaries, came from the upper echelon of society. In keeping with their social station, they believed that people got exactly what they deserved in this life and that God's justice was, therefore, manifest on this earth. They furthermore argued that the Torah does not speak of a life after death, a claim that they were undoubtedly right about, despite Pharisaic claims to the contrary. For a brief treatment of all of this, see *Encyclopedia Judaica*, s.v. "afterlife" and s.v. "resurrection of the dead."

68. B. *Berachot* 7a.

69. B. *Pesachim* 50a.

70. M. *Avot (Ethics of the Fathers)* 2:8.

71. M. *Avot (Ethics of the Fathers)* 6:9. The quotes are from Proverbs 6:22.

72. *Sifrei Devarim* par. 306, 132a. The quotes are from Psalm 82:6–7.

73. M. *Avot (Ethics of the Fathers)* 2:9.

74. Genesis *Rabbah* 11:6 and *Pesikta Rabbati* 22:4.

75. Midrash *Temurrah* as cited in Eisenstein (1915), 2:580–581. Compare also B. *Avodah Zarah* 40b, which contains a story in which the rabbi expresses appreciation for foods that can cure and the human expertise to discover that.

76. B. *Shabbat* 10a, 119b. In the first of these passages, it is the judge who judges justly who is called God's partner; in the second passage, it is anyone who recites Genesis 2:1–3 (about God resting on the seventh day) on Friday night who thereby participates in God's ongoing act of creation. The Talmud in B. *Sanhedrin* 38a specifically wanted the Sadducees *not* to be able to say that angels or any being other than humans participate with God in creation.

77. Some famous examples include Isaiah 2:1–4 (parallel to Micah 4:1–3, although with changes in the vision in verse 5) and Isaiah 11:1–13.

78. S. Greenberg (1977), 223–24, and chap. 4 generally. See also p. 99 and chap. 2 generally, in which he shows how the Declaration of Independence came to be interpreted as the goal for American history and law against which individual acts and laws could be appropriately judged.

79. J. *Kiddushin* 4:12 (66d). See also Rabbi Isaac's sarcastic question "Are not the things prohibited in the Torah enough for you that you want to prohibit yourself other things?" in J. *Nedarim* 9:1 (41b). Voluntary asceticism was actually classified as a sin; see, for example, B. *Nedarim* 10a; B. *Nazir* 3a, 19a, 22a; B. *Bava Kamma* 91a; B. *Ta'anit* 11a. Compare also M.T. *Laws of Attitudes (De'ot)* 3:1. As Schulweis (1995), 25–37, esp. 27–31, points out, at the same time some of the classical Rabbis practiced asceticism, including Rabbi Judah the Prince (B. *Ketub-*

bot 104a) and Mar, son of Ravina (B. *Pesachim* 68b), and ascetic tendencies gained ascendance among Jews living under difficult times. Thus it would be unfair to depict Judaism as totally devoid of asceticism or pessimism about the ability of human beings to improve their lives. Still, as I go on to argue in this paragraph, classical Jewish theology and the rubric of the Torah's commandments led Jews to integrate the physical with the ideal and even engendered a certain optimism about the potential results of doing that.

80. Compare Konvitz (1980), 21, 31, chap. 7.

81. Konvitz (1980), 15–18, 50–51.

82. Psalm 90:10, 12, 17.

83. M. *Avot* (*Ethics of the Fathers*) 2:20, 21.

84. Exodus 2:12.

85. B. *Megillah* 10b.

86. B. *Sotah* 37a and Numbers *Rabbah* 13:9.

87. For example, Leviticus 26 and Deuteronomy 11:13–25, 28.

88. Exodus 19:6.

89. B. *Kiddushin* 40b and M.T. *Laws of Repentance* 3:2, 4.

90. A land flowing with milk and honey: see, for example, Exodus 3:8, 17; 13:5; 33:3; Leviticus 20:24; Numbers 16:14; and Deuteronomy 6:3; 11:9; 26:9, 15; 27:3. See also Deuteronomy 8:7–10. The Land, as God's gift to the Israelites: Genesis 15:7, 17:8; Exodus 3:7–8; and Deuteronomy 1:8, 4:1, etc. But it continues to be God's ongoing possession (Leviticus 25:23) and dwelling place (Deuteronomy 12:4 and Jeremiah 7:7); it is holy, and God continues to watch over it (Deuteronomy 11:12). Therefore, the Israelites had to be careful not to violate its holiness by defiling it through abhorrent acts (Leviticus 18:24–28).

91. Isaiah 2:2–4.

NOTES TO CHAPTER TWO

1. Although the term "pluralism" has historically been used to define a philosophical position affirming that ultimate reality is not one (monism) but many, this is not my concern here.

2. There are also people, of course, who espouse no faith at all. For that matter, many Jews identify ethnically but not religiously. I suggested a series of grounds for religious belief in another book (Dorff, 1992), so I will not deal with the relationships between religious and avowedly secular people here. Suffice it to say that many of the epistemological points on which I build my case for pluralism in this chapter and for good interfaith relations in the next apply equally as well to the relations between religious and secular Jews or non-Jews.

3. Compare, for example, I. Greenberg (1986), 1.

4. *Sifrei Devarim* 96, 346.

5. Ibid., 346.

6. Rashi (Rabbi Shelomoh Yitzhaki, 1040–1105) ascribed the fear of disunity to the worry that it would appear as if Israel had two Torahs: B. *Yevamot* 13b, s.v. "*lo ta'aseh aggudot aggudot.*" Ritba (Rabbi Yom Tov ben Abraham Ishbili, c.

1250–1330) feared that disunity would look as if Israel had two gods: *Hiddushei Haritba* on B. *Yevamot* 13b.

7. The image of Israel as a light to the nations is in Isaiah 42:6; 49:6; compare 60:3. Three times daily, in the *Aleinu* prayer, Jews express their hope that God will perfect the world, and Israel is God's covenanted partner in that task. See Chapter One herein.

8. M. *Shabbat* 1:4 and J. *Shabbat* 1:4 (3c); compare also B. *Shabbat* 17a and Josephus, *The Jewish War,* Book IV, *passim.*

9. Deuteronomy 17:11.

10. Deuteronomy 1:17. Dishon (1984) suggests this juxtaposition of the two verses in Deuteuronomy, and he collected and analyzed many of the rabbinic sources discussed in this section of this chapter and the two following it.

11. Numbers *Rabbah* 13:15–16 and J. *Sanhedrin* 4:2 (22a).

12. M. *Eduyot* 1:4–5.

13. *Pesikta de-Rav Kahana,* "*Massekhet Bahodesh Ha-shlishi,*" on Exodus 20:2. Compare also Exodus *Rabbah* 5:9 and 29:1.

14. Hartman (1978), 130–161, stresses these features of the *aggadah* and the *halakhah* in demonstrating the acceptability of pluralism.

15. B. *Avodah Zarah* 19a.

16. T. *Hagigah* 2:9 and B. *Hullin* 7b; see also Rashi's commentary on this there. Compare T. *Sotah* 14:9 (Erport MSS.).

17. Maimonides, Introduction, *Commentary to the Mishnah* (Hebrew), ed. Kafah, 1:11–12.

18. Meiri, *Commentary to Avot (Ethics of the Fathers)* on M. *Avot (Ethics of the Fathers)* 5:17.

19. B. *Eruvin* 13b.

20. M. *Avot (Ethics of the Fathers)* 1:12, 3:21 and B. *Berachot* 64a.

21. See, for example, Leviticus 24:10–23 and Numbers 15:32–36, 27:1–11.

22. Jeremiah 6:13–15, 14:4, 23:23–40, 27:9–18, 28:1–17, and 29:21–32. To make matters worse yet, a true prophet might be misled by a false one (1 Kings 13), and false prophecy might even be inspired by God to deceive and entice Israel (1 Kings 22:21ff.) God might even seduce a true prophet to deliver a false message (Ezekiel 14:9–11).

23. Jeremiah 17:19–27 announces for the first time that carrying objects within the public domain or from private property to public property constitutes a violation of the Sabbath, and Isaiah 58:13–14 (reiterated by Nehemiah 10:32, 13:15ff.) declares that doing business is not allowed on the Sabbath. Other rules declared in the Prophets and Writings: a prohibition against working on the New Moon (Isaiah 1:13 and 1 Samuel 20:18–19), the requirements of three prayer services per day (Daniel 6:11 and Psalms 55:18); the form and instruments of sale (Jeremiah 32:6–15, 42–44; Ruth 4:7–12); and the rites for mourning (2 Samuel 1:11–12, 13:30–31, 14:1–2; Ezekiel 24:15–18; and Job 1:18–20).

24. Jeremiah (22:19) predicted an ignominious end for King Jehoiakim, but 2 Kings 24:6 belies that. Ezekiel (26:7–14) predicted the destruction of Tyre by Nebuchadnezzar, but he himself later acknowledges that the king's siege of the city was unsuccessful (Ezekiel 29:17–20). The glorious anticipations and designs for Zerubbabel of both Haggai (2:21–23) and Zekhariah (4:6–7) never materialized.

25. Amos 8:11–12; Micah 3:4, 6, 7; Jeremiah 18:18, 23:29–40; and Ezekiel 7:26.

26. Zekhariah 13:3–4.

27. B. *Bava Batra* 12a. For a more detailed discussion of the rabbinic move from revelation to study and interpretation as the way to know God's will, see Dorff and Rosett (1988), 123–132, 185, 187–245, and Dorff (1996a), 69–95.

28. *Avot d-Rabbi Natan* 18:3; T. *Sotah* 7:7; B. *Hagigah* 3b; and Numbers *Rabbah* 14:4.

29. Compare, for example, M. *Rosh Hashanah* 2:8–9.

30. B. *Kiddushin* 29a–b, 40b; later codified in, for example, *Arukh Hashulhan, Yoreh De'ah* 240:12. Compare Goldman (1975), esp. 31–68.

31. Numbers 16:1–35 and M. *Avot (Ethics of the Fathers)* 5:17. Compare the commentaries of Rabbi Obadiah of Bertinoro (c. 1450–before 1516) and Rabbenu Jonah ben Abraham Gerondi (c. 1200–1263) to that Mishnah.

32. For example, Buchler (1956), 245–274.

33. Rashi on B. *Hagigah* 3b, s.v. *"kulan."*

34. *Sifrei Devarim* 96; 346.

35. J. *Pesachim* 4:1 (30d); B. *Yevamot* 14a.

36. J. *Yevamot* 1:6 (3b); B. *Yevamot* 14a–b. Compare also T. *Yevamot* 1:12.

37. Kimelman (1987), 136, put it this way.

38. Compare S. Cohen (1983), 56, 82, 88, 91, 94.

39. Lamm (1986), 56.

40. Wurzburger (1986), 11.

41. B. *Sanhedrin* 44a.

42. Wurzburger (1986), 7.

43. Shafran (1986), 55.

44. Lamm (1986), 59–60.

45. Ibid., 60–61.

46. Wurzburger (1986), 8; compare p. 11.

47. I. Greenberg (1986), 28.

48. That is the message especially of the famous story in B. *Bava Metzi'a* 59b.

49. I. Greenberg (1986), 29.

50. I. Greenberg (1987) phrased it this way.

51. Staub (1986), 4–5; compare 10.

52. Ibid., 5.

53. Hartman (1978), 143–155.

54. Kimelman (1987), 144.

55. Lipman (1986), 1.

56. Kook (1962), 1:330.

57. Kimelman (1987), 145–147. He uses the metaphor of an orchestra whose harmony depends on all the instruments playing their different parts but for a common goal.

58. S. Greenberg (1986), 23; compare also p. 27, where he links pluralism to the absence of violence in transforming another person's opinion.

59. This is indicated by the sentence that follows immediately after Greenberg's definition of validity quoted above. That sentence begins, "This implication of the term legitimate . . ."

60. Numbers 24:16.

61. S. Greenberg (1986), 24, 26. The Mishnah cited is M. *Sanhedrin* 4:5. The blessing cited is in B. *Berachot* 58a. The Midrash cited is in Midrash *Tanhuma* on Numbers 24:16. The source granting righteous gentiles a place in the world to come is T. *Sanhedrin* 13:2, based on Psalms 9:18.

62. *Sifra* to Leviticus 19:18. Ben Azzai (second century C.E.) instead cites "This is the book of the generations of Adam . . . in the likeness of God He made him" (Genesis 5:1)—a principle that extends love beyond Jews ("your neighbor") and ties it directly to God, whose image should be appreciated in every person.

· 63. B. *Eruvin* 13b.

64. B. *Menahot* 29b.

65. Compare Exodus *Rabbah* 29:1 and *Pesikta de-Rav Kahana, "Bahodesh Hashlishi,"* on Exodus 20:2.

66. Proverbs 21:2.

67. See Dorff (1992), chap. 7.

68. Numbers *Rabbah* 19:6; *Tanhuma* Solomon Buber, Devarim 1a.

69. Albo (1946), 2:206.

70. Deuteronomy 6:4.

71. 1 Chronicles 17:21; B. *Berachot* 6a.

NOTES TO CHAPTER THREE

1. In a metaphorical sense you can have a relationship with yourself, but that is only because you are thinking of yourself in two different ways.

2. Judah Halevi, a medieval Jewish philosopher, emphasized that God interacts with Jewish people in history—that God's presence in Revelation and in history, in fact, are the chief evidence for God (Halevi, 1960, sec. 3, pp. 33–37). Emil Fackenheim is a contemporary Jewish philosopher who has focused on the historicity of the Jewish God and the Jewish people (Fackenheim, 1972, 1978).

3. Because of the centrality of the covenant in these crucial matters of definition and relationship, I devoted three articles to the theological and legal implications of the covenant idea for contemporary Jewish self-understanding (Dorff, 1978, 1979, 1988a). In another article I examined and evaluated important efforts by two modern Jewish theologians to reshape the covenant idea to account for past and present relations with non-Jews (Dorff, 1982).

4. Deuteronomy 6:7, which is part of the *Shema,* one of the two central prayers in daily and holiday Jewish liturgy.

5. These themes occur often in the Bible. The promises begin with the Patriarchs (Genesis 15; 17; 26:1–5, 23–24; 28:13–15; and 35:9–12); and they are repeated, along with the curses for not fulfilling the terms of the covenant, many times, perhaps most explicitly in Leviticus 26 and Deuteronomy 6–7, 11:13–25, chap. 28. That God will punish disobedience not only with physical deprivation and affliction but also with His absence is probably most clear in the Bible's prophetic writings, specifically, Isaiah 29:10; Jeremiah 7:1–15; Ezekiel 7:23–27; Amos 8:11–12; Hosea 3:4, 5:6; Micah 3:6–7; and Lamentations 2:9.

6. This theme is expressed in several forms. The People Israel is to be "My treasured possession among all the peoples" and "a kingdom of priests and a holy nation" (Exodus 19:5–6); "a people consecrated to the Lord your God: of all the peoples of the earth the Lord your God chose you to be His treasured people" (Deuteronomy 7:6); "the Lord's portion" and "His own allotment" (Deuteronomy 32:9); and "My chosen one, in whom I delight," who "shall teach the true way to the nations" and thus be "a light of nations" (Isaiah 42:1, 49:6). See also the Messianic visions cited later in this chapter.

7. Exodus 19–24 (note especially 24:7) and Deuteronomy 5 (note 5:24).

8. *Sifrei Devarim* par. 343 and Numbers *Rabbah* 14:10.

9. B. *Shabbat* 88a and B. *Avodah Zarah* 2b.

10. *Sifra,* "Shemini" 12:4 on Leviticus 11:45 (Jerusalem: Sifra Publications, 1959), 57b.

11. B. *Sanhedrin* 44a.

12. Konvitz (1978), 139–159, has explicated this well;. See also Dorff (1987a). One striking image of Jews trying to hide their identity is in the movie *Europa, Europa,* in which a Jewish teenager mistaken for a German Aryan tries to undo his circumcision. Most Jews who try to hide their identity do so in less dramatic, but pervasive, ways that affect their social, cultural, religious, and marital ties.

13. This phrase appears in the traditional prayer announcing the new month, recited on the Sabbath before it occurs. See Harlow (1985), 418–419, where he links the phrase to the previous one and translates, "gather our dispersed from the four corners of the earth in the fellowship of the entire people Israel."

14. This was evident, for example, in the *Los Angeles Times* survey cited in Chapter One, where it was noted that fully half of Jews listed a commitment to social equality as the quality most important to their sense of Jewish identity, whereas only 17 percent cited religious observance (Scheer 1988). So, for example, Jewish lawyers in hugely disproportionate numbers are among those who do pro bono work for the indigent (Arzt, 1986; Auerbach and Arzt, 1987). Similarly, the percentage of Jews who contribute to charity and the proportion of their income they contribute far outstrip the norm in the United States (Shapiro 1987, Krefatz 1982).

15. Mark Twain, for example, wrote in an article in *Harper's* in 1899 that the Jew's "contributions to the world's list of great names in literature, science, art, music, finance, medicine, and abstruse learning are . . . out of proportion to the weakness of his numbers. . . . [The Jew] is now what he always was, exhibiting no decadence, no infirmities of age, no weakening of his parts, no slowing of his energies, no dulling of his alert and aggressive mind" (quoted by *Encyclopedia Judaica* 15:1570).

16. Rubenstein (1966), chaps. 1–3, esp. pp. 58, 69–71. As I point out later, well before Greenberg and even before the Holocaust, Mordecai Kaplan warned of the dangers of the Chosen People doctrine and proposed that we see each nation as having its own "vocation" to live out its unique values and traditions (Kaplan, 1934, 258f., and 1956, 501f.). In response to the Holocaust, contemporary Orthodox rabbi Irving Greenberg (1988), esp. 87–93, developed a three-tier theory of the covenant according to which in the first (biblical) stage, God set the terms

of the covenant; in the second (rabbinic) stage, after the destruction of the two Temples, God and the Jews were on a more equal footing in negotiating the terms of their ongoing relationship; and now, after the Holocaust, with its major questions of why God did not intervene, it is the Jews who have the right to determine the nature of their relationship with the God who has so deeply disappointed them. This is clearly not the mainstream view of contemporary Jews, but it indicates exactly how thoroughly the Holocaust has led Jews to rethink the nature of their covenant with God.

17. The Decalogue: Exodus 20:3–6 and Deuteronomy 5:7–10. Examples of other places that mention this prohibition: Deuteronomy 4:15–19, 23–24, 28; 7:25; and 8:19.

18. Genesis 15:16 and Deuteronomy 9:4–5.

19. See, for example, Leviticus 18, which lists a number of prohibitions against having sex with one's relatives, with someone else's wife, and with animals as well as sacrificing one's child to Molech as practices that the Canaanites did and that the Jews should spurn. In 2 Kings 21:3–7 and 23:4–12, these practices are tied specifically to idolatry; see also Jeremiah 7:30–31.

20. The Rabbis made fun of idolatry in a number of places, for example, B. *Avodah Zarah* 2ff. The prayer thanking God for not being among the idolaters is at J. *Berachot* 7d, a version of which is included in the ceremony celebrating the completion of the study of a tractate of Talmud (*siyum*).

21. *Sifra*, "Shemini" 12:4 on Leviticus 11:45 (Jerusalem: Sifra Publications, 1959), p. 57b. Compare also *Sifrei Devarim*, Ekev on Deuteronomy 11:22, and B. *Sotah* 14a.

22. Numbers 25.

23. B. *Berachot* 28b. In another passage, the Rabbis depicted God mocking the Romans' and Persians' protestations of virtue and of care for Israel. God instead says that the Romans established marketplaces, for example, only so that they could have brothels in them and that the Persians built bridges only to exact tolls. Israel, in contrast, occupied itself with Torah. The nations protest that they were never offered the Torah, and so God offers it to them, but each refuses when it finds out that the Torah forbids something that it was known for doing. B. *Avodah Zarah* 2b–3b.

24. See, for example, Birnbaum (1949), 15–16. The Conservative movement, beginning with the Silverman prayer book of 1946 and in all subsequent forms of Conservative liturgy, changes this to the positive, "Blessed are You . . . who has made me an Israelite" (Silverman, 1946, x, 45; Harlow, 1985, 10). The reason for this change is that those unfamiliar with the liturgy would probably presume that this is simply an expression of chauvinism, but actually the intention of this blessing and the two accompanying it (thanking God for not making me a slave or a woman) is for the free Jewish man to thank God for being responsible for fulfilling all the commandments rather than only some of them, as is the case with the other three categories of people. The traditional form of the blessings, though, sounds both sexist and triumphalist. That led the Prayer Book Commission of the Conservative Movement to rephrase these blessings in the positive to avoid that misinterpretation of the blessings.

25. Deuteronomy 7:7.

26. Exodus 32–34 and Numbers 13–14. See also Deuteronomy 9, where the Torah says specifically (v. 5): "It is not because of your virtues and your rectitude that you will be able to possess their country; but it is because of their wickedness that the Lord your God is dispossessing those nations before you, and in order to fulfill the oath that the Lord made to your fathers, Abraham, Isaac, and Jacob." And that verse is followed by a retelling of the story of the Golden Calf and a reminder of other places where the Israelites provoked God.

27. On God's words to the People Israel: Exodus 19:5–6. On Israel dwelling alone, see Numbers 23:9; Deuteronomy 32:12, 33:28; Jeremiah 49:31; and Micah 7:14.

28. Exodus 19:5–6.

29. Leviticus 20:24, 26. Compare also Exodus 34:10; Leviticus 25:39–46; Deuteronomy 7:1–11, 10:12–22, 33:4; and Jeremiah 11:1–13.

30. Psalms 147:19–20

31. Cf. J. *Nedarim* 38b and Exodus *Rabbah* 25:12.

32. Exodus 31:16–17

33. *Mekhilta de-Rabbi Yishamael*, Ki Tissa on Exodus 31:17.

34. T. *Avodah Zarah* 8:4; B. *Sanhedrin* 56a, 60a.

35. According to rabbinic law, this includes giving charity to the non-Jewish poor and personal obligations like burying their dead, attending their funerals, eulogizing their deceased, and consoling their bereaved; compare M. *Gittin* 5:8, T. *Gittin* 5:4–5, and Dorff (1986a) 37–40 and Dorff (1999), 20–21.

36. See, for example, *Sifra*, "Shemini" 12:4, on Leviticus 11:45 (57b) and M. *Berachot* 2:2.

37. John 3:18. Compare also John 15:1–6, Acts 4:12, 1 Corinthians 1:18, and 2 Corinthians 2:15.

38. Sheler (2000), 74. The Vatican document is called *Dominus Iesus*, and it was issued on September 6, 2000. For a description and analysis of previous Vatican documents that led to much progress in Catholic–Jewish relations, see Dorff (1988b).

39. See, for example, Deuteronomy 7:9–11, Birnbaum (1953), 95, and Rabinowicz (1982), 66–67.

40. *Sifra* on Leviticus 19:18.

41. Kaufman (1958), 243–255, wrote a biting critique of the doctrine that all non-Christians inherit hell, questioning the seriousness of Christian love in the light of that doctrine.

42. B. *Megillah* 10b.

43. T. *Sanhedrin* 13:2; and in regard to the children of Gentiles, T. *Sanhedrin* 13:1. Later Jewish tradition follows Rabbi Joshua in both passages. See also M. *Avot* 4:29 and Lamentations *Rabbah* on Lamentations 3:23, both of which seem to ensure life after death to people generally, and B. *Eruvin* 19a and Ecclesiastes *Rabbah* to Ecclesiastes 3:9, both of which promise the Garden of Eden to the righteous and *Geihinnom* to the wicked, without mention of any restriction to Jews. One source, in fact, specifically limits the punishment of *Geihinnom* to the children of *wicked* gentiles: "With respect to the children of wicked gentiles, all agree that they will not enter the World to Come" (B. *Sanhedrin* 110b). Some rabbinic sources express the opposite extreme: "The Resurrection is reserved for [the People] Israel" (Genesis *Rabbah* 13:6; compare M. *Sanhedrin* 10:1). These undoubt-

edly reflect times in which gentiles were oppressing Jews and the consequent need during such times to reinforce Jewish commitment with the promise of future reward; they may also reflect the concern of Jewish leaders that some of their number would be attracted to Hellenistic or Christian beliefs and practices. Restricting the reward of the world to come to Jews alone would encourage Jews to persevere in their faith, despite oppression or the lures of foreign ideas. That does not erase, though, the remarkably universalistic passages that appear in rabbinic literature, some of which are listed at the beginning of this note, and the clear aversion to missionizing embedded in Jewish law and practice for at least the last two thousand years.

44. The Tosafists said outright that "we are certain that the Christians do not worship idols" (Tosafot to B. *Avodah Zarah* 2a, s.v. "*asur*"); but they did not see them as full monotheists due to their trinitarianism, classifying them instead as Noahides who are not enjoined against trinitarian belief (Tosafot to B. *Sanhedrin* 63b, s.v. "*asur*"; Tosafot to B. *Bekhorot* 2b, s.v. "*Shema*"). On R. Menahem Meiri's thoughts of Christians as monotheists: *Beit Ha-Bechirah* to B. *Bava Kamma* 113b and to B. *Avodah Zarah* 20a. Maimonides, on the other end of the spectrum, applied all the strictures against idolatry to Christians: M.T. *Laws of Idolatry* 9:4 (deleted by censors in the ordinary editions). A good summary of this discussion can be found in the *Encyclopedia Judaica*, s.v. "gentile." Ultimately, all commercial activity with Christians was allowed "because they are not expert in the nature of idolatry!" (S.A. *Yoreh De'ah* 148:12 and Isserles there; compare the Rashba and Tosafot on B. *Avodah Zarah* 2a).

45. One early-twentieth-century American rabbi, though, said that only American Catholics should be seen as monotheists because, unlike their European coreligionists, American Catholics did not really believe that the statues to which they bowed or the Eucharist that they swallowed contained the saints or the body or blood of Christ but were only symbolic of them; I am sure that the Vatican would love to hear that! See Ginzberg (1923).

46. Shimon bar Yohai's statement: J. *Kiddushin* 4:11 (66c) and Samuel's statement: J. *Rosh Hashanah* 1:3 (57a). Compare *Encyclopedia Judaica*, s.v. "gentile," which notes that the Jew's attitude toward the gentile was largely conditioned by the gentile's attitude toward the Jew (see, for example, Esther *Rabbah* 2:3). Moreover, to the extent that there was Jewish antipathy toward gentiles, it was never based on racial prejudice but rather motivated by gentiles' idolatry, moral laxity, cruelty to Jews, and rejection of the Torah.

47. Isaiah 11:6; compare generally Isaiah 2:2–4, 11–12.

48. Isaiah 49:1–6 and 51:4.

49. Isaiah 2:2–4, 19:23–24; Zephaniah 2:11, 3:8–9; and Zekhariah 14:9.

50. Leviticus *Rabbah* 36:2. The biblical quotes are from Psalms 80:8 and Isaiah 49:23, respectively.

51. B. *Avodah Zarah* 3b.

52. For a discussion of Rosenzweig and Buber on this issue, see Dorff (1982), esp. 484–493. For a discussion of Kaplan's notion of vocation, see Dorff (1979), 40–46.

53. According to the Talmud (B. *Bava Metzi'a* 59b), the commandment to love the stranger and not to wrong him occurs thirty-six times in the Torah, including,

for example, "You shall not wrong a stranger or oppress him, for you were strangers in the land of Egypt" (Exodus 22:20); "You shall not oppress a stranger, for you know the feelings of the stranger, having yourselves been strangers in the land of Egypt" (Exodus 23:9); "You shall love the stranger, for you were strangers in the land of Egypt" (Deuteronomy 10:19); and, perhaps most explicitly, "When a stranger resides among you in your land, you shall not wrong him. The stranger who resides with you shall be to you as one of your citizens; you shall love him as yourself, for you were strangers in the land of Egypt: I am the Lord your God" (Leviticus 19:33-34). Furthermore, "There shall be one law for the citizen and for the stranger who dwells among you" appears often in the Torah (for example, Exodus 12:49, Leviticus 24:22, and Numbers 15:15-16). These principles, together with the need to avoid the enmity of non-Jews, made Jews treat non-Jews with the same principles of justice that they used for themselves and even to bury the non-Jewish dead and to provide for the basic needs of the non-Jewish poor. See also n. 54 to this chapter.

54. B. *Gittin* 61a, M.T. *Laws of Gifts to the Poor* 7:7, *Laws of Idolatry* 10:5, *Laws of Mourning* 14:12, *Laws of Kings* 10:12, and S.A. *Yoreh De'ah* 335:9, 367:1.

55. For some other modern Jewish formulations of Jewish–Christian relationships, see Rothschild (1990), which includes excerpts on the subject by Leo Baeck, Martin Buber, Franz Rosenzweig, Will Herberg, and Abraham Heschel; see also Neusner (1993).

56. Some modern Christian attempts to reformulate Jewish–Christian relationships include Hick and Meltzer (1989, 197–210) and Van Buren (1995, 1998).

57. Halevi made this point. He had the Kuzari say that he did not believe the arguments presented for Christianity and Islam and that the only way he could would be if he had grown up with them:

> Here is no logical conclusion; nay, logical thought rejects most of what you [the Christian] say. It is only when both appearance and experience are so palpable that they grip the whole heart, which sees no way of contesting, that it will agree to the difficult, and the remote will become near. . . . As for me, I cannot accept these things, because they have come upon me suddenly, seeing that I have not grown up with them. My duty is, therefore, to investigate further.

See Halevi, *The Kuzari*, book I, par. 5. Compare also par. 6, where the Kuzari tells the Muslim scholar, among other things, that "if your book [the Koran] is a miracle, a non-Arab, like me, cannot perceive its miraculous character because it is written in Arabic"!

58. Ayer (1936), 114–120, and Braithwaite (1955), two nonperspectivists, share the view that religion does not make true or false assertions but rather motivates one emotionally; but the former thinker sees this as a major limitation on religion, whereas the latter thinks that this description is both accurate and fine.

59. McClendon (1974) and Goldberg (1981), esp. 66–70, 91–95, among others, have emphasized the role of biography—one's own and that of others—in theology, along with other stories that inform a tradition. See also Goldberg (1985).

60. Boudreaux and Stamer (2000). In a subsequent editorial, Cardinal Mahoney (2000) of Los Angeles notes that at one point (p. 20) the document affirms that

people who are not formally part of the Roman Catholic Church can, indeed, be saved. It is not clear to me, though, whether that sentence applies to non-Christians as well. In any case, he rightfully reminds his readers that "In the greater Los Angeles area, Roman Catholics have enjoyed a long-standing and valued relationship with Christians of other churches and peoples of other religious traditions." He further says that he "would like to reassure our partners in dialogue that our mutually beneficial conversations and joint pursuit of the truth will continue"; indeed, he pledges his "unyielding support for these efforts." He also correctly points to all the efforts on the part of Pope John Paul II to reach out to non-Catholic Christians and to people of other faiths as the context in which the document must be read. He admits, though, that "the tone of 'Dominus Iesus' may not fully reflect the deeper understanding that has been achieved through ecumenical and inter-religious dialogues over these last 30 years or more" after the Second Vatican Council. Moreover, he himself understands the document as "a firm critique of those theological views that appear to relativize the Christian faith and the Roman Catholic Church." It is to that issue that this section on the epistemological groundwork of dialogue is addressed.

61. Harvey (1966), 205–230; compare also McClendon and Smith (1975), 6–8.

It is interesting to note that even a medieval, hard-line antirationalist like Judah Halevi was open to considering the claims of other faiths and recognized that part of his inability to accept them stemmed from the fact that they were not *his* faiths, that he had not had personal experience with them; compare *Kuzari*, book I, secs. 5, 6, 25, 63–65, 80–91 (reprinted in Heinemann, 1960, 31–32, 35, 37–38, 41–45).

62. Putnam (1987), esp. 17–19. Nozick (1989), 49–51.

63. Tucker (1999), esp. 93–95.

64. Tucker (1999) made this point, and, in discussions with me, Dr. Hanan Alexander emphasized it. I would like to thank them both for making me aware of these philosophical (and political) limits of pluralism. See Alexander (2001), esp. chap. 6.

65. According to Job 2:11, Eliphaz is a Temanite, Bildad is a Shuhite, and Zophar is a Naamathite. Only the fourth interlocutor, Elihu, bears a name that appears Jewish (Job 32:2). On the religious status of Job and his friends, see Gordis (1965), 65–67 and chap. 6 generally. On the international influences on the Book of Job, see Gordis (1965), 53–64; Pope (1962), 2:911–925, esp. 2:914–917; and Matthews and Benjamin (1991), 201–226, esp. 219–226.

66. As the biblical scholar M. H. Pope (1962), 2:914, says,

> The recovery of the literatures of the ancient Near East, of Egypt, Mesopotamia, Syria, and Anatolia has shed much light on the OT [Old Testament]. It is no longer possible to study the OT in isolation from the larger world in which it originated. Wisdom literature of the OT in particular has so much in common with similar literatures of Egypt and Mesopotamia that international influence appears likely.

67. For example, B. *Bava Batra* 10a, on whether God would support human efforts to help the poor; B. *Sanhedrin* 65b (= Genesis *Rabbah* 11:5 and *Tanhuma*, Ki Tissa 33), on whether the Sabbath is incumbent on non-Jews in the hereafter;

and *Tanhuma,* Tazria 5 and 7, on whether God's creations or man's are more beautiful, given that a male human is born uncircumcised.

68. For example, Midrash Psalms on 50:1 (139b, par. 1) and J. *Berachot* 9:1 (13a), in regard to the Bible's multiple names for God; Numbers *Rabbah* 19:8, in regard to the mysterious ability of the ashes of the red heifer to purify, making the process look like sorcery; B. *Hullin* 27b, in regard to whether birds were created from water or earth.

69. Micah 4:5. Compare Micah 4:1–3 with Isaiah 2:2–4.

70. Micah 4:2 and Isaiah 2:3.

71. S. Greenberg (1986), 23. See also p. 27, where he links pluralism to the absence of violence in transforming another person's opinion.

72. T. *Sanhedrin* 13:2. See also n. 43 to this chapter.

73. Father Edward Flannery (1965) provides an extensive and, indeed, a landmark presentation of the evidence by a Christian. Compare also Ruether (1974) for a more theological treatment of the subject by an important Christian theologian.

74. The full titles of these documents are *Guidelines and Suggestions for Implementing the Conciliar Declaration "Nostra Aetate" (n. 4),* published in December 1974 by the Vatican Commission for Religious Relations with the Jews, and *Notes on the Correct Way to Present Jews and Judaism in Preaching and Catechesis in the Roman Catholic Church,* published by the same body in June 1985.

75. John 3:16–18.

76. Declaration *Dignitatis Humanae (Guidelines* I).

77. Cited at the end of section I, paragraph 7 of the *Notes* and more extensively in paragraph 29F.

78. In paragraphs 9, 13, and 17.

79. J. *Peah* 2:6 (17a), J. *Megillah* 4:1 (74d), J. *Hagigah* 1:8 (76d), Leviticus *Rabbah* 22:1, and Ecclesiastes *Rabbah* 21:9.

80. The four pairs of concepts are outlined in paragraph 5.

81. Sura 5, sections 18–20, 51, 64–65, 78; Sura 9, section 34.

82. I discuss this at some length in the context of training rabbinical students, in Dorff (1987a). The phenomenon, however, pervades the Jewish community, as I indicate there.

83. For a good survey of the Jewish material on this, see Agus (1981).

84. Siegel (1967). Rosenzweig (1971). I discuss Rosenzweig's theory in Dorff (1987a). Unlike Rosenzweig, however, I do not want to build in a decidedly secondary status to Christianity's role.

85. The biblical quotes are from Jeremiah 31:33–34 and Malachi 3:24, respectively.

86. Psalms 105:6–10.

NOTES TO CHAPTER FOUR

1. Deuteronomy 17:14–20.

2. 1 Samuel 8.

3. *Everson v. Board of Education of Ewing Township,* 330 U.S. 1 (1947).

4. M. *Avot* 3:2; B. *Avodah Zarah* 4a; B. *Zevahim* 102a. One was even supposed to pray for the welfare for non-Jewish (as well as Jewish) kings: B. *Berachot* 58a.

5. M. *Avot* 1:10; 2:3.

6. For a thorough treatment of this episode from the point of view of Jewish sources, see Graff (1985).

7. Notable among this group are Novak (1993) and, especially, Praeger (1993).

8. Wikler (1983), 2:48.

9. The Aspen Declaration was formulated in the summer 1992 Aspen Summit Conference on Character Education. According to the Josephson Institute's publicity materials, the member organizations include, as of July 1, 1997, fifty-five individual educational schools and regional school boards (for example, Toledo, Ohio, Public Schools). Furthermore, the institute has conducted ethics seminars for government groups and the staffs of a number of corporations. It has also trained the personnel of participating schools to educate their students in the six values outlined in paragraph 4 of the Aspen Declaration. Books on character education include Thomas Likona's *Educating for Character* and Michael Josephson's *Teaching Ethics in the 90s*. I would like to thank Dr. Michael Zeldin, professor of education at Hebrew Union College in Los Angeles, for his help with the educational example of my point here.

10. Cited by Raab (1993).

11. See Dorff (1998a), chap 2, for more description and discussion of this and other fundamental principles of Jewish medical ethics.

12. For a thorough treatment of this matter, see Feldman (1974), chaps. 14 and 15.

13. It was published in Dorff (1998c) and in Dorff (1998a), 176–198.

14. B. *Nazir* 48b, B. *Sotah* 37b, and B. *Zevahim* 115b. This dispute was the subject of a major study by Heschel (1962).

15. Dorff (1996a), 96–150.

16. B. *Sanhedrin* 34a.

17. Numbers *Rabbah* 14:4.

18. Exodus *Rabbah* 29:1, also 5:1. See also *Mekhilta de-Rabbi Yishmael*, "Yitro," chap. 9; *Pesikta de-Rav Kahana*, "Bahodesh Hashlishi," end of chap. 12, on Exodus 20:2 (ed. Mandelbaum, 1:224); and *Tanhuma*, "Shemot," #22 (ed. Buber, 7b) and "Yitro," #17 (ed. Buber, 40b).

19. B. *Eruvin* 13b.

NOTES TO CHAPTER FIVE

1. Deuteronomy 16:20.

2. Deuteronomy 17:6 and 19:15.

3. Exodus 20:13; see also Exodus 23:1–2 and Deuteronomy 5:17.

4. Leviticus 5:20–26.

5. Deuteronomy 19:15–21.

6. Exodus 23:8; see also Deuteronomy 16:19.

7. Deuteronomy 24:16.

8. It was not until about 1830 that the possibility of attaint, under which descendants would suffer for their ancestors' treason, was abolished in Great Britain. Corruption of blood and attaints and forfeitures that extend beyond the life of the criminal were banned by article 3, section 3 of the U.S. Constitution in 1789 in direct response to one feature of English law that the new Americans disliked.

9. Deuteronomy 1:17; see also Exodus 23:2–3, 6.

10. Deuteronomy 1:16.

11. For the requirements of a fair and just trial, see B. *Shavuot* 30a; compare also T. *Sanhedrin* 6:2; B. *Ketubbot* 46a; and M.T. *Laws of Courts* 21, esp. pars. 1–3. That the judges must know the language(s) of the litigants, see M. *Makkot* 6a, M.T. *Laws of Evidence* 21:8–9, and S.A. *Hoshen Mishpat* 28:6. For those unfit to testify due to their criminal or immoral actions, see M. *Sanhedrin* 3:3 (24b) and M.T. *Laws of Evidence,* chaps. 10–12. That relatives are unfit to testify for, against, or with each other, see M. *Sanhedrin* 3:4 and M.T. *Laws of Evidence,* chaps. 13ff.

12. Deuteronomy 24:17.

13. Exodus 22:21.

14. Deuteronomy 14:29 and 16:11,14.

15. See, for example, Isaiah 1:17, 23 and 10:1–2; Jeremiah 5:28; and Ezekiel 22:7.

16. See, for example, Deuteronomy 24:10–15 and Jeremiah 22:16.

17. See, for example, Deuteronomy 15:7–11.

18. See, for example, Ezekiel 16:49 and 22:29; and Amos 2:6–7 and 8:4–7.

19. See, for example, Exodus 21–24 and Deuteronomy 20–25.

20. See, for example, Deuteronomy 30:15 and Psalms 19:8–10 and 119:33–40.

21. See, for example, Leviticus 18; 20.

22. Deuteronomy 6:18.

23. *Mekhilta de-Rabbi Yishmael,* "Amalek," "Yitro," on Exodus 18:20 (H. S. Horovitz and Israel Abraham Rabin, eds. [Jerusalem: Bamberger & Wahrman, 1960], 198, parashah 2; and J. Z. Lauterbach, ed. [Philadelphia: Jewish Publication Society, 1933–1935], 2:182, parashah 4); and B. *Bava Metzi'a* 83a.

24. *Commentary on the Torah,* on Deuteronomy 6:18.

25. B. *Bava Metzi'a* 30b; 88a (end).

26. Leviticus 19:2.

27. For a more thorough discussion of these factors, together with the rabbinic sources that express them, see Dorff and Rosett (1988), 286–302, esp. 286–292.

28. B. *Sanhedrin* 2b–3a.

29. M.T. *Laws of Courts (Sanhedrin)* 22:4; he based this on B. *Sanhedrin* 6b. The biblical quote is from Zechariah 8:16.

30. Dolan (2000), A10.

31. Deuteronomy 10:17–18.

32. Deuteronomy 32:3–4.

33. Genesis 18:25.

34. See for example, Job 9:22.

35. Job 40:8.

36. See for example, the binding of Isaac (Genesis 22), God's hardening of Pharaoh's heart (Exodus 12), the permission to enslave gentiles (Leviticus 25:35–46), the vicarious punishment inflicted on Moses (Deuteronomy 4:20–22), the fate of the seven Canaanite nations (Deuteronomy 20:10–18; see also Exodus 34:11–16 and Deuteronomy 7:1–6), and the incident of Saul's mercy and God's anger (1 Samuel 15).

37. For a discussion of the biblical and rabbinic views of the matter, see Dorff and Rosett (1988), 110–123, 249–257; for my own view, see Dorff (1992), 129–148.

38. Deuteronomy 24:14–15.

39. B. *Berachot* 7a.

40. So, for example, R. Rubenstein (1992), 19–20, 293–306, maintains that the Holocaust proves once and for all that we cannot rationally believe in a God who acts in history, enforcing the rules of justice, but must rather believe only in the God of nature. I. Greenberg (1988, 320–326) and chapter three note above.

41. Dorff (1992), 129–148.

42. Deuteronomy 7:6–11.

43. Deuteronomy 11:1.

44. Leviticus 19:18.

45. That is the Talmud's count: B. *Bava Metzi'a* 59b.

46. Deuteronomy 6:5 and 11:1.

47. Deuteronomy 6:24–25.

48. Deuteronomy 8:5–6.

NOTES TO CHAPTER SIX

1. An earlier form of this chapter was published as Dorff (1986a). A revised version of that material was published as Dorff (1999). Thus this chapter is a third version of my thoughts on this topic.

2. For a discussion of some of the sources on this, see Dorff (1987c) and Chapter Seven herein.

3. M.T. *Laws of Gifts to the Poor* 9:3.

4. M.T. *Laws of Gifts to the Poor* 7:5, 10. Maimonides' sources: B. *Ketubbot* 50a (one-fifth maximum), *Sifrei Devarim* on Deuteronomy 14:22 (tithe applied to money), B. *Bava Batra* 9a (a third shekel minimum), B. *Gittin* 7b (poor must give), and B. *Bava Batra* 8b (compulsion applied, but compare Tosafot there for minority views). Compare also S.A. *Yoreh De'ah* 248:1–2.

5. M.T. *Laws of Gifts to the Poor* 9:12. Compare T. *Pe'ah* 4:9, J. *Bava Batra* 1:4, and B. *Bava Batra* 8a.

6. B. *Bava Batra* 8b and M.T. *Laws of Gifts to the Poor* 9:5.

7. Neusner (1982), 32, 67ff.

8. *Sifrei Devarim* on Deuteronomy 15:7, M.T. *Laws of Gifts to the Poor* 7:13, and S.A. *Yoreh De'ah* 251:3.

9. Goitein (1971), 2:139–142; compare also 128.

10. Deuteronomy 24:17–18, 21–22.

11. Compare Exodus 21:2–11 and Leviticus 25:39ff.

12. Goitein (1971), 2:143.

13. Ibid., 99.

14. See, for example, Deuteronomy 10:14 and Psalms 24:1. See also Genesis 14:19, 22 (where the Hebrew word for Creator [*koneh*] also means Possessor and where "heavens and earth" is a merism, including everything in between as well); Exodus 20:11; Leviticus 25:23, 42, 55; and Deuteronomy. 4:35, 39, 32:6. I discuss the medical implications of this belief in Dorff (1998a), 15–18.

15. T. *Pe'ah* 4:20.

16. Compare Deuteronomy 8:7–10, 15:4.

17. Compare Leviticus 27:30–33, Numbers 18:8–24, and Deuteronomy 18:1–5. The analogy between the poor and the priests is suggested by the inclusion of the Mishnah's tractate *Pe'ah* in its Order *Zera'im*, along with the tractates dealing with the priests' portions; and the analogy is made explicit in T. *Pe'ah* 4:4, 6–8.

18. Compare Brooks (1983), 17–19, and Brueggemann (1977), 48–50.

19. Leviticus 25:42. Compare Leviticus 25:55, Exodus 21:2–11, Deuteronomy 15:12–18, and B. *Kiddushin* 22b.

20. Genesis 1:27.

21. There are other Jewish interpretations of this doctrine, but this moral reading of the phrase fits the biblical contexts in which it is announced best, and so it is probably the plain meaning of the phrase (the *peshat*). See Dorff (1998a), 18–20.

22. It is, of course, not a guarantee of good action. For a discussion of how it helps, see Dorff (1980); see also my discussion there of the talmudic phrase *talmud torah keneged kulam*: "study is the underpinning of them all [that is, of all the good deeds listed previously in this source]" (B. *Shabbat* 127a).

23. M. *Avot* 3:18.

24. Deuteronomy 24:10–11, M. *Ketubbot* 13:3, S.A. *Yoreh De'ah* 251:8, *Even Ha-Ezer* 112:11, B. *Ketubbot* 43a, and S.A. *Even Ha-Ezer* 112:16, 93:4.

25. M. *Bava Kamma* 8:1.

26. B. *Bava Kamma* 86a.

27. B. *Bava Kamma* 119a, B. *Gittin* 7b, M.T. *Laws of Gifts to the Poor* 7:5, and S.A. *Yoreh De'ah* 248:1, 251:12.

28. B. *Bava Batra* 9a and S.A. *Yoreh De'ah* 250:3–4.

29. Hosea 2:4–22 and Jeremiah 2:2 are two famous examples that link the metaphor of marriage to the relationship between God and Israel. Furthermore, Deuteronomy 6:4–8, 7:6–11, 11:1,22, for example, speak of obedience out of love.

30. B. *Sanhedrin* 26b, B. *Bava Batra* 10b, M.T. *Laws of Gifts to the Poor* 8:9, and S.A. *Yoreh De'ah* 254:1. If a non-Jewish king gives Jews money for charity, Jews may take it "for the sake of peace" (that is, so as not to offend the ruler), but they are to give it discreetly to non-Jewish poor people in such a way that the king does not hear of it (M.T. *Laws of Kings* 10:10 and S.A. *Yoreh De'ah* 254:2, 259:4). Moses Isserles, at 254:2, noted that this applies only to money, the transmission of which to non-Jewish poor can be kept secret, but not to objects the king donates to the synagogue. Those must be accepted and retained.

31. God will not forget the poor: for example, Psalms 9:12 and 10:12. God pities and comforts the poor: for example, Psalms 34:6 and Isaiah 49:13. God cares for the poor: for example, Jeremiah 20:13, Psalms 107:41 and 132:15, and Job 5:15.

32. God seeks social justice for the poor: for example, Deuteronomy 10:17–18, 2 Samuel 22:28, Isaiah 25:4, and Amos 2:6 and 4:1. God forbids oppressing the poor: for example, Exodus 23:3, Leviticus 19:15, Isaiah 1:23, Ezekiel 22:7, Micah 2:2, and Malachi 3:5.

33. B. *Sotah* 14a. The quote is from Deuteronomy 13:5.

34. See M. Katz (1925), 80. Compare also B. *Rosh Hashanah* 12b and Rashi thereon.

35. Most of these laws appear in the passages cited at the beginning of this paragraph. Third-year tithes are also mentioned in Deuteronomy 14:28–29 (in addition to 26:12–13). That Sabbatical produce should be given to the poor is in Exodus 23:11 (although in Leviticus 25:6–7 it is the owner of the land together with his slaves and hired workers who are entitled to it), and the Jubilee laws appear in Leviticus 25:8ff.

36. Deuteronomy 24:14–15.

37. Exodus 22:24, Leviticus 25:36–37, and Deuteronomy 23:20.

38. Deuteronomy 15:1–2 and 7–11.

39. Exodus 22:25–26 and Deuteronomy 24:10–15.

40. Exodus 23:6–9. Compare, for example, Deuteronomy 16:18–20, 23:17–18 and Psalms 82:3. The poor, though, were not to be preferred in their cases just because they were poor any more than the rich were to be given special consideration just because they were rich; rather, fairness to all litigants was to be the rule: Leviticus 19:15, and Deuteronomy 1:17.

41. The closest we have to anything like that is not in a law code but rather in *The Instruction of Amen-Em-Opet,* a letter from sometime between the tenth and the sixth centuries B.C.E. similar in tone to the biblical Book of Proverbs. The *advice* given there is to permit the widow to glean unhindered and to give gifts of oil to the poor as conduct approved by the gods, but this is *not* required by them—and certainly not by human governing authorities. See Pritchard (1955), 424.

42. For a brief account, see *New Illustrated Columbia Encyclopedia* (1979), s.v. "debt."

43. M. *Pe'ah* 8:7. Compare T. *Pe'ah* 4:8,10, J. *Eruvin* 3:1 (20d), B. *Shabbat* 118a, B. *Bava Metzi'a* 8b–9a, and B. *Sanhedrin* 17b.

44. Abrahams (1969), 311.

45. B. *Ta'anit* 21b. Compare Goitein (1971), 2:133.

46. Rabbi Eleazar Fleckeles, *Teshuvah Me'ahavah* III, *Yoreh De'ah* 336.

47. S.A. *Yoreh De'ah* 249:16, 255:2.

48. T. *Pe'ah* 4:9.

49. M. *Pe'ah* 8:8.

50. Compare the gloss of Moses Isserles on S.A. *Hoshen Mishpat* 163:1, *Arukh Hashulhan, Hoshen Mishpat* 163:1.

51. B. *Bava Batra* 9a and S.A. *Yoreh De'ah* 251:7.

52. B. *Ketubbot* 67a and S.A. *Yoreh De'ah* 251:8.

53. *Sifrei Devarim* on Deuteronomy 15:7, M.T. *Laws of Gifts to the Poor* 7:13, and S.A. *Yoreh De'ah* 251:3.

54. S.A. *Yoreh De'ah* 249:16.

55. S.A. *Yoreh De'ah* 251:7–8.

56. S.A. *Yoreh De'ah* 252:1,3.

57. B. *Gittin* 61a and M.T. *Laws of Gifts to the Poor* 7:7. According to B. *Gittin* 59b, obligations that are for the sake of peace have Pentateuchal authority.

58. T. *Pe'ah* 4:10–11.

59. B. *Ketubbot* 67b, M.T. *Laws of Gifts to the Poor* 7:3,4, and S.A. *Yoreh De'ah* 250:1.

60. M.T. *Laws of Gifts to the Poor* 7:3,4 and S.A. *Yoreh De'ah* 250:1.

61. B. *Shabbat* 118a.

62. Goitein (1971), 2:129.

63. Lancelot Addison, *The Present State of the Jews* (London, 1675), chap. 25, quoted in Abrahams (1969), 307.

64. Claude G. Montefiore, "Hebrew Charity," *London Jewish Chronicle*, May 1884, cited in Abrahams (1969), 325.

65. Compare Goitein (1971), 2:191.

66. B. *Kiddushin* 29a.

67. M. *Ketubbot* 6:5. compare B. *Ketubbot* 67a–b, B. *Megillah* 3b, B. *Makkot* 24a, and S.A. *Yoreh De'ah* 250:2, 251:8.

68. B. *Bava Batra* 90a; Falk, *Sma*, to S.A. *Hoshen Mishpat* 231, n. 36. Compare Levine (1980), 91–95. Falk seemed to include clothing and rent as well as food in this rule.

69. B. *Sanhedrin* 3a.

70. Kahan (1975), 68.

71. M.T. *Laws of Gifts to the Poor*, 10:7–14. The biblical quote is from Leviticus 25:35. Compare S.A. *Yoreh De'ah* 249:6. Goitein (1971), 2:142, however, notes that jobs, loans, and investments were generally given first to relatives or those who had not yet taken alms.

72. Rubenstein (1983), esp. chaps. 1, 9, and 10.

73. In April 1997, the Rabbinical Assembly, the organization of Conservative movement rabbis, passed the "Resolution on Global Poverty and the Deteriorating Global Environment," calling for "our governments to scrutinize the dynamics and practices of their respective economies with a view to balancing the battle against poverty with environmental protection so that humankind live within the bounds of the regenerative, absorptive, and carrying capacities of the earth and in such a way that the needs of current and future generations can be met" (Rabbinical Assembly, 1998).

74. Based on God's words to Adam, "By the sweat of your brow / Shall you get bread to eat" (Genesis 3:19), the Rabbis asserted that people have a moral right to eat only if they earn it by their own effort. B. *Bava Batra* 110a; Genesis *Rabbah* 14:10.

75. M. *Pe'ah* 8:8, B. *Ketubbot* 68a, and M.T. *Laws of Gifts to the Poor* 9:14–17.

76. M. *Avot* 1:10. Compare Rav's "pearl" in B. *Berachot* 17a.

77. *Tanhuma*, "Vayetze," sect. 13. The biblical quote is from Job 1:10.

78. M. *Avot* 2:2.

79. Leviticus *Rabbah* 25:5.

80. B. *Nedarim* 49b.

81. J. *Pe'ah* 15c. God's commandment is in Deuteronomy 30:19.

82. S.A. *Yoreh De'ah* 252:6.

83. Deuteronomy 24:10–11.

84. Leviticus *Rabbah* 34:9.

85. M. *Avot* 1:5.

86. Psalms 51:19.

87. B. *Bava Batra* 9b and M.T. *Laws of Gifts to the Poor* 10:5.

88. I am indebted to Jacob Neusner for the idea for this section and some of its substance. See Neusner (1982), 45–52.

89. *New York Times*, December 29, 1996, pp. A1, 22.

90. *Asbury Park* (New Jersey) *Press*, September 11, 1996, A1, A10. A study by Columbia University's National Center for Children in Poverty, based on the 1990 U.S. Census, shows that nearly half of all children under age six have slipped into poverty as a result of the job instability of the 1990s. Former middle-class suburbanites are thus joining the ranks of the poor at a rapid pace. Growth of poverty in urban areas in the same period was 33.6 percent; in rural areas, 45.4 percent.

91. According to the Department of Health and Human Services' 1996 listing, first published in the *Federal Register* of March 4, 1996, 8286–8288, even the current, newly increased minimum wage does not begin to keep a family of three or more safely above the poverty line. The table on those pages was prepared by the U.S. Administration on Aging. The following data are the poverty guidelines listed in that document per number of people in a family: for one person, $7,740; for two people, $10,360 (which is just under one person's wages for a forty-hour week at minimum wage); and for three people, $12,980 (which is already more than $2,000 *over* a minimum-wage earner's annual income). For a family of four this number rises to $15,600. I would like to thank Rabbi Lee Paskind for the information in this note and the previous one.

92. "Though Upbeat on the Economy" (1996).

93. Goitein (1971), 2:121ff., and esp. 128ff. See also Appendix B herein.

94. *Proceedings of the Rabbinical Assembly* (1998), 256. Passed by the assembly in April 1997.

95. Genesis 4:9–10.

96. See n. 87 herein and the text there.

97. The Rabbis understood that verse to apply not only to a physical stumbling block being put before a physically blind person but also to moral stumbling blocks put before a morally blind person—and even to giving false information to someone who can be harmed by it. See, for example, *Sifra* on Leviticus. 19:14 (in regard to giving inappropriate or dangerous advice), B. *Pesachim* 22b (in regard to giving wine to a Nazarite or a limb from a living animal to a non-Jew, thus tempting each of them to violate laws that apply to them), B. *Mo'ed Katan* 5a (commanding that we mark grave sites so as to avoid stepping on them), B. *Mo'ed Katan* 17a (in regard to striking a grown child, thus tempting him to strike his parent back and be subject to the death penalty according to Exodus 21:15), and B. *Bava Metzi'a* 75b (in regard to lending money without witnesses).

98. "Births among Unwed Blacks Hit Record Low," (1998), A13. "The percentage of unmarried black women giving birth dropped to record low in 1996 after seven years of steady decline, the government reported Tuesday. Blacks were

significantly more likely to have a child out of wedlock than whites, though less likely than Latinas. But the rate among blacks was the lowest since the government began keeping the statistic in 1969." The report of the Centers for Disease Control and Prevention put the rate of giving birth among unmarried white women of childbearing age at 2.8 percent, of black women at 7.6 percent (after a high of 9.1 percent in 1989), and of Latinas at 9.3 percent—also a modest decline.

99. Additional Jewish sources that speak further about this theme include Albo (1946), Baron et al. (1975), Gross (1974), Goldenberg (1985), Kimelman (1983), Levine (1985), G. Rubin (1986), A. Shapiro (1971), and D. Siegel (1982).

100. Leviticus 25:35–36 and 26:13.

NOTES TO CHAPTER SEVEN

1. Ecclesiastes 3:1–3,7–8.

2. Rackman (1977), 137.

3. See Harlow (1985), 798 (the end of grace after meals), 120 (the priestly blessing), and 160 (*Kaddish*) and some of the sources for concluding these prayers with the hope for peace in Numbers *Rabbah* 11:7 and Deuteronomy *Rabbah* 5:14.

4. Gittelsohn (1970), 52.

5. Isaiah 11:6; compare generally his Messianic visions in chaps. 2 and 11.

6. Numbers *Rabbah* 11:7.

7. Deuteronomy 20:10.

8. *Sifrei Devarim* to Deuteronomy 20:10, "*Shofetim*," par. 199.

9. M. *Sotah* 8:7 (44b). Note that although Deuteronomy 20:7 refers to only the groom as being exempt, the Mishnah, in defining the limits of this exemption, obligates both the groom *and the bride* to engage in a commanded or obligatory war!

10. M. *Sotah* 8:7 (44b).

11. Compare B. *Sanhedrin* 72a and *Yoma* 85b.

12. For example, Numbers 31:7, 15f. and 33:55 and Deuteronomy 7:2, 20:16f.

13. Exodus 17:14–16 and Deuteronomy 25:17–19.

14. B. *Eruvin* 45a. Compare M. *Eruvin* 4:3; T. *Eruvin* 3:6, 8; J. *Eruvin* 4:3 (21d); and Lieberman (1962), 342–344.

15. For example, B. *Berachot* 58a, *Yoma* 85b, *Sanhedrin* 72a, and Genesis *Rabbah* 21:5.

16. Bleich (1983), 18–19. Compare also Zevin (1957), 13–16.

17. B. *Sanhedrin* 72b–73a; M.T. *Laws of the Murderer* 1:6–7, 9; and S.A. *Hoshen Mishpat* 425:1.

18. *Teshuvot Radbaz* 3:1052; *Pri Megadim, Mishbetzot Zahav*, 328:7; *Arukh Ha-Shulhan, Hoshen Mishpat* 426:4; and *Pithei Teshuvah, Hoshen Mishpat* 426:2. Compare, however, *Kesef Mishneh, Hilkhot Rotzeah*, 1:14 and *Bet Yosef, Hoshen Mishpat* 426.

19. Rashi, B. *Sanhedrin* 72a, s.v. "*hakhi garsinan*" and Rashi, B. *Pesachim* 2b, s.v. "*mi-de-kaamar.*" Also *Teshuvot Koah Shor*, no. 20 and *Teshuvot Ahi'ezer*, I, no. 23, sec. 2.

20. B. *Sanhedrin* 74a.

21. M.T. *Laws of the Sabbath* 2:23.

22. S.A. *Orach Chayyim* 329:6,7.

23. *Sifrei Devarim,* "Shofetim," #203 (Finkelstein edition), 238–239. Also T. *Eruvin* 3:7; J. *Shabbat* 1:8 (4a); B. *Shabbat* 19a; M.T. *Laws of the Sabbath* 2:25 and *Lehem Mishneh,* a standard commentary to the *Mishneh Torah,* there; *Tur, Orach Chayyim* 249; and Rashi on Deuteronomy 20:19.

24. B. *Berachot* 3b and B. *Sanhedrin* 2a, 16a, 20a.

25. Cf. B. *Eruvin* 45a and S.A. *Orach Chayyim* 339:6.

26. Rabbi Solomon Goren (1983), 1:137, former chief rabbi of Israel, is willing to substitute the present Israeli government for the king but not for the Sanhedrin. This is based, in part, on much too narrow a reading of a responsum by Rabbi Abraham Isaac ha-Cohen Kook (1865–1935), who ruled that "At a time when there is no king, all royal prerogatives are transferred to the nation in general, since the rights of a kingdom include that which concerns the general situation of the nation" (337–338). Kook clearly meant for a modern Jewish government, whatever its form, to assume all the governmental duties of Israel's ancient government above and beyond the legitimacy granted to any sovereign state by virtue of the talmudic principle *dina d'malkhuta dina:* "the law of the land is the law." In line with this, Kook himself laid the foundation for the Israeli chief rabbinate and was its first Ashkenazi head. Compare Lewittes (1987), 237.

27. M.T. *Laws of Kings* 5:1.

28. This is based on Bleich (1983), 7–14; and on Zevin (1957), 12–13.

29. This is according to a literal reading of the Ibn Tibbon translation of Maimonides' *Commentary on the Mishnah, Sotah* 8:7.

30. *Hazon Ish, Orach Chayyim-Mo'ed* 114:2.

31. This is according to the Kapah edition of Maimonides' *Commentary on the Mishnah, Sotah* 8:7.

32. Rabbi Menahem Me'iri, *Bet Ha-Behirah* on B. *Sotah* 43a and B. *Sanhedrin* 50.

33. *Shiyurei Korban,* addenda to *Korban Ha-Edah,* a standard commentary to the Jerusalem Talmud, on J. *Sotah* 8:10.

34. *Lehem Mishneh* on M.T. *Laws of Kings* 5:1.

35. Rabbi Yehiel Epstein, *Arukh Ha-Shulhan He-Atid, Hilkhot Melakhim* 74:3–4.

36. That victory must be anticipated: J. *Sotah* 8:10 and Gersonides, *Commentary to the Bible, Judges,* chap 9 (end), conclusion #9. Compare Goren (1964), 179. That suicide is forbidden: B. *Bava Kamma* 91b and compare M.T. *Laws of a Murderer* 11.

37. Gershuni (1983), 58. Also *Sefer Ha-Hinukh,* Mitzvah #425; Nahmanides, *Commentary to Maimonides' Sefer Ha-Mitzvot,* Addenda, Negative Commandments #17.

38. Sidorsky (1979), xl.

39. Wyschogrod (1980), 132, 136–137, 138, 139.

40. Ibid., 136–137, 138, 139.

41. Deuteronomy 12:29–13:1 and 18:9–14. These verses contradict Brichto's (1979), 226, thesis that the Bible never contemplates exporting monotheism beyond Israel's borders in a coercive fashion.

42. Genesis *Rabbah* 16:6, B. *Sanhedrin* 56a, and M.T. *Laws of Kings* 9:1. Compare Novak (1983) for an extensive study of these laws.

43. B. *Sanhedrin* 57a.

44. Deuteronomy 32:4.

45. Numbers 15:15.

46. M.T. *Laws of Kings* 8:9–10.

47. Ibid., 9:14.

48. Compare Rashi on B. *Sotah* 35b (end), s.v. *"v'katbu mi'limtah"*; *Sefer Mitzvot Gedolot,* Negative Command #49; and *Lehem Mishneh* on M.T. *Laws of Kings,* 6:1. I would like to thank Dr. Elieser Slomovic for these references.

49. M.T. *Laws of Kings,* 6:1. *Sifrei Devarim* and Rashi on Deuteronomy 20:10 restrict the demand of that verse to seek peace to discretionary wars, but both Maimonides and Nahmanides applied it to commanded wars, too. Compare Nahmanides on that verse and Maimonides, M.T. *Laws of Kings,* 6:1.

50. See Kimelman (1970).

51. M. *Avot (Ethics of the Fathers),* 3:2; B. *Avodah Zarah* 4a.

52. See, for example, M.T. *Laws of Kings* 6:7–15 and 8:1–9. For a more extensive discussion of these rules and comparisons to the Catholic rules of war, see Dorff (1991).

53. Shapira (1970), 130–135.

54. Kaplan (1970), 7–10.

55. Compare Kimelman (1968).

56. Pipes (2000), B9, citing a poll of Israelis published on Friday, October 13, 2000.

57. Psalms 34:15.

58. J. *Pe'ah* 1:1.

NOTES TO CHAPTER EIGHT

1. These statements were reproduced in Wolf and Vadikan (1989).

2. McCarthy (2000) 50.

3. Exodus 34:7 and *Tosefta, Sotah* 1:4. Compare M.T. *Laws of Repentance* 1:3–4, 7:1–8, qualified, however, in 3:6ff. God thus forgives almost everyone and everything, with, however, some notable exceptions.

In this section and the next, where I briefly review the rudiments of the traditional view of divine and human forgiveness extended to individuals, I cite only a few sources for each of the components of the doctrines, although in most cases many, many more could be cited. Because these doctrines derive from the very roots of Judaism, I generally cite biblical or rabbinic sources rather than later, medieval forms of the doctrine.

When quoting classical sources, I have left the male language for God intact, simply because that is how they read. I use inclusive language for God (and human beings!), however, when expressing my own views.

4. That God will discipline us: Deuteronomy 8:5. That God hopes that we will return to Him so that He can forgive: for example, Jeremiah 3:14, 22.

5. Genesis 9:8–17.

6. Leviticus 26:44–45 and Psalms 106:45.

7. God's relationship with the Patriarchs as a motive for forgiveness: Deuteronomy 9:27. God's promises to the Patriarchs as a motive for forgiveness: Exodus 32:13.

8. Exodus 32:12, Numbers 14:13–20, Deuteronomy 32:26–27, and Psalms 79:8–9.

9. For example, 1 Kings 21:27–29, Isaiah 1:10–20 and 29:13, and Joel 2:13.

10. For example, Isaiah 1:15–17, 33:14–15, 58:3ff; Jeremiah 7:3ff, 26:13; and Amos 5:14–15.

11. M. *Yoma* 8:9.

12. See Dorff (1998b) for a thorough discussion of the process of forgiveness of one person by another.

13. M. *Bava Kamma* 8:7; B. *Yoma* 85b, 87b; and M.T. *Laws of Repentance* 2:9–10.

14. B. *Bava Kamma* 92a; *Tanhuma, Hukkat* 19; M.T. *Laws of Forgiveness* 2:10.

15. Genesis 20:17, B. *Bezah* 32b, B. *Yevamot* 79a, and Numbers *Rabbah* 8:4.

16. B. *Shabbat* 151b.

17. B. *Shabbat* 133b.

18. Leviticus 19:17–18.

19. Students rebuking their teachers, even a hundred times over: B. *Bava Metzi'a* 31a. Some (Rab) include permission to strike the offender, and some (the *baraita* toward the top of the page and, probably, Samuel) do not, but all agree that one may not publicly embarrass the offender (B. *Arakhin* 16b). Scold only those who will listen: B. *Yevamot* 65b and Rashi there.

20. M. *Avot* 1:8.

21. M. *Bava Metzi'a* 4:10 and B. *Kiddushin* 40b; compare M.T. *Laws of Repentance* 1:3.

22. M. *Avot* 1:12.

23. Jeremiah 46:28. The longest and fiercest expositions of the punishments God has in store for Israel are in Leviticus 26 and Deuteronomy 28. That God, even after those punishments, will not utterly destroy Israel is made clear in Leviticus 26:44–45. The times when God wanted to obliterate Israel but was restrained from doing so: Exodus 32:1–14 and Numbers 14:11–45.

24. Deuteronomy 25:17–19.

25. B. *Megillah* 18a and *Sifrei Devarim*, "Ki Teze," par. 296; compare M.T. *Laws of Kings* 5:5.

26. Exodus 17:16.

27. Genesis 15:13–21 and Deuteronomy 7:1–11.

28. M. *Sotah* 8:7 (44b) and M.T. *Laws of Kings* 5:1–5. For general discussions of this topic, cf. Bleich (1983), and Dorff (1987c), and Chapter Seven herein.

29. Numbers 31 and 1 Samuel 15.

30. For example, Amos 1:3–2:5 and Jeremiah 46–51.

31. B. *Avodah Zarah* 2aff.; the nations are asked to build a sukkah, specifically because it is an "easy commandment" to fulfill, as indicated at the bottom of p. 3a.

32. Jonah 1:2, 3:8.

33. 2 Kings 17–19, Zephaniah 2:13ff., and the entire Book of Nahum.

34. Deuteronomy 23:8. On Ammon and Moab, compare Deuteronomy 23:4–7.

35. Golding (1984–1985), 121–137.

36. Ibid., 133.

37. B. *Sanhedrin* 44a and the codes on that passage. Compare also Nahmanides' comment on Deuteronomy 29:14, in which he explains this as a result of the fact that we were all at Sinai, including even "those who are not with us here today"— presumably later generations of Jews as well as converts. A good summary of these laws can be found in *Encyclopedia Judaica,* s.v. "apostasy."

38. B. *Sukkah* 53a.

39. A good discussion of these differing views of the individual and their legal implications for American Jews can be found in Konvitz (1980), chap. 5.

40. The fact that Jews, through most of their history, have been scattered worldwide rather than inhabiting one geographic space also, of course, was a factor. It is interesting, though, that cognitive or moral commitments, or even actions in accordance with the commandments, were not chosen as the defining factors. This is not entirely fortunate; see Wyschogrod (1983) and my review of it, Dorff (1986b).

41. Ozick (1989), 19.

42. Ibid., 21.

43. B. *Yoma* 87a; compare M.T. *Laws of Forgiveness* 2:11.

44. Between 1947 and 1951, the United States spent more on aid to Europe than it had in the entire federal budgets of the last prewar years, 1937 and 1938. In addition, between 1945 and 1951, it spent nearly two billion dollars in aid for Japan. See Bragdon and McCutchen (1958), 657, 661.

45. Maimonides, as usual, gives a good summary of the tradition's view of this process: M.T. *Laws of Repentance,* chap. 2.

46. Jacobs (1965), chap. 8, esp. 90–92, describes this process well. As he points out, this is, after all, simply the doctrine of the Oral Torah.

47. I analyzed the implications of these documents for Catholic–Jewish relations more fully in Dorff (1988b).

48. *Columbia Encyclopedia* (1979), 19:5814.

49. Levi (1984), 218, 221–223. I am indebted to Professor Lenn Goodman for this reference.

50. T. *Bava Kamma* 9:29–30.

Appendix A:
The Right in Contrast
to the Good

W HAT DO WE MEAN WHEN WE SAY THAT X IS THE *RIGHT* thing to do? How is that different from saying that x is a *good* thing to do? Similarly, what is the difference in saying that Nora is a "righteous person" in contrast to saying that she is a "good person"? (Nora may also be "the right person" for the job, for example, but that simply means that she fits the qualifications for the job; when describing people, "right" is usually not a moral category.)

These questions are discussed at length in philosophical literature, but for our purposes it is sufficient to note briefly the following differences:[1]

The Different Ways in Which We Use the Terms "Right" and "Good"

THE AGENT'S MOTIVES   The "right action" describes a duty that I have, often deriving from a relationship that I have from times past. The right thing to do is thus almost always the right thing *for me* to do; judgments of right involve a personal reference. This does not necessarily mean that duties are restricted to a given person or community (moral relativism); they may be duties that apply to all human beings as human beings (moral absolutism). A judgment of the right thing to do, though, is an evaluation of what an individual should do given his or her relationships to others (however broadly "others" is construed).

So, for example, I have a series of moral duties to my parents simply because they are my parents; these duties, if rightfully performed, are not in payment for whatever they did for me or in hope that my own children will treat me in the same way some day. That is, they are not pragmatically grounded. Filial duties arise simply from the existence of a relationship between children and parents. The same is true for parental duties, for sibling duties, and for the duties of good friends to each other.

All of these duties are, as W. D. Ross put it, "*prima facie* duties"—that is, presumed duties until and unless something arises to cancel them.[2] In Ross's theory, it is a conflicting duty or set of duties that might cancel a given, prima facie duty; I would add that situations that undermine the relationship on which a given duty is based can also cancel a prima facie duty. So, for example, if my parents abused me repeatedly in my childhood, I may no longer have filial duties to them because they undermined the presumed nurturing relationship between parents and children. They, in that case, did not perform their parental duties, and that may free me from seeing myself as their child and from the attendant filial duties toward them. Similarly, if a good friend fails to invite me to his wedding, then he had better have a good excuse if I am going to continue to regard him as a friend, with all the duties involved in friendship.

The burden of proof, however, is always on the one who claims that a prima facie duty is to be ignored, because the very relationship establishes the expectation that such duties exist. In legal language, the presumption of my having a duty to someone to whom I am related in some way is a "rebuttable presumption," but not easily rebuttable, since the relationship does establish prima facie duties. Thus, even if my parents were not the best of parents, as long as they were not downright abusive I still have filial duties to them.

The relationship underlying our moral duties is also evident in the following feature of duties: The depth and scope of duties depends on the depth and scope of the relationship that establishes them. Thus I have far more numerous and demanding duties to close friends than I do to casual acquaintances, and more to them than I do to strangers who ask me for directions. Family obligations are notoriously burdensome precisely because family relationships are not easily broken. Thus, even if I do not particularly like the members of my family, I still feel obligations toward them (for example, showing up at their weddings and at family Thanksgiving dinners), and those obligations can be very burdensome (such as supporting them financially in time of need). As noted earlier, in extreme cases, such as abuse, even family relationships may disintegrate and their attendant duties may thereby dissolve, but that does not usually happen. Indeed, it is precisely because blood relationships are generally immune to dissolution that the duties that apply to family members are so durable and demanding.

That personal reference is usually absent from judgments of the morally good thing to do, which stem more often from an assessment of goals: The good thing is that which will produce future desirable consequences, whereas the bad thing is that which will produce bad results. This is true for whoever does these things: The relationship, or lack thereof, of the actor to the beneficiary makes no difference. In fact, in some ways an act of charity toward someone unknown to me is more admirable than one done out of a sense of duty to those I morally must support. Maimonides' famous hierarchy of charity makes this point clearly, for, short of helping people help themselves, the highest rungs of charity are those in which the benefactor and the beneficiary are unknown to each other.[3]

A goal becomes a moral good (rather than simply a good for me) when it is, at least partially, other-directed. Thus it may be good for me to get a promotion, but that is not a moral good; it is solely a practical good. (It may also be a manifestation of justice if I worked hard for the promotion, did my job with skill, and thus deserve the advancement, but that is another matter.) Moral goods involve the welfare of others. I too might benefit, but if the good is moral, I alone cannot benefit. In general, then, it is a moral good to donate time, energy, and money to the benefit of others beyond what any call of duty may require. So, for example, while we may have some degree of duty to people unrelated to us in any way, simply because they are fellow human beings, spending considerable time, resources, and effort on their behalf would not be a morally required obligation but rather a good thing, an act of charity. Indeed, if working for humanity in general prevents you from fulfilling your duties toward those who are near and dear to you, your efforts on behalf of those unrelated to you may actually be immoral, for fulfilling your duties takes precedence over doing voluntary acts of moral goodness.[4]

This difference between the right and the good also manifests itself in the converse way: We may well feel insulted if we were trying to do our duty and someone misconstrues our motives, thinking that we had some pragmatic end in mind, some ulterior motive, even if it is a good one. Duty is personal in its call on us and in our motive for performing it; and its nobility is sullied, we think, if it is admixed with some pragmatic aim.

THE AGENT'S FEELINGS   I can want to do my duty, either through being acculturated to doing so (that is, I do it out of habit) or because I want something that depends on doing my duty. So, for example, I may avoid having an affair because the prohibition of adultery has been ingrained in me since childhood, even before I knew what the word meant. Alternatively, I may adhere to my duty to remain faithful, despite temptations to the contrary, because I know that doing the right thing will contribute to having a good relationship with my spouse. Whether or not I want to do my duty, though, I feel duties as a burden on me that I must do. In contrast, I usually want to do what is morally good, for such actions, by definition, lead to a desirable state. Moreover, what is desirable may not be desired, but it often is.

I may not know what the right thing is to do, for I may be subject to several conflicting duties. In such circumstances, I will be in a quandary that I must resolve to determine which of those duties takes precedence over the rest. Once my duty is clear, though, it feels completely and compellingly obligatory; indeed, all my duties feel that way. That is the nature of duty.

The Rabbis noted a similar thing in regard to the Torah's commandments. The Torah promises the reward of long life for fulfilling two commandments: The duty to honor your parents and the duty to shoo away the mother bird before taking her eggs. The former obligation lasts for a person's entire life, while the latter takes but a second. This teaches you, said the Rabbis, that while some commandments may be more difficult than others to fulfill and while they may even carry with them different rewards according to their respective difficulty, they all are equally obligatory.[5]

In contrast, we experience varying degrees of intensity in our desires for various goods: We want our children to be educated, but we want them to be healthy first, for only if they are healthy does their education matter. Our moral goods thus form a hierarchy, with some of them desired more intensely than others.

CRITERIA OF JUDGMENT   When we move now from the perspective of the agent to the viewpoint of the outside observer and judge, we find that, by and large, the "right" is judged primarily in terms of acts while the "good" is judged with significant reference to motives. Neither "right" nor "good" is *solely* a matter of acts or motives, but acts are in the forefront in judgments of right, whereas motives dominate our judgments of good.

For example, if I give to charity beyond what duty requires because I want to contribute to the welfare of society as much as I can, I am acting in a morally good way. If I contribute the same amount of money to impress my friends, my act is not as morally good. Here again, I should do the good thing even with the wrong motive so that the habit of doing the good thing may ultimately induce me to be inspired to act for the morally good reason; but in the meantime, my act, while morally good, is not nearly as good as if it were prompted by the moral reason.

Moral goodness, in other words, is very significantly a function of the agent's motive.

As these examples illustrate, to say that right is solely a matter of actions while goodness is exclusively a matter of motives states the matter too bluntly, for acts and motives are related, and, therefore, so are our judgments of the right and the good. For one thing, good motives are more likely than bad or neutral ones to produce right acts. For another, both the best action and the right act take all consequences into account and thus often coincide. Finally, there is a duty to cultivate good motives, and, conversely, there is type of goodness known as moral goodness— namely, goodness attached to acting out of a sense of duty.

Therefore, a more accurate way to describe this difference in the criteria of judgment of the right and the good is this: When we judge the rightness of an act, we evaluate the act against our principles of duty; people who fulfill the requirements of a right act are credited with doing the right thing, and people who fail to accomplish those ends do not do the right thing. Those who do the right thing, however, may differ in the moral purity of their actions, depending on their motive: Those who act out of the motive of duty act morally with purity of purpose, whereas those who fulfill their moral obligations with other than moral motives act morally but with impurity of motive.

Conversely, people who intend to benefit others act in a morally good way even when they aid others only slightly or fail to aid others altogether; their intention is what counts in judging the moral goodness of their actions. (If they should have known how to succeed better in fulfilling their moral intentions, they may be considered a fool. Moreover, if in the process of trying to do a good thing, they instead caused harm, we might say that they violated their duty to stay out of matters that they cannot control. In such circumstances, we would still see their intended actions as morally good, though, and most American states have recently stripped good samaritans of liability for any injury they cause in the effort to do good.)

On the other hand, if I intend to harm someone and fail to do so, my attempts to harm the person would be morally bad despite my lack of success in carrying out my intentions. It is interesting, on this matter, that the Talmud maintains that God is kinder than we normally are; for while God ascribes merit to people for intending to do the morally good thing even when they fail, as we would, God does not count it to our detriment if we intend to do something bad to someone else but fail in that effort.[6] In any case, then, the right and the good are distinct in their criteria of judgment, with acts the primary concern in judgments of right and motives playing a more significant role in judgments of goodness.

THE REFERENTS OF THE TERMS "Right," "duty," "obligated," and similar terms denoting moral duty refer only to acts as done by specific people. This, in some ways, is a corollary of the first distinction made earlier—namely, that duties stem from relationships, whereas goodness refers to social goals. Along those lines, talk of "duties" makes sense only within the context of specific people who have particular relationships to other people requiring that they act in certain ways. An act by itself, without any reference to the person who is supposed to do it and that person's relationships, cannot be obligatory, for I have moral duties only toward those who are related to me in some way as part of my family, friendship circle, religious group, neighborhood, state, country, and so on. Thus educating others, for example, is not a duty that I have in the abstract; I have it, first and foremost, toward myself and my children, then toward the other members of my family, and then to the members of my community. Thus moral duty makes sense only in regard to acts done by and for specific people.

Moral goodness, in contrast, can be predicated on people, motives, or acts independently. That is, "good" can refer, in its moral sense, to acts without referring to the people who do them or to people without referring to the acts that they do or to motives alone. Thus we can talk meaningfully about Sam as a morally good person without referring to any specific morally good acts that he has done. We mean, simply, that he routinely intends to help others and tries to act on those intentions.

We may also talk of an intention as being morally good without referring to the person or people who have that intention or to the acts that result from it. So, for example, we may say that it is a good thing to resolve to educate yourself and to give to the poor; and, conversely, it is a bad thing to aim to harm someone else. It is, of course, a better thing to act on your good intentions and a worse thing to act on your bad ones, but the intentions themselves carry a moral valence.

Finally, we can also speak of acts as being good or bad, independent of who does them or their intentions (although not independent of their contexts). Thus most human moral systems begin with the assumption that killing someone else is a bad thing, whoever is the perpetrator and whoever is the victim. Killing may be excused and even justified by the need for self-defense or the context of war, but that is the point: Killing needs a justification or at least an excuse for us to think of it as anything but bad, and the justification or excuse most commonly comes from the context in which the killing takes place. Conversely, giving aid to the poor is normally classified as a good act. It may become a bad act if the poor people in question can work and instead depend on the dole for a livelihood, but it is precisely that kind of analysis of the larger context of an act of charity that must be completed to convince us that helping the poor is anything but a good thing to do.

THE NATURE OF THE JUDGMENTS   Finally, statements of the "right" are closer to action than assertions of the "good." That is, when I say that it is right to treat two people of equal skills but of different races fairly and wrong to discriminate on the basis of race, I am saying something that has the air of being put into action soon. In contrast, when I say that it is good to educate yourself, that is a declaration of an ideal that has more long-term consequences. As a result, judgments of right versus wrong are expressed in the imperative mood, or, at least, have an imperative tone to them, while pronouncements of what is morally good or bad are articulated in, and have the tone of, the indicative mood.

*A Theory Explaining the Differences between
the Right and the Good*

Various theories have been advanced to account for these differences between the right and the good. Each competing theory is based, in turn, on a specific understanding of what we mean by each term and how judgments of the right and assertions of the good are justified. These topics occupy a prime place in the philosophical specialty called "ethics" or "moral theory."

For the present purposes, I will suggest just one such theory. Judgments of "the right," it seems to me, are assertions of what must be done to advance *the basic needs of a society as that society envisions them.* Those needs include both physical and spiritual requirements. By "spiritual requirements," I mean values that the society regards as necessities of character and that it may even prefer over life itself in extreme cases. "The good," in contrast, is a declaration of *the less basic needs or the ideals of a society.* I explain this thesis in the following paragraphs.

The view of morality I just outlined locates it in *relationships.* That is, moral duties emerge from our linkages to others and from the societies or social groupings that we establish; they are not, in my view, inherent in individuals or in nature. This explains why we feel a greater sense of duty to those who are near and dear, for the depth and scope of our duties mirrors the depth and scope of our relationships. This social view of morality also explains why we have specialized duties to particular people. So, for example, beyond the obligations we have to all people, we have additional duties to those in our profession and to our clients, as articulated in codes of practice of many professions and the code of honor of the armed forces. We similarly take on additional duties when we join or are otherwise part of specific subgroups within society, such as the group of Jews, Boy Scouts or Girl Scouts, a football team, and the like.

Every society or social grouping, though, views the world in its own way. Such a view we might call an "ideology," in contrast to an individual's personal philosophy. Ideologies may or may not be articulated formally, but they do find expression in the judgments of the right and the good made by the members of the group.

Individuals may choose to affiliate with a variety of different groups, but they probably choose to disaffiliate with any group whose viewpoint differs in important respects from their own. As a result, ideologies come to express the general viewpoints of a given group's members—or else the group dissolves or it changes its ideology.

One important exception to this voluntaristic view of communities is our families. Familial relationships created by law, like marriage or child custody, can be dissolved by law. Familial relationships created by birth, though, are harder to undo. While recent court cases have raised the possibility of children legally divorcing their parents, that happens, if at all, only in extreme cases. Normally, birth creates relationships and their attendant obligations that we cannot terminate, whether we like the members of our family or not, and whether we agree with their basic commitments or not.

As I discussed in Chapter One, modern nation states are based on the view of the nation as a voluntaristic community, but classical Jewish sources assert a much stronger, organic view of the Jewish community. Jews cannot, according to Jewish law, abdicate their responsibilities as Jews or forsake their Jewish identity because they are linked by blood and by covenant to the Jewish people, a tie that they do not have the authority or power to break. Families, then, and extended families of organic communities like the Jewish people, do not necessarily share an ideology as clearly and coherently as voluntary groups do, for family members do not have the option of disaffiliating. Nevertheless, families and organic communities often do share a wide variety of ideological commitments as well as the ties of relationship that link and obligate them.

Each time individuals make a decision, they may call into question their whole range of group associations and ideological commitments. Even a decision to follow the will of God is a decision that has to be constantly reaffirmed, especially when believers live among many who do not share their conviction.

Nevertheless, as individuals develop, their convictions tend to become more or less stabilized, and their affiliations follow suit. So while ideologies do not cause differences in viewpoint, they do express them.

Every society's ideology must account for the requirements of human survival, for otherwise the group committed to it will face its own dissolution and the collapse of the moral system to which it is committed. A moral theory that is self-destructive in that way is not what we mean to talk about when we talk about morals.[7] We do, of course, expect more from admirable people than merely adhering to the basic norms of right and wrong. But we expect at least that minimum standard of all people. We, therefore, consider such minimally acceptable behavior, that which is required to provide for our basic human needs, to be "right" and its lack "wrong," in contrast to the desirable but less necessary traits that we term "good" or "bad."

In general we assume that the functions of providing for physical survival will be taken care of by the larger societies (states) that have the political, economic, and military means to do so. As a result, social groups that exist within such states usually do not take specific measures for physical survival, but even they implicitly assume that the needs of physical survival are met, albeit by another agency.

On the other hand, even larger societies often tolerate and even encourage certain breeches in the quest for human survival for purposes that they consider to be equally as necessary to them as biological survival is. That is, many societies would forego survival, either of the individual or even of the entire group, rather than see certain values violated. Which values have this importance depends on the ideology of the society, and certainly human survival must be a high priority in the ideology of any society; but for many societies death is preferable to life under certain conditions. The Hanukkah story and Massada are dramatic examples of this in Jewish history, but any time a nation chooses to go to war (rather than simply defending itself) it has made a decision that the lives of its own citizens may be sacrificed to attain a social goal.

Moreover, there are certain judgments of right and wrong that are not directly connected to survival at all. Some are not even required by less basic utilitarian considerations, as, for example, our judgment that exposure of the genitals in public is wrong. How can these types of judgments be explained?

Moral language, like language in general, is a creation of society and reflects what its members think about life. But we are not just physical animals; we have certain notions about what human beings should be like, how they should behave, and even perhaps how they should think and feel. These ideas get expressed in our moral language just as much as our physical needs do because, as human beings, we are both physical and (for lack of a better word) spiritual. Indeed, we are integrated wholes, such that our physical, mental, cognitive, and emotional faculties all interact and influence each other.[8]

As a result, the inclinations that moral discourse assumes include not only those for preserving human survival but also those that produce and protect specific forms of behavior, feeling, and association. Furthermore, in our assessment of our needs and our desires, the physical aspects of our being do not always win out over the nonphysical elements of who we are. That is why it was a genuine and hotly debated issue for the Rabbis when they were faced with the case of a besieged city that had been given the choice by the enemy of either surrendering one of their number or all dying: Contributing to the death of innocents is simply not what a Jew should do, even at the cost of his or her own life.[9] That is also the conviction behind the Talmud's rule that Jews should generally violate Jewish law to save their own lives but not when they are forced to do one of three things—namely, commit murder, commit adultery or incest, or commit idolatry.[10] Life, in the Talmud's estimation, is not worth living if one must sacrifice that much of one's moral integrity.

This social evaluation of what is required in society is also behind much less drastic decisions about right and wrong. It is simply wrong, the United States has said in its court decisions and laws since the 1950s, to discriminate in education, housing, or employment on the basis of race or gender or creed, and we punish those who do any of those things even though no life is at stake. It is even wrong to expose your genitals in public, and punishable as such, even though absolutely no physical harm has befallen anyone else. These acts simply do not fit our image of how people should conduct themselves. Conversely, it is right, as viewed in the United States, to respect freedom of religion, but in some societies (for example, Inquisition Spain and contemporary Afghanistan) no such right exists; in fact, it is deemed downright wrong in those societies to believe in anything but the established religion.

Of course, there are many dangers with morals derived from our image of what is right rather than from strictly utilitarian considerations. People can even become fanatics if they totally disregard the consequences, and they can be downright dangerous if they do not temper their ideal image with sympathy and toleration. For better or for worse, though, people do make moral judgments on the basis of their images of proper behavior (the right) and ideal behavior (the good), considering actions that undermine or attack the fundamental parts of those images to be "wrong" and actions that fly in the face of social ideals or make them harder to attain to be "bad"—unless, of course, the social image itself is in the process of changing.

The important thing to note here is that the right must be defined in terms of the needs of human survival *as a particular society sees them*. Each society, in its ideology, must determine what *it* considers necessary for human survival and what *it* considers valid grounds for giving up survival in the name of another value.

Obviously, some features and needs of human existence must be accounted for in every human society as a function of the biological nature of the human being. That is why theorists who argue that our moral values are based on natural laws or intuitions can understandably come to think that certain acts are right or wrong intrinsically and universally.

A comparison of societies across the globe, however, immediately reveals that they do *not* agree in their interpretation and application of values, even those as basic as person and property. Thus Western societies classify the intentional, malicious killing of any human being as murder, but killing one's own slave did not constitute "murder" in ancient Mesopotamia or Rome, and, much more recently, killing a Jew did not constitute "murder" in Nazi Germany. Similarly, individual societies determine the definition of property. In some, paying money for an object makes you the owner, and in others signing a contract effects ownership. There certainly are some general similarities in the needs and norms of all societies brought about by our common physical requirements, our common social tasks, and our common psychological processes, but even these are tempered in form and content by the differing ideologies among societies.

The same social lenses are at work in defining the good. The ideal in classical Judaism, for example, is to restrict sexual intercourse to marriage, but many Americans today think that limiting oneself in that way is strictly a matter of choice and others think that it is actually unwise and morally perverse to wait to have sex until marriage. My point here is not to evaluate the arguments for any of these positions; I am simply trying to underscore that what counts as the ideal form of behavior depends on the vision of the ideal held by a particular society—or, as in this case, by subgroups within a given society. Similarly, granting the right of free speech is considered the "obviously" moral thing to do in some societies (most Western democracies), and in others it is deemed not only dangerous but wrong, at least when that speech challenges the political structure (China) or commonly accepted norms of thought and behavior (Afghanistan).

On the other hand, notions of right and wrong are not merely expressions of our whims or emotions. However we view the basic requirements of existence (both biological and moral), we see them *as fundamental* and thus as completely and authoritatively binding on us. But it is *we* who perceive those requirements. That is why notions of the right and the wrong, while considered binding in every society, differ in content from society to society. In sum, then, the right and the wrong are functions of how a society *sees* the *basic requirements* of existence;

the "seeing" makes the content of the terms relative to the particular society, and the "basic requirements" gives the terms their authority and objectivity.

Now we can understand how the non-moral uses of "right"—as in "He is the right man to marry Susan" or "That is the right tool for the job"—are related to the moral uses. "Right" in its moral sense consists in what *fits* an image of what is necessary for physical or spiritual survival, just as the non-moral use of "right" consists in what fits the image or needs of the user of the term.

Furthermore, this analysis nicely explains the ritual aspect of ethics. Rituals are usually differentiated from acts that have direct, pragmatic goals, and the common way of speaking about them is to say that some act is "fitting" or "not fitting" to do. Thus it is not considered "ritually fitting" (*kasher*) in Jewish law for Jews to eat pork, and it is not considered "fitting" at certain tennis clubs to appear on the court in anything but white shorts. Presumably the speaker who declares an act appropriate or inappropriate in each case has some notion of a framework in terms of which of these acts are fitting or not; for it certainly is quite proper for a Christian to eat pork or for someone playing on a public tennis court to don blue shorts. Thus rituals function in a way that is directly parallel to ethics: In both cases, acts are considered right or wrong according to whether they fit, or fail to fit, the social ideology that governs the situation.

Thus it should not be surprising that Margaret Macdonald, in a very suggestive essay, has shown that moral decisions can be illuminated by seeing them as analogous to rituals. Specifically, she writes, "Ceremonial invests the performance with authority and binds the adherents to whatever further action may be required of them by this allegiance."[11] Ethical judgments too, she claims, are practical (that is, directed toward action), authoritative, and public.

Like rituals, ethical statements are practical. Declarations of what is right or wrong are not theoretical propositions or emotional expressions but are rather performatory sentences, giving directions for action and thereby assisting in it. Thus ritual and ethical statements are not "true" in the same sense that theoretical sentences are true when they *describe* reality accurately; ritual and ethical assertions rather *make a claim* that a given act is right or wrong, good or bad, fitting or not fitting, appropriate or inappropriate, depending on whether it matches up well with the society's vision of the fundamental (the right) and ideal (the good). Moreover, the connection of assertions of right and wrong—and also assertions of good and bad, although, as I noted, to a somewhat lesser extent—to specific acts helps explain why moral judgments are more effectively spoken than written, just as rituals are.

In fact, the only important reason that ethics is only *analogous* to rituals and not precisely like them is that rituals are usually clearly connected to specific times and places, while ethical norms apply to a wide variety of contexts.[12] In this, ethics is closer to law, which is another ceremonial use of language.

It is not enough, in criminal law, for the prosecution and defense to submit their arguments in writing to the jury (or judge) for an opinion that is rendered in writing. Even though those procedures may fulfill the functions of trials to investigate and evaluate the facts and to declare and apply the law, for trials to be authoritative, they must be public and oral. Only an actual trial can enable the litigants to have their day in court so that they can be convinced that the tribunal heard their case, deliberated about it carefully, and explained the decision to them in language they can understand. This procedure not only produces the appearance of justice but actually makes justice possible. (This, by the way, is also part of the reason that the Rabbis were reticent to transform the Oral Torah to written form.[13]) Similarly, the authority of ethical statements lies in their authoritative, public, and practical nature. When I say that something is right, I am not just saying that I, personally, believe it to be so or that I like it; I am saying that the hearer or reader should see it that way too. Thus religion, law, and ethics all have a ceremonial character in that all three are intended to be authoritative, public, and practical; and all three, as I have been arguing, depend on a social ideology for their justification and meaning.

This analysis also explains the different levels of moral obligation that come with the various social groupings of which we are a part. The right and the good describe two different levels of relationship, and to confuse the two, as philosopher Helen Oppenheimer noted, is similar to what philosophers call "a category mistake." The lower level, the level of right and wrong, is the level of rule morality. Its central concept is fairness, of what in justice may be required of people. Except when relevant differences among people can be demonstrated and justified, universalizability—that is, that the same norms should apply to everyone—is a prime characteristic of this level of morality. On this level there is the required, the optional, and the forbidden. We are, after all, dealing with what must be expected of people if the society is going to exist physically and spiritually.

People, though, do not relate to each other in this minimal way alone. They form friendships, professional relationships, marriages, families, and communities. According to the depth and scope of these relationships, the people in them expect to do for each other well beyond what a rule morality could reasonably require of them. The lower level claims, of course, remain valid, but the very nature of the relationship assumes that the parties will and can reasonably expect more of each other.

Those expectations, for example, are built into professional codes of ethics. Friends do not generally spell out their mutual responsibilities to each other in detail, but as soon as one person fails to perform a commitment of friendship that the other party assumes, the aggrieved friend will let him or her know about it. As Oppenheimer says, "the word is 'ought' and not 'may' "—that is, friendships involve real duties that I must do, not just optional deeds of kindness that I may do if I so choose. On the other hand, if one member of a friendship continues to complain about what the other fails to do, the likelihood is that that friendship will not last. For a friendship to work, both parties must understand and fulfill their mutual obligations out of their own acknowledgment of the relationship, their own desire to continue it, and their own acceptance of the obligations that it entails; "to compel is to destroy." In the most intense human relationships—namely, those between spouses and with other close family members—the scope and the depth of moral obligations becomes all the greater. There too the minimal obligations still apply, and so spouses or family members may not lie to each other or steal each other's property. But insofar as their relationship is fully personal, to talk to them about duty is beside the point and even destructive of the relationship.

> The mutual help, society and comfort that the one ought to give to the other is neither optional, for the word is "ought" not "may," nor compulsory, for here to compel is to destroy. . . . Certain situations fundamentally alter what can be morally expected of one. If "I ought" implies "I can," a radical enlargement of "I can" may well engender a radical enlargement of "I ought."[14]

This last point that Oppenheimer makes is also crucial. We simply cannot sustain multiple close relationships. In part, that is because we have neither the time nor the physical or psychic energy to do that. Another part of the reason, though, is that close relationships bring with them numerous obligations, and when I accept the benefits of a close relationship, I also accept its burdens: "A radical enlargement of 'I can' may well engender a radical enlargement of 'I ought.' " We may not be able to ignore or set aside those close relationships created by birth, together with their familial (and, within Judaism, national) duties; but any relationship that I freely take on always involves the judgment of whether I can manage to fulfill the obligations that that relationship entails. Indeed, friends and lovers often have to negotiate exactly how close they each intend their relationship to be precisely because they need to know what they can expect of each other.

In all of these latter cases—professional colleagues, friends, spouses, family members—we are not just in the realm of the right and the wrong any longer; we have crossed over into the arena of the good and the bad. In that domain, at its ultimate ends, are the ideal—what J. O. Urmson, in a seminal article, called the "saints and heroes."[15] Saints are those who suppress desire and self-interest beyond the call of duty, and heroes are those who resist fear and the claims of self-preservation beyond the normal bounds of obligation. Just as the vision of a particular society is critical in identifying its understanding of the right and the wrong, so too a society's vision of its ideals underlies its understanding of its saints and heroes. However a society conceives of its ideal, its members cannot frivolously ignore or abandon it as long as it accurately expresses their aspirations.

> Here we have something more gracious, actions that need to be inspired by a positive ideal. If duty can, as Mill said, be exacted from persons as a debt, it is because duty is a minimum requirement for living together; the positive contribution of actions that go beyond any duty could not be so exacted . . . [but] are clearly equally pressing *in foro interno* on those who are not content merely to avoid the intolerable.[16]

So one must learn about ideals to understand truly good behavior—which, I think, is not as unusual as Urmson's words "saints" and "heroes" suggest. People often do have an altruistic streak in them, if only so that they can think of themselves as truly good people, and ideology teaches them how to direct those inclinations while it also teaches them how to understand them.

Whenever we use words like "good" or even more laudatory forms of praise such as "excellent," "outstanding," or "ideal," we may simply be expressing our own opinion, in which case we are making no call on the listener to agree with us. We may, however, be invoking our particular society's vision of the ideal, in which case we are making a claim on the listener to agree with us and even to do something about it, although not nearly as strong a claim as when we assert that something is right or wrong.

So, for example, if I were to say that it is good to exercise every day, I could simply be saying that I like to do that, that it makes me feel good, and I may even be implying or saying that you might like it too. On the other hand, I could be invoking the American ideal of fitness, based, as usual for American ideology, on its pragmatic benefits. I might even justify my positive evaluation of daily exercise with statements from a long line of American presidents supporting fitness programs. In this latter usage, I would be appealing to standards endorsed by the society. As a result, the *burden of proof* about the value of exercise no longer rests with me but rather with any American who denies its goodness.

That, of course, does not mean that my listener will act on my statement or even that I think that he or she must. After all, I did not say that it is *right* to exercise (which would imply that I thought that there really could be very few good excuses not to do so, unless there were conflicting duties) but only that it is *good* to exercise (implying that, barring other conflicting goods or duties, my listener should consider it seriously). This is one instance of the more general point made earlier that judgments of the right are closer to action than assertions of the good. Moreover, my claim, like any assertion about the good, is open to being disproved if my listener can show me that exercise does things contrary to the American ideal. So, for example, if it leads to heart attacks, or if the presidents mentioned advocated it only to get a kickback on sneakers, I might reevaluate the role of exercise in attaining the American ideal—unless, of course, I am a fanatic about exercise, in which case no argument will convince me otherwise and I may not even be willing to listen to an argument for the contrary position.

According to the convictions of Jewish ideology, though, I might even say that it is *right* to exercise every day and that you are doing something *wrong* if you do not. Health in the Jewish tradition, after all, is not just an ideal that one should, if one can, take steps to attain and retain; it is rather, in the Jewish conception, a prerequisite for our ability to fulfill our divine mission in life. As a result, maintaining our health is nothing less than a commanded act as well as continual service to God. Maimonides states this explicitly:

> He who regulates his life in accordance with the laws of medicine with the sole motive of maintaining a sound and vigorous

physique and begetting children to do his work and labor for his benefit is not following the right course. A man should aim to maintain physical health and vigor in order that his soul may be upright, in a condition to know God. . . . Whoever throughout his life follows this course will be continually serving God, even while engaged in business and even during cohabitation, because his purpose in all that he does will be to satisfy his needs so as to have a sound body with which to serve God. Even when he sleeps and seeks repose to calm his mind and rest his body so as not to fall sick and be incapacitated from serving God, his sleep is service of the Almighty.[17]

This illustrates my final point about the right and the good—namely, that what may be considered good in one society may be what is expected of everyone (that is, right) in another, and vice versa. Thus, while it may be good to be clean about yourself in general society, it is your duty to be so if you are a physician administering care to patients; in other words, medical ethics requires a degree of cleanliness that general ethics would consider beyond the bounds of duty and either unusually good or, with a tone of disdain, much too fastidious. Among automobile mechanics a doctor's degree of cleanliness would be considered unrealistic and inappropriate.

Our use of ethical terms, then, must be flexible enough to accommodate different social and professional groupings and varying contexts. We use the terms "right" and "good" with relative stability only in regard to those obligations required by any society for it to exist. Thus it is almost universally considered "wrong" to lie or steal, but in most societies it is only "bad" to be lazy. Even the definition of the duties of minimal morality, though, depends crucially, as I discussed, on different societies' *perspectives* on their fundamental physical and spiritual needs. (This should recall the discussion of relativity, as against relativism and absolutism, in Chapter Three.) But in each society one can usually determine what it considers to be crucial to its interests (physical or spiritual) by checking which acts it considers right and wrong, in contradistinction to those it classifies as retrograde ("bad") or approaching the ideal ("good").

Appendix B:
Comparative Ways for Identifying the Moral Course of Action

ALTHOUGH PEOPLE AROUND THE WORLD AFFIRM THAT THEY would like to be seen as good people, Friedrich Nietzsche challenged the soundness of that desire. He maintained that aspirations for goodness—with their attendant idealization of sympathy, empathy, loyalty, cooperation, and altruistic action—were rooted in the slave morality foisted on the world by the Jews. Oppressed people abhor the powerful who set values and rule them, getting even by calling them names like "evil." Slaves valorize those who are safe, "good-natured, easily deceived, perhaps a little stupid." Instead, he claimed, we should adopt a master morality in which we try to be noble, defining values ourselves as an act of power and taking control over others no matter who or what gets trampled under foot in the process. The ideal should be the *ubermensch*, the superman, who rules anyone he can subject in any way he chooses.[1]

Nietzsche's thesis is remarkable for its novelty and its challenge to commonly accepted norms; he certainly makes one think. In the end, though, the vast majority of the world's peoples, both religious and secular, and their political and intellectual leaders have rejected Nietzsche's point of view. They all recognize the dangers inherent in the rule of dictators, even benign ones. Justice and fairness are replaced by one person's whims; the body politic depends on the wisdom and power of one person; and life itself is threatened by the arbitrariness of dictatorial rule. Nobility may be a virtue, but certainly not as Nietzsche describes it and surely not as a replacement for goodness.

Goodness, though, is not our only moral ideal. We also seek to do the right thing. After all, the Torah demands that we do both "the right and the good in the eyes of God."[2] The differences between the right and the good were discussed in Appendix A, and we clearly want to do both in our private lives and on the social plane.

How, though, do we determine what is the right and/or good thing to do? The Jewish tradition has depended primarily on a legal method of identifying the right and the good, all the while acknowledging that there are moral duties "beyond the letter of the law." Because Jews tend to think that the whole world thinks and acts as Jews do, it is helpful to note that other traditions have chosen very different ways of discovering the right and/or the good. The differences could be found by exploring and comparing the methods that all the religious and secular traditions around the world use to discover the right and the good. However, because this is a book on Jewish social ethics and this methodological discussion is but groundwork, I consider here only the other traditions likely to be familiar to North American Jews—namely, Catholicism, Protestantism, and American secularism.

Catholicism

Catholics depend on their clerical hierarchy and, ultimately, on the pope to define what is right and good. Indeed, the First Vatican Council declared in 1870 that in matters of faith and morals, the pope has the right to declare something "infallibly." Popes have done that only rarely, but through their papal statements they have effectively defined Catholic doctrine and morality. Individual Catholics might disagree with the pope or the bishops on a given issue, either vocally or by "voting with their feet," but even those who take another stand acknowledge that once the pope has ruled on something, that is, for better or worse, the Catholic stand on the matter.

This method has all the strengths and weaknesses of any system that trusts an authority. On the positive side, the authority—whether it be one person, as in the case of the pope or a dictator, or a group of people, as in the case of an oligarchy, and whether it be benign or malevolent—provides clear directives about what people may and may not do. The authority also delineates the ideals that people should aspire to attain. This eliminates the need for individuals to wonder about moral matters or to struggle with them, at least in theory. (One cannot help but recall the Nuremberg Trials here, in which acting on clear legal authority issued by the person in charge was *not* considered a sufficient defense for committing "crimes against humanity.")

In this method, all the authority of the person or people trusted with this defining role attaches to the moral directives that he, she, or they issue, including the right and, often, the ability to enforce them. Authority figures may attempt to persuade their followers of the wisdom of their decrees, as popes and bishops have done through their pastoral letters; ultimately, though, what they say establishes the right and the good for their followers simply by virtue of the position they hold. People who like clarity, order, and a sense of strong authority will like these features of the authoritarian way of defining morality.

This way of determining the right and the good, though, has some distinct drawbacks. First, the entire system is based on trusting those in authority for moral wisdom. Why should they be so trusted? Even if they have personal and professional qualifications to be a good guide for moral judgment, no human being or group, one would suppose, should have absolute power, for none of us shares in God's omniscience. Minimally, the authority figure's decisions should be subject to criticism, challenge, and change by those who look up to him or her. This position instead encourages people to be docile and submissive.

Furthermore, this method of defining the right and the good relieves individuals of too much moral responsibility. Nuremberg notwithstanding, far too many of those who follow an authoritarian system rely on the authority figure for their moral direction without question, and that is at the least morally irresponsible and is sometimes downright dangerous. Becoming an adult, after all, requires sharpening one's own moral sense, learning how to act on it, and taking responsibility for one's own actions. Advice from others is often appropriately considered, but authoritarian ethics provides not only advice but orders.

Third, for all its appearances of affording definite and stable positions, there is an inherent chaos involved in this method. An authority figure like the pope, after all, could change his mind at any moment, and even if he does not, the next pope could. The pope has a vested interest, of course, in retaining the allegiance of his followers, and since he represents tradition and even God to them, there is very good reason for him to adhere to precedent. That is the conservative side of this position. The other, chaotic side, however, is just as real: There are no systematic limitations on the pope's authority to prevent him from changing any of the Church's instructions on faith and morals.

Protestantism

Protestant theorists place strong emphasis on individual conscience in defining the right and the good. They expect that individual Protestants should be guided in their moral perceptions and actions by Scripture, in particular the stories of Jesus. Some Protestant theologians also recommend the stories of other ancient and modern exemplars of how a person should act. Protestant leaders also expect that church members be guided by the traditions, doctrines, and practices of their particular denomination. In the end, though, it is the individual's conscience that reigns in moral matters.

This Protestant methodology emerged as a reaction to the Catholic placement of moral authority in institutional representatives and some of the abuses of that system. If each person were instead to read Scripture on his or her own, the theory was and continues to be, then people will interact with the word of God directly, without the distortions of human intermediaries. Thus even though most Protestant traditions maintain that all human beings are born with Original Sin and deserve divine damnation, the most effective way for us to know the right and the good is to use our own conscience, chastened, prodded, and tutored by Scripture.

In placing great trust in the individual, the Protestant system has the advantage of avoiding all the pitfalls of the various forms of authoritarianism. Relying on conscience stimulates individuals to think about moral matters on their own and in conjunction with others of their faith community, knowing all along that in the end they will have both the right and the responsibility to decide for themselves. This tends to instill respect for oneself and for all others, because each person has a conscience. Communities need to establish laws to govern society, but the Protestant theory implies that the widest possible berth should be given to individuals to exercise their own senses of right and wrong. Calvinist circles, in which Original Sin is especially stressed, did not draw that particular implication in past centuries, but it has become a dominant theme of much Protestant thought today. Thus individual freedom, producing individual responsibility, is an important boon of the Protestant methodology and, indeed, an important legacy of Protestantism for Western democracy.

The disadvantages of the Protestant methodology, though, stem from the same factors that make it attractive. First, if all of us are born with Original Sin and deserve to be damned to hell, then why should we trust ourselves to know the right and the good? Granted that we are supposed to use Scripture as our guide, but how can we trust our sinful sense of right and wrong to interpret it? This very problem has led a significant segment of Protestantism to adopt a fundamentalist stance toward Scripture. Such people cannot abide the thought that Scripture itself was mediated by human beings and has a history; it must be the direct, infallible, word of God for it to be able to guide the sinful souls that we are.

Other Protestant denominations that do not stress Original Sin as much have been willing to take a historical approach to Scripture. Nevertheless, evangelicals, who make up the middle Protestant camp between the fundamentalists on the right and the liberals on the left, maintain that the text of the Bible may have a history, but its underlying message is the infallible word of God. Only liberal Protestants are keenly aware of the problems of interpretation (called "hermeneutics") imbedded in Bible study, and they, therefore, put more emphasis on individual conscience as guided by the biblical traditions and less on Original Sin. This very discrepancy, though, illustrates the tension between the core Protestant doctrines of Original Sin and respect for individual conscience.

Moral and communal chaos is another problem inherent in this system. There is ultimately no way in the Protestant method to determine that some act is definitively right or wrong; the best that one can do is to say that I, or the members of a particular church community, *think* that it is right or wrong. If others in my community do not agree and we can live together despite that difference, then fine; but if not, the only alternative is for me to join another denomination or to create one of my own—one important factor in the history of Protestant splintering, which today counts more than 250 denominations in the United States alone.[3] Put in more abstract terms, Protestant methodology leads to moral relativism, if not moral individualism, with its inherent difficulties for defining the right and the good with any authority or clarity and for creating a cohesive community.

American Secularism

American secular thought, with strong roots both in Protestantism and in Enlightenment thought, places great faith both in individual conscience and in rule by the majority in a government with checks and balances. Some Enlightenment theorists and some of the Founding Fathers of the United States accepted the Calvinist doctrine or the doctrine of Thomas Hobbes that people are inherently selfish and evil; for them a balanced form of government, with nobody having too much power, is the best defense against human perversity. Other Enlightenment thinkers, like John Locke, had a much more positive view of humanity, conceiving of us as inherently rational beings; for them, too, a balanced government is the best way to make decisions, but that is because nobody has the right to trample on individuals' natural rights until and unless an individual rationally and deliberately gives up specific rights in the name of gaining some of the benefits of living in a community. Thus, to quote the quintessential Enlightenment American document—the Declaration of Independence—some rights, "endowed by their Creator," are "unalienable" by any governmental authority. As a result, defining the right and the good is a matter, first, of individual conscience and, second, of majority vote with protections for minority rights.

The tension between individual conscience and majority vote is evident in such contemporary moral issues as abortion and school prayer. These matters gain the attention and difficulty they do in the United States precisely because of the conflicting pulls of individual choice and majority vote.

I noted the advantages and disadvantages of individual conscience as the guide earlier, when I discussed Protestantism. The other factor in American secular thought, majority rule, has its own pluses and minuses.

The advantages of deciding moral issues by majority vote is that those presumably ruled by the decision get the chance to influence it. This is a matching of freedom with responsibility, a clearly desirable thing. Another advantage of this methodology is that if the majority wills a policy, its chances of becoming effective within that society are rather good; morals produced by other systems that ignore the will of the majority may be honored, but they incur the danger of being overwhelmingly neglected in practice. Finally, although the will of the majority is not as easy to determine as one may suppose, as the 2000 presidential election in Florida amply illustrates, it nevertheless is easier to discover than, say, the will of God.

Ever since Thucydides warned us in *The Peloponnesian Wars*, however, of the reality that the rule of the majority can very easily become the rule of the mob—with emotion ruling decisions rather than information, expertise, and reason—moral theorists have rarely invoked the will of the majority as the criterion of what is right or good. What, after all, provides the majority with the requisite, special knowledge to make an informed and reasoned moral decision in a specific case or the philosophical knowledge to understand more theoretical moral issues? On the contrary, the greater the expertise required, the less likely the majority will have it. Moreover, what is the basis of the majority's decision? Their own desires? That raises the standard ethical problem that the desired is not necessarily the desirable, that, in other words, the criteria for judging the right and the good are not necessarily—and maybe even not often—identical with the criteria for deciding what we want. Furthermore, what kind of stability can be ensured through such a moral system? The majority can presumably change its mind at any time, and then what is construed to be moral today may be deemed immoral tomorrow, or vice versa. Thus, despite its attractions, the American secular methodology for determining moral policy has significant difficulties, just as the Catholic, Protestant, and, as I will point out, the Jewish approaches do.

Different Methods, Different Results

In any case, this brief survey and evaluation of competing moral methodologies for identifying the right and the good should make it clear that the Jewish legal methodology is definitely not the only possible one for intelligent, morally sensitive people to adopt, nor even the most popular one. Indeed, the most followed religions and secular systems of thought and action in North America have chosen very different ways to determine the right and the good. Although I did not explore this in detail here, Chapter One describes how the three systems just discussed and Judaism arrive at different results, depicting the moral person and the moral society in significantly different ways.

Moreover, my brief review should also demonstrate that each system has its own benefits and drawbacks; that is true for the

Jewish method as well, as I explore next. We Jews may value the benefits of the Jewish system beyond those of the alternatives, and we may be willing to tolerate the weaknesses of the Jewish methodology more than other people would. We may even think that the Jewish system is the one formulated and commanded by God and that the others are not divine, or at least not as fully so—but, of course, Catholics and Protestants would say similar things about their own methods and norms vis-à-vis Judaism. The important things to note, though, are that the various religions and secular philosophies of the world have adopted very different systems for defining the right and the good, with very different results, and that, although any group may value its own method and content the most, none can reasonably say that the only possible way for a morally sensitive, intelligent person to think and act morally is the way that it has chosen.

Judaism

What, then, are the specific benefits and pitfalls of defining the right and the good in the legal way that Judaism largely does? And how can the benefits be strengthened and the pitfalls be avoided—or at least mitigated?

Christianity, of course, has historically objected to Judaism's insistence on using law as one of religion's forms, claiming that law makes a person meticulous about the details and blind to the law's larger meanings—to the point, at least in some cases, of downright meanness. (It is from the New Testament that the word "Pharisee" gets its negative connotations along these lines.[3]) In any case, for Christians, the advent of Jesus means that the Holy Spirit has replaced the reign of the law in directing our lives.

Even if most contemporary Jews reject these Christian claims, many modern Jews are influenced by the Western emphasis on individualism and autonomy and thus understand Jewish laws as guidelines at most.[4] Hence the popularity of Reform Judaism, which, like American ideology, stresses the role of individual choice in deciding when and how to live by the tradition.

The Jewish tradition itself was painfully aware of some of the chief dangers in using law to live morally. One such risk is that for some people acting in accordance with the law becomes an end rather than a means. In performing the required actions out of habit rather than out of conviction, people become "religious behaviorists,"[5] doing what they are required to do but blind to the phenomena and meanings the law was intended to reveal. In traditional Jewish terms, they sacrifice all concern for *kavanah* (intention, meaning) in their quest to make sure that the *keva* (the fixed Jewish practice) is done correctly.

In philosophic terms, such people adopt a *legalistic* approach to the law, concerning themselves with the details to the exclusion of the broader aims and spirit of the law, rather than an appropriately *legal* approach, by which the aims and spirit of the law shape one's view of the details. Becoming legalistic is a serious risk not only for laypeople who seek to abide by the law but even for some of the rabbis who interpret and apply it. Knowing the peril of slipping into the legalistic mode, the Rabbis of the Talmud and Midrash repeatedly raised the question in a variety of contexts of whether fulfillment of the commandments requires appropriate intention, and if so, what the nature of that intention must be.[6] Moreover, they constantly interwove their legal discussions with moral and theological points. Still, this concern remains.

A legal approach to moral issues is inherently conservative, and that can be a benefit or a burden. The law can change, of course, but it does not change often. This, in fact, is one of the reasons people want a legal system in the first place—namely, to ensure a continuity in what they can expect of each other together with the physical, legal, and psychological security that such continuity affords. If a legal system constantly changes, these advantages disappear. But this conservative feature of law means that if the morals of a culture are encased in its laws, as is largely the case in Judaism, the moral norms will not change very much over time. There are some good aspects to that: We then have the sense that Judaism's moral norms have staying power, that they express genuine and deep commitments of

Judaism and of Jews, and that, therefore, we Jews can know what we stand for and what we can expect each other to do—or at least what we can expect each other to aspire to do. The inherent conservatism of law, though, also has some distinct disadvantages: It means that Jewish moral thinking and action may lag behind contemporary moral sensitivities and become downright reactionary in those areas where it does not change when it really needs to do so.

In light of all these pitfalls, why would classical Jewish sources depend so heavily on law to define and inculcate moral norms? Part of the reason, of course, is that the tradition presents the laws as the will of God; we are bound to those laws, including the moral norms among them, even if we do not understand why God has given moral norms to us in that form. Even if we cannot discern God's purposes in this, we can look at the way in which law actually functions in society—that is, the *results* of putting moral norms into legal form. Then, just as we have described some of the major drawbacks of this approach, we can also analyze the *advantages* of Judaism's linking matters of the conscience and the spirit to law. So, then, what are those advantages? Or, put theologically, how is law supposed to help us find the right and the good that God demands of us and, in the process, to find God?

LAW ESTABLISHES MINIMUM MORAL STANDARDS   The most obvious contribution of law to morality is that law establishes a minimum standard of practice. This is important from a moral standpoint because many values can be realized only through the mutual action of a number of people, and a minimum standard that is enforced as law enables the society to secure the cooperation necessary for such moral attainment. Furthermore, there is an objective value to a beneficent act whether or not it is done for the right moral reason.

In spelling out minimal standards of moral conduct, there is always the danger that people will interpret the minimum requirements legalistically as the total extent to which they need to extend themselves for others. That, however, would involve

a serious blindness to the realm of morality that would probably not be cured by removing the legal trappings from the minimum standards. Moreover, Judaism guards against such an
abuse through its requirements of public and private study of
the Bible and other morally enriching literature, through the
liturgy and sermons, and through making the minimal requirements of action rather demanding in the first place.

LAW GIVES MORAL VALUES AND IDEALS CONCRETE APPLICATION AND
REALITY   It is not just on a minimal level that the law is important for morality; law is crucial at every level of moral aspiration in order to translate moral values into specific modes of
behavior. The Prophets enunciated lofty values, and we rightly
feel edified and uplifted when we read their words or those of
other great moral teachers in other generations, including our
own. At the other end of the spectrum, when we hear "fire and
brimstone" sermons or go through the painful self-examination
of a confessional procedure such as Yom Kippur, we come away
feeling chastened and purified. But the vast majority of life is
lived between those two extremes of moral awareness as we
pursue our daily tasks. Consequently, if that edification or chas-
tening is to contribute to a better world in any significant way,
it must be translated into daily activities. We ordinarily do not
have sufficient time or self-awareness to think seriously about
what we are doing, and, hence, a regimen of specific laws that
articulate what we should do in a variety of circumstances can
often enable us to act morally when we might not do so. Morris Adler articulated this point well:

> Religion is not a matter of living on the "peaks" of experience.
> This is for the saint and the mystic. More fundamentally, reli-
> gion must mean transposing to a higher level of spiritual aware-
> ness and ethical sensitivity the entire plateau of daily living by
> the generality of men. Idolatry is defeated not by recognition of
> its intellectual absurdity alone, but by a life that expresses itself
> in service to God. Selfishness and greed are overcome not by
> professions of a larger view but by disciplines that direct our
> energies, our wills, and our actions outward and upward.[7]

Another way to look at the same point is to note that values and ideas are at the heart of what it means to be a person and a Jew, and yet we live in a world of objects and forces. Thoughts and values can become part of our lives only if they are somehow translated into the world of concrete objects. Law does that. It coordinates ideas and values with specific patterns of action that express them. In so doing, law enables us to make them an active part of our lives.

So, for example, providing for the poor, as demanded and delineated in Jewish law, is no longer exclusively a matter of emotion or a pious but an ephemeral ideal; it is instead the value that requires us to provide food, shelter, and clothing for others as we teach them how to support themselves. Obeying this command can be a reminder of our obligations to God and of the ways in which the Jewish tradition pushes us toward its ideals.

Ritual laws function in the same way. So, for example, God's creation of the world is not restricted to the world of metaphysical principles when the Sabbath laws transform that tenet into a special day to experience its import in what we say and do. The laws requiring Jews to perform specific acts on the Sabbath and refrain from others make up the principal part of our consciousness and behavior. We not only think about God's continuing ownership of everything and everyone but experience the ramifications of it. With that principle embedded in our minds throughout the week, we are less likely to take the world for granted and more likely "to use it and safeguard it."[8]

LAW DEFINES THE REQUIREMENTS AND THE LIMITS OF MORAL DEMANDS   In providing specific details and demands, law defines principles, spelling out what is required and, at least as important, what is not. "Justice, justice shall you pursue," for example, *could* be interpreted to require merely a specific attitude. Alternatively, it *could* prescribe total adherence to principles of justice with no room for compassion. Similarly, the Jewish Sabbath *could* be like the Christian or the Muslim one. By requiring certain activities and prohibiting others, Jewish law defines (literally, "sets limits to") the Sabbath by establishing what behavior is within it and what is outside its boundaries. Without that kind of definition both the ideas of the Jewish Sabbath and the experience of it would become vague and amorphous. The distinctively Jewish character and message of the Jewish commands to pursue justice and observe the Sabbath are thus largely the products of Jewish law.

LAW PROVIDES A PUBLIC FORUM FOR ADJUDICATING MORAL CONFLICTS   Until now I have spoken about areas in which the moral norm is more or less clear and the problem is one of realizing it. There are many situations, however, in which there is a conflict of values and it must be determined which will take precedence and in what circumstances. Nonlegal moral systems usually offer some mechanism for treating moral dilemmas, but they often depend on the sensitivity and analytic ability of one individual, whether that be the pope (Catholicism) or every person (Protestantism). Law, in contrast, provides a format for deciding such issues *publicly,* thus ensuring that many minds of different convictions will be brought to bear on the issue. This procedure does not guarantee wisdom, but it does at least provide a greater measure of objectivity and, hence, a more thorough consideration of the relevant elements.

Moreover, issues are often joined more clearly in court than they are in moral treatises because the realities are more dramatically evident there and a decision must be reached. Moral essayists or theorists, on the other hand, do not face the immediate responsibility of having people act on their decisions, and hence they tend to be somewhat "ivory towerish." Actually, much of the sheer wisdom of the Jewish tradition can be attributed to the fact that the Rabbis who shaped it served not only as scholars and teachers but also as judges.

LAW AFFORDS CONTINUITY WITH FLEXIBILITY   Continuity with flexibility is the positive side of the moral conservatism that I mentioned earlier. Because law operates on the basis of precedent, there is a greater sense of continuity in a moral tradition that is structured legally than in one that is not. On the other hand, through standard legal techniques like differentiation of cases, the law preserves a reasonable amount of flexibility and adaptability. By contrast, moral decisions made on the basis of conscience often have little public effect or staying power, whereas moral decisions made on the basis of natural or divine law lack sufficient malleability to retain relevance to new situations and to take advantage of new knowledge. A legal tradition like that of Judaism, despite the believed divinity of its foundational document, can accommodate needed changes because rabbis in each generation have the right and the responsibility to adjust it appropriately. Therefore, for all of its problems in practice, a legal tradition attains the best balance that can be achieved between tradition and change.

LAW PROVIDES ONE IMPORTANT WAY TO TEACH MORALITY   Theories of education are obviously many and diverse, but the Jewish tradition has a clear methodology for moral education:

> Rab Judah said in Rab's name: A person should always occupy himself with Torah and good deeds, even if not for their own sake, for out of [doing good] with an ulterior motive he will [do good] for its own sake.[9]

That is, you should do the right thing, even if not for the right reason, for by forming the habit of doing the right thing, the tradition trusts, you will come to understand and adopt the right motivation.

Part of the reason for that trust is that over the course of time people doing the right thing may well be confronted with situations in which it is not so easy or in which one right thing comes into conflict with another. Then a person may be motivated to engage in some self-reflection on why and in what context a given act is right and how it is to be balanced against other duties and ideals. That is, a life of living morally and facing moral conflicts may engender deepening in moral thought and motivation. Patterns of action, though, are easier to under-

stand and inculcate than proper understanding and motivation—or so, at least, the tradition believes, and hence the emphasis is on training people to do the right thing first. This largely behavioristic approach to moral education, though, is not
totally so: Study of the tradition is also an integral part of Jewish moral education, as I will explore at greater length below.
In the end, though, the emphasis in Jewish moral education is
on action:

> An excellent thing is the study of Torah combined with some
> worldly occupation, for the labor demanded by both of them
> causes sinful inclinations to be forgotten. All study of the Torah
> without work must, in the end, be futile and become the cause of
> sin.[10]

The Rabbis applied the same educational theory to moral de-
generacy and repentance:

> Once a person has committed a sin and repeated it, it appears to
> him as if it were permitted.[11]
>   Run to fulfill even a minor precept and flee from the slightest
> transgression; for precept brings precept in its train, and trans-
> gression draws transgression.[12]
>   If a transgression comes to a person a first time and second
> time without his sinning, he is immune from the sin.[13]

If one accepts this approach to moral education in whole or
in part, the formulation of moral norms in terms of law is very
important educationally, for in doing so you *require* people to
act in accord with moral rules as a step in teaching them how
to do the right thing for the right reason.

Logically, of course, principles precede the actions that express them, but what comes first logically is not necessarily
what comes first in education or practice. We discover, for example, that we may not steal Johnny's marbles long before we
learn the general theories of ethics that explain why. At first we
may refrain from stealing the marbles simply because we do not
want to make Mommy or Daddy—or Johnny—angry; it is only
later that we acquire general notions of property, divine and

social expectations, and action on principle. When that time comes, the experience we have had in interacting with people and their property helps us considerably in mastering the abstract idea because we can relate it to situations and actions that we have already experienced.

The two examples I used earlier are no exceptions. We learn the meaning of justice when we discover that certain behaviors toward others are condemned and others are expected. We may not even be able to understand the meaning of the word "justice" until we have had such experiences. Similarly, when we begin to observe the Sabbath, we may not fully comprehend all of its ideas and values, but the law at least directs our actions to be in consonance with them. It does more: It establishes a framework of special actions that begs us to ask why. It thereby encourages us to probe the meaning of the Sabbath legislation and to become more conscious of the Sabbath's themes. Ultimately, we can come to appreciate its messages of God's creation, Revelation, and redemption, with the Sabbath experiences serving as a guide to their specific Jewish meaning. The law thus teaches us what to do, it stimulates us to ask questions so that we can more fully understand the meaning of life, and it provides a framework to understand some answers.

LAW PRESERVES THE INTEGRITY OF MORAL INTENTIONS   We all think of ourselves as having good intentions, but we can only clarify and verify our intentions in action. Heschel articulated this point well:

> The dichotomy of faith and works which presented such an important problem in Christian theology was never a problem in Judaism. To us, the basic problem is neither what is the right action nor what is the right intention. The basic problem is: what is right living? And life is indivisible. The inner sphere is never isolated from outward activities. . . .
>
> It would be a device of conceit, if not presumption, to insist that purity of heart is the exclusive test of piety. Perfect purity is

something we rarely know how to obtain or how to retain. No one can claim to have purged all the dross from his finest desire. The self is finite, but selfishness is infinite.

God asks for the heart, but the heart is oppressed with uncertainty in its own twilight. God asks for faith, and the heart is not sure of its own faith. It is good that there is a dawn of decision for the night of the heart; deeds to objectify faith, definite forms to verify belief.[14]

Concretizing moral values in the form of law is, thus, an important method for testing the nature and seriousness of our intentions so that we may avoid hypocrisy. It also graphically shows us the effects of our intentions, so that we all alter those that are knowingly or unknowingly destructive. Law brings our intentions out into the arena of action, where we can see them clearly and, if necessary, work with them.

Law Contributes to Creating a Moral Community On the most obvious of practical grounds, one cannot have a community if people merely assent to a list of moral principles; they must also agree to abide by rules governing their behavior toward each other, rules that may be based on those moral principles but that have the full authority of law. Moreover, communities need law not only to establish minimally acceptable behavior but also to motivate their members to accomplish social ideals.

The pursuit of justice is a good example of this communal function of law. The law specifies the behavior required of people to make justice a living value in society, and it communicates the group's insistence that its members follow its rules to accomplish that end. This contributes mightily to both group identity and group spirit.

Communities also need rituals to express their social cohesion and character. The Sabbath certainly functions in that way for Jews. Those who abide by the laws of the Sabbath feel an immediate kinship with others who do so. Such people know the same enriching experiences, and their observance of the

Sabbath indicates that they hold many of the same values and beliefs. This, of course, excludes others who do not obey the Sabbath laws, but not out of prejudice; any Jew who decides to join the club may do so by simply obeying the rules, and non-Jews can do likewise by converting to Judaism and observing the Sabbath. In the meantime, Sabbath legislation and custom create the structure for Jews to share a day each week in fellowship, worship, study, and family and communal gathering, making for a powerful element in Jewish group identity.[15] Even Asher Ginsberg (Ahad Ha-Am; 1856–1927), a secular Zionist, wanted to maintain the Sabbath for communal, if not religious, reasons:

> A Jew who feels a real tie with the life of his people throughout the generations will find it utterly impossible to think of the existence of Israel without the Sabbath. One can say without exaggeration that more than Israel has kept the Sabbath, the Sabbath has kept Israel. Had it not been for the Sabbath, which weekly restored to the people their "soul" and weekly renewed their spirit, the weekday afflictions would have pulled them farther and farther downward until they sank to the lowest depths of materialism as well as ethical and intellectual poverty. Therefore one need not be a Zionist in order to feel all the traditional sacred grandeur that hovers over this "good gift," and to rise up with might against all who seek to destroy it.[16]

In all of these ways, then, law contributes to morality, and the interaction between them has an influence in both directions. This is especially important when we are trying to understand Judaism, which went so far in trying to deal with moral issues in legal terms.

The Jewish legal system, though, is specifically a *religious* legal system. Its laws are embedded in a broader, theological context that assigns to law both a moral and a theological purpose. Even with a number of instances that challenge this doctrine, the Bible assumes that God's commandments are binding not only because God is powerful, but also because God is just:

> The Rock!—His deeds are perfect,
> Yea, all His ways are just;
> A faithful God, never false,
> True and upright is He.[17]

Given that overriding biblical view of God, the biblical verse that motivated the title of this book ("Do the right and the good in the eyes of the Lord") states Jewish law's theological context and its moral and theological purposes explicitly. Some practitioners of Jewish law fail to keep these underlying tenets and goals in mind when interpreting and applying it. In their hands, Jewish law is likely to incur the disadvantages of a legal approach to morality and to miss many of its benefits. Thus the decision to take a legal approach to moral matters is only the beginning of the story; one then has to adopt a philosophy and methodology of Jewish law that minimizes the risks of using law for moral decisions and maximizes its benefits. I discuss the parameters of such an approach elsewhere.[18]

Can one, though, gain the advantages of a legal approach to morality without law altogether? Paul, especially in the New Testament's Book of Romans, thought so. He actually went further, claiming that law is in some ways detrimental to attaining spiritual goals. Much of Christendom has adopted his view.[19] In practice, however, Christian denominations often have specific rules. Historically these canons have been enforced with punishments as harsh as torture and death, and some groups of Christians still impose excommunication.

The Jewish tradition, in contrast, has consistently and unreservedly maintained that law is essential for the life of the conscience and the spirit, in part for the reasons delineated earlier. Moreover, from the Jewish perspective, God demands obedience of the law. The content of the law may change over the course of time, but the corpus of the law, however it is defined in a given time and place, is obligatory.

The modern Reform Movement does not accept this binding character of Jewish law, and many contemporary Jews do not abide by it. For these people, Jewish law clearly cannot function in the ways described here. Only those who obey it can expect to reap its rewards.

For those who do abide by it, though, Jewish law remains a powerful mechanism through which one can learn of God's ways, be motivated to follow them, and come into contact with God. It transforms one's actions into a quest for the right and the good—and, indeed, for the holy.

Notes to Appendix A

1. This section is based primarily on a small section of my doctoral dissertation in philosophy; see Dorff (1971).

2. Ross (1930).

3. M.T. *Laws of Gifts to the Poor* 10:7–14, esp. 10:8. There is, of course, a counterprinciple in Jewish law—namely, "One who is commanded to do something and does it is preferable to one who is not commanded to do that thing and does it" (B. *Kiddushin* 31a) because, according to the comment of Tosafot there, the one who is commanded will be careful to fulfill the duty and do it completely, whereas those who act out of a sense of charity feel—rightly—that they may choose to do it today but not tomorrow and that they may choose the extent to which to carry out the act. In this way, duties, with their foundation in relationships, are more imperative than good acts, grounded in pragmatic goals, a point that I make at greater length later in this appendix. When judging the moral goodness of acts, however, we are precisely assessing the degree to which a person did a morally good thing *without* having a moral duty to do so, and thus the moral goodness of an act increases when the parties are unknown to each other.

4. This is another aspect of the principle discussed in note 3. Those who act out of a sense of commandedness are to be preferred to those who do not both because people who feel commanded are more trustworthy and reliable to continue to act in that way, as stated there, and also because such people are correctly doing first what they must do morally before turning to what it would be morally good for them to do.

5. The reward of long life for honoring parents: Exodus 20:12 and Deuteronomy 5:16. For shooing away the mother bird before taking her eggs: Deuteronomy 22:6–7. The Rabbis' lessons from this: B. *Kiddushin* 39b and B. *Hullin* 142a. Both of these sources include R. Jacob's comment that the reward for fulfilling the commandments must be in the world to come, for if a boy obeys his father's command to climb up a tree and shoo away the mother bird before taking her

eggs, and then falls on the way down and dies, the Torah's promise of life for fulfilling each of these two commandments must be understood as referring to life after death. In sharp contrast to Rabbi Jacob's conclusion, this is the story that, in Steinberg (1939), 248–250, leads Elisha ben Abuya to assert instead, "There is no justice and no Judge." This is a major step on the road to his apostasy.

The last mishnah in *Hullin* (12:5) uses the Torah's promise to teach yet a different lesson: "If in respect to that which is worth just an *issar* [that is, the mother bird], the Torah said, 'That it may be well with you and that you may prolong your days,' how much more [must be the reward] for the observance of the more difficult precepts of the Torah!" The commandments may all be equally obligatory, but their rewards vary according to their difficulty.

6. B. *Kiddushin* 40a: "R. Assi said [after Malachi 3:16 was quoted]: Even if one [merely] thinks of performing a precept but is forcibly prevented [from accomplishing that good end], Scripture ascribes it to him as though he has performed it. [On the other hand,] evil intention is not combined with an action [that is, there is no punishment for mere intention to do evil], for it is said, 'Had I an evil thought in my mind, the Lord would not have listened' (Psalms 66:18). [That is, when the evil intention remained in my heart and did not issue into action, God overlooked it.] Then how do I interpret, "Hear O earth! I am going to bring disaster upon this people, the outcome of their own schemes [thoughts]" (Jeremiah 6:19)? Evil intention that bears fruit [that is, is followed by action] the Holy One, blessed be He, combines with the deed [punishing both]; evil intention that does not bear fruit [in action] the Holy One, blessed be He, does not combine with deed [to punish either]."

7. This, I think, is the kernel of truth in natural law theory: Many of our basic notions of duty stem from basic human requirements for survival. This tenet also underlies the truth in intuitionist moral theory: Our expectation that people act to further human survival is so obvious to all people that the intuitionists were understandably led to suspect that the obligation to carry out such duties is something that a person must just see or else give up all pretensions of being moral. Freud's "death wish" notwithstanding, the will to survive is certainly a fundamental inclination of individuals and of groups. Indeed, because the fulfillment of any other inclination assumes that you are alive to achieve it, those who lack the desire to live probably fall outside the group of people with whom there can be moral argument.

8. For more on this, see Dorff (1998a), 20–24, 134–138; see also Chapter Seven herein.

9. J. *Terumah* 7:20 (47a); Genesis *Rabbah* 94:9. See my discussion of these sources in Dorff (1998a), 291–299; see also Schochet (1973).

10. B. *Sanhedrin* 74a.

11. Macdonald (1963), 213.

12. Ibid., 214.

13. The Rabbis wanted the Oral Law to be specifically announced by judges in each generation so as to give it authority. Writing it down would sever it from its judicial base of authority, as delineated in Deuteronomy 17:8–13. For a list of the Rabbis' five reasons for keeping the tradition oral, see Dorff and Rosett (1988),

219–223. That people understand the justice of a legal verdict better if it is announced orally is illustrated by *Megillat Ta'anit*, mishnah 10 and *scholium ad locum*, translated and quoted on p. 220 there.

14. Oppenheimer (1966), 229–230.
15. Urmson (1958).
16. Ibid., 209, 216.
17. M.T. *Laws of Ethics (De'ot)* 3:3.

Notes to Appendix B

1. Nietzsche (1956), 166–168.

2. Deuteronomy 6:18.

3. Dillenberger and Welch (1954), 284, 316. The denominations are separated not only on moral grounds but also on theological doctrines and even ethnic origins.

4. On the New Testament's view of the Pharisees, see, for example, Matthew 3:7; 23; Luke 18:9ff, in which they are variously called "hyocrites" and "offspring of vipers." The Rabbis themselves recognized the insincere among their numbers, whom they called "sore spots" or "plagues on the Pharisaic party" (M. *Sotah* 3:4; B. *Sotah* 22b). With the exception of the relatively favorable depiction of Rabban Gamliel in the Acts of the Apostles, though, the New Testament paints the Pharisees with quite a broad, negative brush, particularly for being legalistic in their approach to Jewish law—and then, to make matters worse, for hypocritically acting in violation of that law (at least as the New Testament writers see things). For the dispute between Jesus and the Pharisees over the details of Sabbath laws, see Matthew 12:9–14; Mark 3:1–6; Luke 6:6–11; 13:10–17; 14:1–6; John 5:1–18. For Jesus' dispute with the Pharisees over divorce, see Matthew 19:1–14; Mark 10:1–14. For the replacement of law with spirit, see, in particular, Paul's Letter to the Romans 7:1–8:8, 9:30–33, and his Letter to the Galatians 5:16–26.

5. This is particularly true in the United States, where individualism is perhaps most in evidence in both ideology and practice. Compare Dorff (1987a), esp. 11–19. Roman Catholicism, of course, has developed a sophisticated legal system of its own—that is, Roman Catholic Canon Law—and Protestant churches have instituted rules of practice in varying degrees of specificity. Canon law is rarely invoked or even studied by diocesan priests, however, and Protestant denominations, whatever the extent of their rules, still stress individual autonomy over law. In any case, Christianity as we know it began with the rejection of Jewish law by Paul in Romans 7–11.

6. This is Heschel's phrase; see Heschel (1955), chap. 32 and see generally chaps. 28–34.

7. See, for example, B. *Berachot* 13a (in regard to saying the *Shema*); B. *Eruvin* 95b–96a (in regard to the use of phylacteries); B. *Pesachim* 114b (in regard to the need for two dippings at the Seder); B. *Rosh Hashanah* 27a–29a, esp. 28b (in regard to blowing the shofar); and see the discussion in Dorff (1992), on *keva* and *kavanah* in prayer. See also B. *Shabbat* 72b in regard to the related question of whether one needs to have intention to be held liable for violating a law. A further development of that question: Even those who claimed that unintentional violation did not make one liable nevertheless held that one would be liable if one's violation of the law in doing an act was, though unintentional, an inevitable consequence of acting as one did; compare B. *Shabbat* 75a, 103a, 111b, 117a, 120b, 133a, 143a; B. *Bezah* 36a; B. *Sukkah* 33b; B. *Ketubbot* 6b; and B. *Bechorot* 25a.

8. Adler (1963), 64.

9. Genesis 2:15. For a more detailed treatment of what the Sabbath laws teach us about God and what God wants of us, see Dorff (1992), 60–70, 77–78.

10. B. *Pesachim* 50b; B. *Sanhedrin* 105a; B. *Arakin* 16b; B. *Sotah* 22b, 47a; B. *Horayot* 10b; B. *Nazir*, 23b.

11. M. *Avot (Ethics of the Fathers)* 2:1.

12. B. *Yoma* 86b.

13. M. *Avot (Ethics of the Fathers)* 4:2.

14. B. *Yoma* 38b.

15. Heschel (1955), 296–297.

16. From the twelfth century to the twentieth, the community that assembled on the Sabbath even acted as a court of last resort. Members who felt that justice had not been done in their cases could interrupt the prayers and have the community sit as a court of the whole. As time went on, restrictions were imposed on this right to ensure that it was not used frivolously, but the use of Sabbath services for judicial matters shows clearly the extent to which the Sabbath was and is an occasion for the community. Compare Finkelstein (1964), 15–18, 33, 125, 138. For a description of the practice in Eastern Europe in modern times, see Zborowski and Herzog (1952), 217–218.

17. Ahad Ha-Am, *Al Parashat Derahim*, 3:30.

18. Deuteronomy 32:4. For a discussion of this doctrine and its challenges in biblical literature, see Dorff and Rosett (1988), 110–123.

19. Dorff (1998a), 404–417.

20. For a conspectus of Christian views on this matter and an argument for the traditional, "Lutheran" interpretation of Paul as making salvation depend not on deeds but on faith alone, see Westerholm (1988).

Bibliography
of Cited Modern Sources

Abrahams, Israel. 1969. *Jewish Life in the Middle Ages*. New York: Atheneum.

Adler, Morris. 1963. *The World of the Talmud*. New York: Schocken.

Agus, Jacob. 1981. "The Covenant Concept—Particularistic, Pluralistic, or Futuristic?" *Journal of Ecumenical Studies* 18:217–230.

Albo, Joseph. 1946. *Sefer Ha-Ikkarim*. Trans., Isaac Husik. Philadelphia: Jewish Publication Society.

Alexander, Hanan A. 2001. *Reclaiming Goodness: Education and the Spiritual Quest*. Notre Dame, IN: University of Notre Dame Press.

Arkin, Marcus. 1975. *Aspects of Jewish Economic History*. Philadelphia: Jewish Publication Society.

Arzt, Donna. 1986. "The People's Lawyers." *Judaism* 35, no. 1 (winter): 47–62.

Astor, Carl. 1985. *". . . Who Makes People Different": Jewish Perspectives on the Disabled*. New York: United Synagogue of America.

Auerbach, Jerold S., and Donna Arzt. 1987. "Profits or Prophets: An Exchange." *Judaism* 36, no. 3 (summer): 360–367.

Ayer, Alfred J. 1946. *Language, Truth, and Logic*. London: Dover.

Birnbaum, Philip. 1949. *Daily Prayer Book*. New York: Hebrew Publishing.

Birnbaum, Philip, ed. 1953. *The Haggadah of Passover*. New York: Hebrew Publishing.

"Births among Unwed Blacks Hits Record Low." July 1, 1998. *Los Angeles Times*, p. A13.

Bleich, J. David. 1983. "Preemptive War in Jewish Law." *Tradition* 21, no. 1 (spring): 3–41.

Boff, Leonardo. 1997. *Cry of the Earth, Cry of the Poor*. Trans., Philip Berryman. Maryknoll, NY: Orbis.

Boudreaux, Richard, and Larry B. Stamer. September 6, 2000. "Vatican Declares Catholicism Sole Path to Salvation." *Los Angeles Times*, pp. A-1, A-8.

Bragdon, Henry W., and Samuel P. McCutchen. 1958. *History of a Free People*. New York: Macmillan.

Braithwaite, R. B. 1955. *An Empiricist's View of the Nature of Religious Belief* (The Eddington Memorial Lecture for 1955). Cambridge, UK: Cambridge University Press.

Brichto, Herbert Chanan. 1979. "The Hebrew Bible on Human Rights." In *Essays on Human Rights: Contemporary Issues and Jewish Perspectives* (215–233). Ed., David Sidorsky. Philadelphia: Jewish Publication Society.

Brooks, Roger. 1983. *Support for the Poor in the Mishnaic Law of Agriculture: Tractate Peah*. Chico, CA: Scholars Press.

Brueggemann, Walter. 1977. *The Land: Place As Gift, Promise, and Challenge in Biblical Faith*. Philadelphia: Fortress.

Buber, Martin. 1948. *Tales of the Hasidim*. 2 vols. New York: Schocken.

Buchler, A. 1956. "The Minim of Sepphoris and Tiberias in the Second and Third Centuries." In *Studies in Jewish History* (245–274). Eds., I. Brodie and J. Rabbinovitz. Oxford, UK: Oxford University Press.

Cohen, Steven M. 1983. *American Modernity and Jewish Identity*. New York: Tavistock.

Cone, James. 1997. *God of the Oppressed*. Maryknoll, NY: Orbis.

Dalin, David, ed. 1993. *American Jews and the Separationist Faith*. Washington, DC: Ethics and Public Policy Center.

Devorkes, Elyokum. 1974. *Aspakloryat Hatzedakah* (Hebrew). Jerusalem: np.

Dillenberger, John, and Claude Welch. 1954. *Protestant Christianity Interpreted through Its Development*. New York: Charles Scribner's Sons.

Dishon, David. 1984. *Tarbut Ha-Mahloket B'Yisrael* (Hebrew). Tel Aviv: Schocken.

Dolan, Maura. August 25, 2000. "State High Court Limits Companies' Use of Arbitration." *Los Angeles Times*, pp. A-1, A-10.

Dorff, Elliot. 1971. "The Right and the Good" Ph.D. disseration, Columbia University. (Available through University Microfilms, Ann Arbor, MI.)

Dorff, Elliot N. 1978. "Judaism As a Religious Legal System," *Hastings Law Journal*, 29, no. 6 (July): 1331–1360.

Dorff, Elliot N. 1979. "The Meaning of Covenant: A Contemporary Understanding." In *Issues in the Jewish-Christian Dialogue* (38–61). Eds., Helga Croner and Leon Klenicki. New York: Paulist Press (Stimulus Books).

Dorff, Elliot N. 1980. "Study Leads to Action." *Religious Education* 75, no. 2 (March–April): 171–192.

Dorff, Elliot N. 1982. "The Covenant: How Jews Understand Themselves and Others." *Anglican Theological Review* 64, no. 4 (October): 481–501.

Dorff, Elliot N. 1986a. "Jewish Perspectives on the Poor." In *The Poor Among Us: Jewish Tradition and Social Policy* (21–55). Ed., Gary Rubin. New York: American Jewish Committee.

Dorff, Elliot. 1986b. *Review of Michael Wyschogrod*, The Body of Faith. *Journal of Reform Judaism* 33, no. 1 (winter): 95–97.

Dorff, Elliot N. 1987a. "Training Rabbis in the Land of the Free." In *The Seminary at 100: Reflections on the Jewish Theological Seminary and the Conservative Movement* (11–28). Eds., Nina Beth Cardin and David Wolf Silverman. New York: Rabbinical Assembly.

Dorff, Elliot N. 1987b. " 'A Time for War and a Time for Peace': A Jewish Perspective on the Ethics of International Intervention" (*University Papers*, 6, no. 3). Los Angeles: University of Judaism.

Dorff, Elliot N. 1988a. "The Covenant: The Transcendent Thrust in Jewish Law." *The Jewish Law Annual* 7:68–96.

Dorff, Elliot N. 1988b. "Catholic/Jewish Dialogue: A Jewish Perspective on Vatican Documents." *Ecumenical Trends* (September): 116–120.

Dorff, Elliot N. 1989. *Mitzvah Means Commandment*. New York: United Synagogue of America.

Dorff, Elliot N. 1991. "Bishops, Rabbis, and Bombs." In *Confronting Omnicide: Jewish Reflections on Weapons of Mass Destruction* (164–195). Ed., Daniel Landes. Northvale, NJ: Jason Aronson.

Dorff, Elliot N. 1992. *Knowing God: Jewish Approaches to the Unknowable*. Northvale, NJ: Jason Aronson.

Dorff, Elliot N. 1996a. *Conservative Judaism: Our Ancestors to Our Descendants.* 2nd ed. New York: United Synagogue of Conservative Judaism.

Dorff, Elliot N. 1996b. *"This Is My Beloved, This Is My Friend" (Song of Songs 5:16): A Rabbinic Letter on Intimate Relations.* New York: Rabbinical Assembly.

Dorff, Elliot N. 1997. "Custom Drives Jewish Law on Women." *Conservative Judaism* 49, no. 3 (spring): 3–21.

Dorff, Elliot N. 1998a. *Matters of Life and Death: A Jewish Approach to Modern Medical Ethics.* Philadelphia: Jewish Publication Society.

Dorff, Elliot N. 1998b. "The Elements of Forgiveness: A Jewish Approach." In *Discussions of Forgiveness: Psychological Research and Theological Perspectives* (29–55). Ed., Everett Worthington Jr. Philadelphia: Templeton Foundation.

Dorff, Elliot N. 1998c. "Teshuvah on Assisted Suicide." *Conservative Judaism* 50, no. 4 (summer): 3–24.

Dorff, Elliot N. 1999. *"You Shall Strengthen Them": A Rabbinic Letter on the Poor.* New York: Rabbinical Assembly.

Dorff, Elliot N., and Arthur Rosett. 1988. *A Living Tree: The Roots and Growth of Jewish Law.* Albany: State University of New York Press.

Eisenstein, Judah David, ed. 1915. *Otzar Midrashim.* New York: Hebrew Publishing.

Epstein, Barukh Halevi. 1969. *Torah Temimah.* Tel Aviv: Am Olam.

Fackenheim, Emil. 1972. *God's Presence in History: Jewish Affirmations and Philosophical Reflections.* Reprint ed. New York: Harper & Row.

Fackenheim, Emil. 1978. *The Jewish Return into History: Reflections in the Age of Auschwitz and a New Jerusalem.* New York: Schocken.

Feldman, David M. 1974. *Marital Relations, Birth Control, and Abortion in Jewish Law.* Reprint ed. New York: Schocken.

Finkelstein, Louis. 1964. *Jewish Self-Government in the Middle Ages.* New York: Jewish Theological Seminary of America.

Flannery, Edward. 1965. *The Anguish of the Jews: Twenty-Three Centuries of Anti-Semitism* New York: Macmillan.

Gershuni, Y. 1983. "War and Bravery" (Hebrew). In *Tehumin* (54–67). Vol. 4. Ed., Ithamar Warhaftig. Jerusalem: Tzomet.

Ginzberg, Levi (Louis). 1923. "A Response to the Question Whether Unfermented Wine May Be Used in Jewish Ceremonies." *American Jewish Year Book* 25:401–425.

Gittelsohn, Roland B. 1970. "Judaism on War, Peace, and Conscientious Objection." *Jewish Digest* 15, no. 4 (April): 52.

Goitein, S. D. 1971. *A Mediterranean Society: The Jewish Communities of the Arab World As Portrayed in the Documents of the Cairo Geniza.* 2 vols. Berkeley: University of California Press.

Goldberg, Michael. 1981. *Theology and Narrative: A Critical Introduction.* Nashville, TN: Abingdon.

Goldberg, Michael. 1985. *Jews and Christians: Getting Our Stories Straight.* Nashville, TN: Abingdon.

Goldenberg, Robert. 1985. "Economic Justice and Rabbinic Tradition." *Sh'ma* 16, no. 303 (December 13): 17–18.

Golding, Martin. 1984–1985. "Forgiveness and Regret." *The Philosophical Forum* 16, nos. 1–2 (fall–winter): 121–137.

Goldman, Israel M. 1975. *Life-Long Learning among Jews.* New York: KTAV.

Gordis, Robert. 1965. *The Book of God and Man: A Study of Job.* Chicago: University of Chicago.

Goren, Shelomo. 1964. *Torat Ha-Mo'adim.* Tel Aviv: Tsiyoni. Reprint ed. 1996, Jerusalem: Ha-Idra Rabbah.

Goren, Shelomo. 1983. *Masheev Milhamah.* Jerusalem: Ha-Idra Rabbah.

Graff, Gil. 1985. *Separation of Church and State: Dina de-Malkhuta Dina in Jewish Law, 1750–1848.* Birmingham: University of Alabama Press.

Greenberg, Irving. 1985. "Will There Be One Jewish People by the Year 2000?" In *Perspectives* (1–8). Ed., Nina Beth Cardin. New York: CLAL, The National Jewish Center for Learning and Leadership.

Greenberg, Irving. 1986. "Toward a Principled Pluralism." In *Perspectives* (20–31). Ed., Nina Beth Cardin. New York: CLAL, The National Jewish Center for Learning and Leadership.

Greenberg, Irving. 1987. "Theological Models for a Plural Covenant." Lecture presented on March 8, at Camp Ramah (Ojai, CA).

Greenberg, Irving. 1988. *The Jewish Way.* New York: Summit Books.

Greenberg, Simon. 1977. *The Ethical in the Jewish and American Heritage.* New York: Jewish Theological Seminary of America.

Greenberg, Simon. 1986. "Pluralism and Jewish Education." *Religious Education* 81 (winter): 19–28.

Gross, Nachum, ed. 1975. *Economic History of the Jews.* New York: Schocken.

Gutierrez, Gustavo. 1973. *A Theology of Liberation: History, Politics, and Salvation*. Trans. and ed., Sister Caridad Inda and John Eagleson. Maryknoll, NY: Orbis.

Harlow, Jules. 1985. *Siddur Sim Shalom: A Prayerbook for Shabbat, Festivals, and Weekdays*. New York: Rabbinical Assembly and United Synagogue of America.

Hartman, David. 1978. *Joy and Responsibility*. Jerusalem: Ben-Zvi Posner.

Harvey, Van A. 1966. *The Historian and the Believer*. New York: Macmillan.

Heinemann, Isaak, ed. 1960. *Three Jewish Philosophers*, Part III: *Halevi*. Philadelphia: Jewish Publication Society.

Heschel, Abraham Joshua. 1955. *God in Search of Man*. New York: Harper & Row.

Heschel, Abraham Joshua. 1962. *Torah Min Ha-Shamayim B'Aspakloria Shel Ha-Dorot* (The Doctrine of Torah from Heaven from the Perspective of the Generations) (Hebrew). 3 vols. London: Soncino.

Hick, John, and Edmund S. Meltzer. 1989. *Three Faiths—One God: A Jewish, Christian, Muslim Encounter*. Albany: State University of New York Press.

Hopkins, Charles Howard. 1982. *The Rise of the Social Gospel in American Protestantism, 1865–1915*. New York: AMS Press.

Jacobs, Louis. 1965. *We Have Reason to Believe*. London: Vallentine, Mitchell.

Josephson, Michael. 1990. *Teaching Ethics in the 90s*. Santa Monica, CA: Joseph and Edna Josephson Institute of Ethics.

Kahan, Arcadius. 1975. "The Early Modern Period." In *Economic History of the Jews* (55–78). Ed., Nachum Gross. New York: Schocken.

Kaplan, Mordecai M. 1934; rpt. 1967. *Judaism As a Civilization*. New York: Schocken.

Kaplan, Mordecai M. 1956. *Questions Jews Ask: Reconstructionist Answers*. New York: Reconstructionist Press.

Kaplan, Mordecai M. 1970b. "Wage Peace or Else." *Reconstructionist* 35, no. 15 (January 23): 7–10.

Katz, Mordecai. 1925. *Protection of the Weak in the Talmud*. New York: Columbia University Press.

Kaufman, Walter. 1958. *Critique of Religion and Philosophy*. Garden City, NY: Doubleday (Anchor Books).

Kimelman, Reuven. 1968. "Non-Violence in the Talmud." *Judaism* 17, no. 3 (summer), 316–334.

Kimelman, Reuven. 1970. "The Rabbinic Ethics of Protest." *Judaism* 19, no. 1 (winter): 38–58.

Kimelman, Reuven. 1983. *Tsedakah and Us*. New York: National Jewish Resource Center.

Kimelman, Reuven. 1987. "Judaism and Pluralism." *Modern Judaism* 7, no. 2 (May): 131–150.

Kirschenbaum, Aaron. 1970. *Self-Incrimination in Jewish Law*. New York: Burning Bush.

Konvitz, Milton R., ed. 1972. *Judaism and Human Rights*. New York: Norton.

Konvitz, Milton R. 1980. *Judaism and the American Idea*. New York: Schocken.

Kook, Abraham Isaac. 1937. *Mishpat Kohen: Teshuvot Be-Mitzvot Hal-Teluyot Ba-Aretz*. Jerusalem: Ha-Agudah Le Hotza'at Sifre Ha-Reayahkuk. Reprint ed. 1966 Jerusalem: Mosad Ha-Ravkuk.

Kook, Abraham Isaac. 1939; rpt. 1962. *Seder Tefilah Im Perush 'Olat Rayah*. 2 vols. Jerusalem: Mossad Harav Kook.

Krefatz, Gerald. 1982. *Jews and Money: The Myths and the Reality*. New Haven: Ticknor & Fields.

Lamm, Norman. 1971. *Faith and Doubt: Studies in Traditional Jewish Thought*. New York: KTAV.

Lamm, Norman. 1986. "Unity and Integrity." In *Materials from the Critical Issues Conference: Will There Be One Jewish People by the Year 2000?* (53–76). New York: Center for Learning and Leadership.

Levi, Primo. 1984. *The Periodic Table*. New York: Schocken.

Levine, Aaron. 1980. *Free Enterprise and Jewish Law*. New York: KTAV and Yeshiva.

Levine, Aaron. 1985. "Jewish Social Welfare and the Economy." *Sh'ma* 16, no. 303 (December 13): 18–21.

Lewittes, Mendell. 1987. *Principles and Development of Jewish Law*. New York: Bloch.

Lieberman, Saul. 1962. *Tosefta ki-Feshutah*. New York: Jewish Theological Seminary of America.

Likona, Thomas. 1991. *Educating for Character*. New York: Bantam.

Lipman, Eugene. 1986. Untitled presentation. In *A CAJE Symposium: Division, Pluralism, and Unity among Jews*. Ed., Leonard A. Matanky. New York: Coalition for the Advancement of Jewish Education.

Macdonald, Margaret. 1963. "Ethics and the Ceremonial Use of Language." In *Philosophical Analysis: A Collection of Essays* (198–215). Ed., Max Black. Englewood Cliffs, NJ: Prentice-Hall.

Mahoney, Cardinal Roger. September 10, 2000. "Partnership Is Still a Goal of the Catholic Church." *Los Angeles Times,* p. M5.

Matthews, Victor H., and Don C. Benjamin. 1991. *Old Testament Parallels: Law and Stories from the Ancient Near East.* New York: Paulist Press.

McCann, Dennis. 1981. *Christian Realism and Liberation Theology: Practical Theologies in Conflict.* Maryknoll, NY: Orbis.

McCarthy, Terry. 2000. "The Stolen Generation: Aborigines Taken from Their Families in the Name of Assimilation Seek an Apology from White Australia." *Time* (October 2): 50.

McClendon, James William, Jr. 1974. *Biography As Theology.* Nashville. TN: Abingdon Press.

McClendon, James William, Jr., and James M. Smith. 1975. *Understanding Religious Convictions.* Notre Dame, IN: University of Notre Dame Press.

Neusner, Jacob. 1982. *Tzedakah: Can Jewish Philanthropy Buy Jewish Survival?* Chappaqua, NY: Rossel Books.

Neusner, Jacob. 1993. *A Rabbi Talks with Jesus: An Intermillenial, Interfaith Exchange.* New York: Doubleday.

Nietzsche, Friedrich. 1956. *The Genealogy of Morals.* Trans., Francis Golffing. Garden City, NY: Doubleday (Anchor Books).

Novak, David. 1983. *The Image of the Non-Jew in Judaism: An Historical and Constructive Study of the Noahide Laws.* New York: Edwin Mellen Press.

Novak, David. 1993. Untitled essay. In *American Jews and the Separationist Faith* (93–95). Ed., David G. Dalin. Washington, DC: Ethics and Public Policy Center.

Nozick, Robert. 1989. *The Examined Life.* New York: Simon & Schuster.

Oppenheimer, Helen. 1966. "Moral Choices and Divine Authority." In *Christian Ethics and Contemporary Philosophy* (219–233). Ed. Ian Ramsey. New York: Macmillan.

Ozick, Cynthia. 1989. "Why I Won't Go to Germany." *Jewish Journal of Greater Los Angeles* (April 7–13): 19, 21.

Pipes, Daniel. October 17, 2000. "Stop Pressing Israel to Make Concessions." *Los Angeles Times,* p. B9.

Pope, M. H. 1962. "Job, Book of." *Interpreter's Dictionary of the Bible.* Nashville, TN: Abingdon.

Praeger, Dennis. Untitled essay. In *American Jews and the Separationist Faith* (106–109). Ed. David G. Dalin. Washington, DC: Ethics and Public Policy Center.

Pritchard, James B., ed. 1955. *Ancient Near Eastern Texts Relating to the Old Testament*. Princeton: Princeton University Press.

Putnam, Hilary. 1987. *The Many Faces of Realism*. La Salle, IL: Open Court.

Raab, E.1993. Untitled essay. In *American Jews and the Separationist Faith* (110–111). Ed., David G. Dalin. Washington, DC: Ethics and Public Policy Center.

Rabbinical Assembly. 1998. "Resolution on Global Poverty and the Deteriorating Global Environment." *Proceedings of the Rabbinical Assembly 1997* (254–256). New York: Rabbinical Assembly.

Rabinowicz, Rachel Anne. 1982. *The Haggadah of Passover*. New York: Rabbinical Assembly.

Rackman, Emanuel. 1977. "Violence and the Value of Life." In *Violence and Defense in the Jewish Experience* (112–142). Eds., Salo Baron and George S. Wise. Philadelphia: Jewish Publication Society.

Rauschenbusch, Walter. 1978. *A Theology for the Social Gospel*. Nashville, TN: Abingdon.

Rosenzweig, Franz. 1971. *The Star of Redemption*. Trans., William W. Hallo. Reprint ed. New York: Holt Rinehart, & Winston.

Ross, William David. 1930. *The Right and the Good*. Oxford, UK: Clarendon Press.

Rothschild, Fritz, ed. 1990. *Jewish Perspectives on Christianity*. New York: Crossroad.

Rubenstein, Richard. 1983. *The Age of Triage: Fear and Hope in an Overcrowded World*. Boston: Beacon Press.

Rubenstein, Richard. 1992. *After Auschwitz*. 2nd ed. Baltimore: Johns Hopkins University Press.

Rubin, Gary, ed. 1986. *The Poor among Us: Jewish Tradition and Social Policy*. New York: American Jewish Committee.

Ruether, Rosemary. 1974. *Faith and Fratricide: The Theological Roots of Anti-Semitism*. New York: Seabury Press.

Scheer, Robert. April 13, 1988. "Jews in U.S. Committed to Equality." *Los Angeles Times*, A-1, 14, 15.

Schochet, Elijah J. 1973. *A Responsum of Surrender*. Los Angeles: University of Judaism.

Schulweis, Harold. 1995. "Judaism: From Either/Or to Both/And." In *Contemporary Jewish Ethics and Morality: A Reader* (25–37). Eds.,

Elliot N. Dorff and Louis E. Newman. New York: Oxford University Press.

Shafran, Avi. 1986. Letter. *Moment* 2 (January–February): 55.

Shapira, Avraham, ed. 1970. *The Seventh Day: Soldiers Talk about the Six-Day War*. English edition ed., Henry Near. New York: Charles Scribner's Sons.

Shapiro, Aharon. 1971. "The Poverty Program of Judaism." *Review of Social Economy* 9, no. 2 (September): 200–206.

Shapiro, Edward S. 1987. "Jews with Money." *Judaism* 36, no. 1 (winter): 1–16.

Sheler, Jeffrey L. 2000. "Pull Back or Reach Out? Interfaith Statements Seem to Differ Markedly." *U.S. News and World Report* (September 18): 74.

Sidorsky, David, ed. 1979. *Essays on Human Rights: Contemporary Issues and Jewish Perspectives*. Philadelphia: Jewish Publication Society.

Siegel, Danny. 1982. *Gym Shoes and Irises: Personalized Tzedakah*. Spring Valley, NY: Town House Press.

Siegel, Seymour. 1967. "Covenants—Old and New." *Jewish Heritage* (spring): 54–59.

Silverman, Morris. 1946. *Sabbath and Festival Prayerbook*. New York: Rabbinical Assembly of America and United Synagogue of America.

Staub, Jacob. 1986. Untitled presentation. In *A CAJE Symposium: Division, Pluralism, and Unity among Jews* (4–6, 10). Ed., Leonard A. Matanky. New York: Coalition for the Advancement of Jewish Education.

Steinberg, Milton. 1939. *As a Driven Leaf*. New York: Behrman House.

"Though Upbeat on the Economy, People Still Fear for Their Jobs." December 29, 1996. *New York Times*, A1, 22.

Tucker, Gordon. 1999. "Metaphysical Realism: Theoretical and Practical Considerations." *Conservative Judaism* 51, no. 2 (winter): 84–95.

Turner, J. David. 1994. *An Introduction to Liberation Theology*. Lanham, MD: University Press of America.

Udoff, Alan. 1987. "Tolerance." In *Contemporary Jewish Religious Thought* (989–994). Eds., Arthur A. Cohen and Paul Mendes-Flohr. New York: Charles Scribner's Sons.

Urmson, James Opie. 1958. "Saints and Heroes." In *Essays in Moral Philosophy* (198–216). Ed., Abraham Irving Melden. Seattle: University of Washington Press.

Van Buren, Paul. 1995. *A Theology of the Jewish-Christian Reality.* Part 1: *Discerning the Way.* Part 2: *A Christian Theology of the People Israel.* Lanham, MD: University Press of America.

Van Buren, Paul. 1998. *A Theology of the Jewish-Christian Reality.* Part 3: *Christ in Context.* San Fancisco: Harper & Row.

Westerholm, Stephen. 1988. *Israel's Law and the Church's Faith: Paul and His Recent Interpreters.* Grand Rapids, MI: Eerdmans Publishing.

Wikler, Daniel. 1983. "Philosophical Perspectives on Access to Health Care: An Introduction." In *Securing Access to Health Care.* Vol. 2. Ed., Daniel Wikler. Washington, DC: U.S. Government Printing Office.

Wolf, Rabbi Alfred, and Monsignor Royale M. Vadikan, gen. eds. 1989. *A Journey of Discovery: A Resource Manual for Jewish-Catholic Dialogue.* Valencia, CA: Tabor Publishing.

Wurzburger, Walter. 1986. Untitled presentation. In *A CAJE Symposium: Division, Pluralism, and Unity among Jews* (7–8). Ed., Leonard A. Matanky. New York: Coalition for the Advancement of Jewish Education.

Wyschogrod, Michael. 1980. "Religion and International Human Rights: A Jewish Perspective." In *Formation of Social Policy in the Catholic and Jewish Traditions* (123–141). Ed. Eugene J. Fisher and Daniel F. Polish. Notre Dame, IN: Notre Dame University Press.

Wyschogrod, Michael. 1983. *The Body of Faith: Judaism As Corporeal Election.* New York: Seabury Press.

Zborowski, Mark, and Elizabeth Herzog. 1952. *Life Is with People.* New York: International Universities Press.

Zevin, Solomon. 1957. *Le'or Ha-Halakhah.* Tel Aviv: Mosad Ha-Rav Kook.

Index